The Dublin
Book Trade
1801–1850

CHARLES BENSON

The Dublin Book Trade 1801–1850

CHARLES BENSON

———

*A thesis submitted to Trinity College,
University of Dublin*

*With an editorial preface by
David Dickson and an
updated bibliography*

LONDON
THE BIBLIOGRAPHICAL SOCIETY
2021

The Dublin Book Trade 1801–1850

© 2021 The estate of Charles Benson and the Bibliographical Society,
c/o Institute of English Studies, Senate House, Malet Street, London WC1E 7HU

A CIP record for this book is available from the British Library

ISBN 978 0 948170 25 6

DESIGNED AND TYPESET IN 11 ON 13 PT MINION BY DEREK BROWN

PRINTED AND BOUND BY GOMER PRESS LIMITED, LLANDYSUL, CEREDIGION

A NOTE ON THIS BOOK

When Charles Benson died in 2017 he was working on a project, agreed with the Bibliographical Society, to compile a nineteenth-century directory to complement Mary Pollard's *Dictionary of Members of the Dublin Book Trade 1550–1800*, which the Society published in 2000. It was based on the biographical directory which formed an appendix to his thesis on *The Dublin Book Trade 1801–1850*, and on which he worked continuously after 2000, augmenting the original with additional entries. The plan, agreed with Charles, was that this would become an online database, published by the Society.

Unfortunately, this was not sufficiently far advanced by 2017 for it to be feasible to complete the original scheme. Those who recognised the authoritative nature of Charles's work in this field began a discussion about how best to bring at least some of his unpublished work to a wider audience, and this led to the initiative to print his thesis. The detailed overview of the development of many aspects of the Dublin book trade during the first half of the nineteenth century which it sets out is not available anywhere else, and is not likely to be superseded in the foreseeable future.

This book comprises the narrative text of the thesis, with some additional material provided by an editorial group led by Professor David Dickson of Trinity College Dublin. The Bibliographical Society is grateful to him and his colleagues, and also to Charles's son Ralph Benson, for their enthusiasm and help in making this publication possible. Considerations of space, together with the knowledge that this was the part which Charles was revising and augmenting, precluded the printing of the directory in its original version as appended to the thesis, but all his working papers and record cards have been deposited in the Library of Trinity College Dublin and are available for consultation there.

Contents

Table of Figures

Early Printed Books colleagues Charles Benson, Veronica (Vicky) Cremin, Mary (Paul) Pollard and Siobhán Fitzpatrick reunited outside Trinity College's Long Room on 9 June 2005. The occasion was the launch of *That Woman! — Studies in Irish Bibliography: A Festschrift for Mary 'Paul' Pollard*, eds Benson and Fitzpatrick (Dublin: Lilliput Press for the Library Association of Ireland, 2005, photograph and © Raymond Jordan).

Editorial Preface, 2020

WHAT EVENTUALLY BECAME the Department of Early Printed Books and Special Collections was established as a minor division within the Library of Trinity College Dublin in 1967. The team was very small, yet for many years they had full responsibility for the care, management and development of the historic collections housed within Trinity's Old Library. In addition they began to operate as a tiny research laboratory, reviving the dormant field of Irish historical bibliography. Mary Pollard was the inspirational first director for a decade and a half. Then for twenty-three years from 1988 it was led by Charles Benson, and he was assisted for much of that time by his deputy and close collaborator Vincent Kinane.

The Department over these years developed exemplary standards of cataloguing, engaged in an enlightened and imaginative acquisitions policy, and collaborated in innovative multi-disciplinary graduate programmes. The team also built up a remarkable flow of publications and, such was the vision and dedication of those involved, it set the gold standard in Irish historical bibliography, a field that only began to blossom late in the twentieth century. *Long Room*, the journal produced by the 'Friends of the Library' since 1970, provided a platform for their research, and they became the sole editors; its elegant, professional and sometimes subversive tone fully reflected the culture of the Department. Given very limited budgets and the competing demands on their time, what Pollard, Benson, Kinane and their colleagues achieved over a half a century of scholarship, prudent acquisition, and support for the research of many others was outstanding. It is only now coming to be fully appreciated.

Pollard's focus was Dublin's book trade in the glory days of the eighteenth century, and her great ambition was to compile a dictionary of all those involved from its sixteenth-century inception to 1800. The *magnum opus* was completed in retirement and published in 2000, and some measure of its impact is registered in the *festschrift* that appeared in her honour in 2005, edited by Siobhán Fitzpatrick and Charles Benson.[1] The cut-off date for her work was always 1800, and indeed the original remit of the Department had specified 1800 as the end date for its responsibilities

---

[1] *That Woman! — Studies in Irish Bibliography: A Festschrift for Mary 'Paul' Pollard* (Dublin, 2005).

(this was later changed to *c.*1875). There was good reason for seeing 1800 as a boundary line. The Irish book trade was uniquely affected by the Act of Union insofar as British copyright was extended very shortly afterwards to include Ireland. That undermined the great reprint trade that had flourished in Dublin for almost a century. But there were other factors at work changing the character and circumstances of printing and publishing in early nineteenth-century Ireland. The assumption that the end of the reprint trade meant the end of Irish publishing was of course entirely mistaken: it was an era of rising literacy, of the democratisation of politics and of an immense widening of Irish civil society, and as a consequence the demand for print rose sharply. It took many forms: devotional literature, newsprint, educational and juvenile texts, ephemera, and print matter sponsored by public institutions. But new technology (inside and outside the print room) and fundamental changes in the price of print drove many of these market changes. As a consequence, the organisation of Irish publishing, printing and bookselling was transformed during the first half of the nineteenth century. Yet in an era of freer trade and imperial expansion, the Irish industry had less success externally, certainly compared to the exceptional performance of Scottish publishing.

Charles Benson seized on this era as an exciting field of research, capitalising on Pollard's methodologies and exploiting her findings. But whereas a few brave hearts had pioneered Irish book history for the period up to 1800, almost no attention had been paid up to the post-Union transformation of the industry. And where Pollard's focus had rightly been on publishing, book production and sale, Benson broadened his investigations into the social history of all the crafts involved in the printing process. This was entirely sensible as the scale of enterprises involved in printing had grown much larger by the 1840s, and the organisation of the skilled trades had evolved from guild to operative-controlled clubs and societies. And the residual Irish publishing houses of the 1840s were very different in character and composition from the family businesses that had dominated Pollard's world.

Benson's decision to follow the Pollard prototype and produce a dictionary of the printing trade between 1800 and 1850 was taken many years before she completed her monumental project. Like her, he chose to concentrate on Dublin, although he was mindful of the provincial printing industry, which became relatively far busier than it had been in the eighteenth century. He continued to run the Department with great flair while conducting research for the project across a very broad spectrum of sources. He opted to present his study as a doctoral dissertation within the discipline of History, and he brought this to a successful conclusion in 2000, coinciding with Pollard's publication.

The original thesis was a work of two halves: a set of interpretative chapters, and a 'Dictionary' modelled on Pollard's format. It was received very warmly and was immediately recognised as transformational by nineteenth-century specialists. Publication was however postponed until he had the luxury of retirement. But a number of papers based on his doctoral researches appeared during the following decade, most notably his three contributions to James Murphy's nineteenth-century volume for *The Oxford History of the Irish Book* (vol. IV, published in 2011). This stirred up further interest in his unpublished great work, and it was eagerly anticipated at the time of his retirement. But he was cheated by sudden death in 2017.[2]

The work as now presented is the first (interpretative) part of the *magnum opus* of 2000 finally brought to light, together with an updated general bibliography, new illustrations, a bibliography of all of Charles Benson's known publications (including his anonymised contributions to *Long Room*), and an index. Interventions by the editors (Elizabethanne Boran, David Dickson, Siobhán Fitzpatrick, Máire Kennedy and Jason McElligott) have been minimal, and footnotes have mostly been left in the form used in the thesis. It has not been possible to include, in this printed version, either the original Dictionary or the additions which he was planning, partly for reasons of space but also because the supplementary work was in an unfinished state. However, Benson's glosses and notes on the 'Dictionary' entries, together with the collection of record cards that were the building blocks for the 'Dictionary', have now been deposited in Trinity's Department of Early Printed Books by the Benson family, and will be available in the future for scholarly consultation.

David Dickson

---

[2] David McKitterick, 'Charles Benson', in *The Book Collector*, 67 (4) (Spring 2018), 167–68; Derval Conroy, 'Charles Benson: An appreciation', in the *Irish Times*, 23 July 2018; Elizabethanne Boran, 'Dr Charles Benson, 1946–2017', in *An Leabharlann / The Irish Library*, 27 (2) (October 2018), 38–39.

Acknowledgements

I wish to express my thanks to the many individuals and institutions who have assisted me in this work.

In the first place I wish to thank my supervisor Dr David Dickson for advice and encouragement during the long preparation of the work. I wish to thank my colleagues in the Department of Early Printed Books in Trinity College Library, Vincent Kinane, Lydia Ferguson, Caroline Gray, Shane Mawe and particularly Rose Reddy who put my scribbles into neat shape. I am particularly grateful to M. Pollard, whose own *Dictionary of the Dublin Book Trade to 1800* provided the jumping off point for my dictionary, for her enormously valuable advice on all aspects of bibliography. I wish to thank Dr Julia Walworth of the University of London Library for her considerable help; Mary Clark, Dublin City Archivist, for advice on the City Records; Ray Refaussé and Susan Hood of the Representative Church Body Library, Siobhán O'Rafferty of the Royal Irish Academy Library, Dr Máire Kennedy of the Gilbert Library and Peter Kenny of the National Library.

I owe a debt to staff of various institutions, particularly to the unsung heroes who work for scholarship, the book and manuscript fetchers, in Trinity College Library, The National Library of Ireland, The Royal Irish Academy, The Gilbert Library of Dublin Corporation Libraries, The Registry of Deeds, Dublin, The National Archives of Ireland, The British Library, The University of London Library, The Modem Records Centre University of Warwick, St Bride's Printing Historical Library, London.

The work would not have come to fruition without the encouragement and support over many years of Norma MacManaway and the extremely hard work by Fiona Fitzsimons, Nicola Morris, Robert Somerville Woodward and the staff of Eneclann who put all the trade entries into disciplined order. The work could not have been completed without the forbearance and support of my wife Gillie and my children Ralph and Caroline who have patiently endured my absences on research and my return to litter the house with paper for several years.

CHARLES BENSON, 2000

Abbreviations

A number of abbreviations are used throughout this book for institutions and reference sources which are regularly referred to:

DTPS   Dublin Typographical Provident Society

NLI   National Library of Ireland

NTA   National Typographical Association

TCD   Trinity College, Dublin

TNA   The National Archives (Kew)

Introduction

HISTORIANS OF THE BOOKSELLING AND PRINTING TRADES in Ireland have concentrated principally on the abundant activity and vitality of the eighteenth century and little attention has been given to business in the early nineteenth century. The eighteenth century ending with the Act of Union is seen as a time of initiative unfettered by copyright legislation, the nineteenth century as of minor importance.

The year 1801 marks a natural break with the conditions of the eighteenth century as the provisions of the Copyright Act were extended to Ireland in July of that year. Subsequently the publishing trade had to operate on a completely different basis to that on which it had hitherto flourished. Where before anything could be printed legally, provided it was not libellous or blasphemous, in the new century the law of copyright crippled the Dublin reprint trade. Although book publishing by way of reprinting literature and drama undoubtedly diminished, and the extinction of the Irish Parliament lessened the quantity of government printing and to some extent pamphleteering, there was still an active book trade with a greatly increased importation of books from Great Britain.

The Irish economy grew quite fast during the first fifteen years of the nineteenth century but suffered a depression in the five years following, though the collapse in agricultural prices was accompanied by a fall in the price of manufactured goods; from the early 1820s when growth resumed, the level of economic activity continued to rise until the early 1840s, although there were some severe but short-lived recessions.[1]

A sense of the drabness and depression of the Irish market was expressed by several contemporary observers, most notably William Carleton, when decrying the tendency of Irish authors to sell their works to London publishers.[2] While this held true so far as literature and drama were concerned, there were other areas in which indigenous activity developed, such as in medicine and law. While medical books and, to a limited extent, Irish law reports had a potential international market, the business for Irish law textbooks and manuals was domestic. There was a very large market, domestic and international, for school text-books, a demand promoted by moves to provide greater access to primary education.

---

[1] C. Ó Gráda, *Ireland: a New Economic History 1780–1939*, Oxford, 1994, pp. 153–70.
[2] W. Carleton, *Traits and Stories of the Irish Peasantry*, Dublin, 1843, v. 1, p. v.

Not enough work has yet been done to enable a proper measure to be taken of the overall quantity of publishing. Whereas for the eighteenth century the *English Short Title Catalogue* draws on the resources of hundreds of libraries, the *Nineteenth Century Short Title Catalogue* draws on the resources of eight. While these include libraries with large Irish holdings it must be admitted that the holdings of one of them, Trinity College Dublin, are poor in comparison with the collections in the National Library of Ireland and the Royal Irish Academy.

Few contemporary business records survive to throw light on the trade. The best one, Graisberry and Campbells' ledger 1797–1806 contains the accounts of sixty-four people and associations and provides bibliographic information on over 300 books printed in the period including the edition sizes.[3] It spans the period of change enforced on the trade by the application of the Copyright Act in 1801. It is significant as the ledger of a firm of jobbing printers of middle size whose range of business ran from placards to multi-volume works and shows the huge volume of jobbing printing which accompanied bookwork in most printing offices. A second volume of the firm's records, the bill book 1812–1815 was presented to TCD in 1999.[4] This has not been examined in any detail, except to extract employees' names, as it had been badly charred in a fire in 1979 and was in need of conservation treatment.

At the other end of the half century the firm of Webb and Chapman was active in Great Brunswick St. The bill book for the period 1846–1850 lists the work done by the employees on a weekly basis.[5] This firm also had a jobbing business though doing much less bookwork than Graisberry and Campbell did, its trade illustrating more the variety of small jobs done in connection with commercial life in the way of advertising placards, labels and railway tickets. A wages ledger survives for the period from R. D. Webb's start of business in 1828 up to 1863.[6] The ledger commences at the start of Webb's partnership with Chapman, with the earlier years added at the end. It demonstrates clearly the annual variation in employment and the amount of casual labour used and has been of enormous use in establishing names and dates of activity of journeymen for periods not covered by trade union records.

The correspondence of two English firms, Longman and Co. and John Murray throw light on the practices of the trade between the two countries.[7] One of the partners in Longman and Co., Owen Rees, was a regular traveller to Ireland observing the state of business, creditworthiness of booksellers and promoting his wares. The correspondence is of considerable importance in establishing trading terms for discounts and credit. John Murray's letters early in the century also help in this

---

[3] TCD MSS 10315.

[4] TCD MSS 11037.

[5] NLI MSS 141.

[6] NLI MSS 139.

[7] Longman Archives, University of Reading Library; John Murray Archive, John Murray, 50 Albemarle St, London (now in the National Library of Scotland).

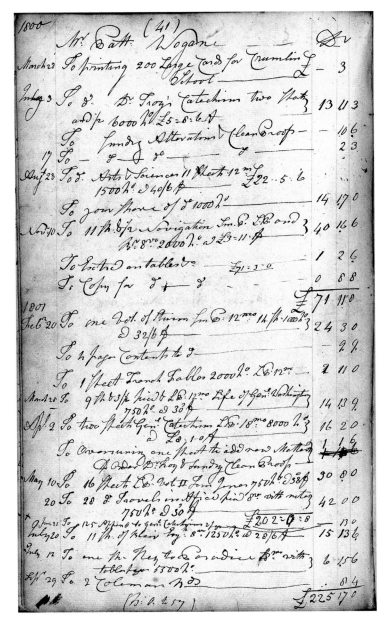

Figure 1. Printers and publishers: a page from Graisberry and Campbell's remarkable business archive. This relates to work carried out by the Back Lane printer/publishers during 1800 and 1801 for Patrick Wogan (*c.* 1740–1816), a veteran of the trade in nearby Old Bridge St. It highlights the great diversity of printing jobs undertaken for such a prolific client — including a catechism by Archbishop Troy, and the supply of sheets for Wogan's edition of John Corry's *Life of George Washington* (1801) and for an unrecorded *Travels in Africa* (possibly a Dublin edition of Mungo Park's account). *Reproduced by permission of the Board of Trinity College Dublin*: TCD MS 10,315, p. 41.

3

respect as well as providing indications on the potential London market for Dublin produced books. Longman and Co. were even then a large London firm while John Murray's prosperity had yet to be firmly established, which was soon to be achieved through his connection with Lord Byron.

Apart from books, there was an expansion (after a couple of economically and politically difficult decades at the start of the century) in the demand for newspapers and periodicals. Initially, heavy taxation and political prosecutions depressed demand and initiative.[8] But reductions in stamp duty brought a revival in the 1830s and at least two magazines, the *Dublin Penny Journal* and the *Dublin University Magazine*, had an international circulation as did one weekly newspaper, *The Nation*.

The growth in the number of Dublin printers recorded between 1833 and 1851 confirms a generally rising trend in demand for print. This was despite a seasonal pattern of employment, extensive underemployment, and several times of slump. Wages for printers remained at the top end of the grades for trades throughout the period. In common with many others, wages rose to unprecedented levels during the Napoleonic Wars and then drifted downwards until the late 1820s, although their purchasing power does not appear to have altered greatly for the worse during the 1820s or 1830s. Although there was some technical change in presses with the invention of the iron hand press in 1800 and the application of steam power to printing in 1814 — not seen in Ireland until 1834 — these innovations were accepted without difficulty. In fact iron presses did not come into general use until the late 1820s, and even as late as 1850 comparatively few printers had steam presses. Compositors were comparatively unaffected by change; all setting of type was still done by hand, although the perfecting of stereotyping limited the amount of resetting for second or subsequent editions.

In the context of the United Kingdom trade overall, Dublin failed to sustain the position it had achieved in the eighteenth century as second publishing centre in the British Isles, being overtaken by Edinburgh and possibly by Glasgow. But it remained a significant producer of unglamorous books through the period, while continuing to be the main distribution centre for a great flow of imported books.

The lack of good dictionaries of the trade has long been regretted by book trade historians and librarians. Such a work has been compiled by M. Pollard for the period up to 1800 and was published by the Bibliographical Society in the year 2000. The appendix here [in the original thesis, but not printed in this version] provides a dictionary for the period 1801–1850 and is assembled on the same bibliographical principles. It includes all persons in any way concerned with the manufacture, sale and distribution of print in its varying forms in the city of Dublin. Early estimates of the numbers involved at about 2,500 people and firms proved to be a gross under-estimate. The total is now about 5,000.

---

[8] B. Inglis, *The Freedom of the Press in Ireland 1784–1841*, London, 1954.

Chapter One: Publishing and Printing

IN TERMS OF THE LONG HISTORY of the book trade in Ireland, the early nineteenth century has been seen as a period of real decline, situated between the glorious and productive eighteenth century and the Irish literary renaissance at the end of the nineteenth century. Although publishing did decline greatly at the beginning of the century, there was a revival in the 1830s and 1840s in certain sectors of the market, especially those of school books and fiction publishing.

THE EIGHTEENTH-CENTURY BACKGROUND

Copyright had been established in Great Britain in 1709, but no equivalent legislation was passed by the Irish Parliament. The absence of a legal framework, apart from statutory protection of the Bible (the authorised version), the Book of Common Prayer, and government publications, had led to the development in eighteenth-century Dublin of a vigorous reprint trade supplying in large measure the domestic demand for fiction, drama, poetry, classical literature and school books.[1] Original publication was not very extensive. M. Pollard notes: 'Even before the passing of the Copyright Act most writers preferred to publish in London — for the sake of reputation and the better circulation of their work among the discerning. After 1709 there was the compelling attraction of payment for copy.'[2]

In an essay presented to the Royal Irish Academy on 29 September 1796 William Preston remarked on the evils arising from the lack of Irish copyright protection:

[it] exposes to a certain loss, from piracy, the author of any original work, who shall publish it, at his own expense; and the greater the merit of the work, the more certainly will the author be exposed to this injury and damage .... It precludes all improvement in the typography of this country, with respect to correctness, or beauty of type. Should any printer, of taste and enterprise in his art, prepare an elegant and costly edition of any work, he is liable to have the sale of it mined, by a spurious and disgraceful republication.[3]

---

[1] The Dublin trade before 1800 has been examined in J. W. Phillips, *Bookselling and Printing in Dublin 1670–1800*, Dublin, 1998; R. C. Cole, *Irish Booksellers and English Writers 1740–1800*, London, 1986; M. Pollard, *Dublin's Trade in Books 1550–1800*, Oxford, 1989.

[2] Pollard, *Trade in Books*, p. 40.

[3] W. Preston, 'Essay on the natural advantages of Ireland', *Transactions of the Royal Irish Academy* IX (1803), p. 404.

Preston castigated the quality of production, 'the type and the paper of these publications are, in general, so execrable, and they are so miserably executed, in point of correctness, that they are a disgrace to the country'.[4] The bulk of the Dublin business was in reprinting in a format generally smaller than the original publication. This represented a saving in the quantity of paper used, and with the added advantage of not having to purchase copy, Dublin printers could price their output competitively.

There was, of course, original production of such things as works of local political controversy — the Wood's Halfpence debate in the 1720s, the money bills in the 1750s, tithes in the 1780s, and the proposed Union in the late 1790s. There was also publication of locally preached sermons and indeed some original publications can be found in almost every subject or literary genre. Publication was primarily for domestic consumption, although a substantial export trade developed in the 1780s and 1790s to the British colonies and the United States.[5]

The Dublin publishing trade went into a decline in the 1790s, caused partly by difficulties in paper supply.[6] Much of the Irish paper had up to the 1790s been supplied from France. The outbreak of war between England and France in 1793 disrupted this commerce. Taxes imposed on paper by the Irish Parliament in 1795 greatly increased costs. Indeed, the journeymen printers petitioning Parliament in 1796 against renewal of the paper duties claimed that their employment on editions for the American market had greatly decreased.[7] Nor were the journeymen printers the only ones to suffer. A very substantial proportion of books for the American market were exported fully bound; indeed it was claimed in 1795 that no unbound books were ever exported there.[8] The compilers of a report on the bookbinding trade in 1834 recalled that American orders for books employed 30 men up to 1800.[9] There had by then been a decline in the number of master printers, booksellers and stationers recorded in Wilson's *Dublin Directory* — from 118 in 1793 to 92 in 1799, but the publishing trade was quite vigorous at the end of the century. A search of the *ESTC* (*English Short-Title Catalogue*) done on 12 November 1999 for Dublin imprints dated 1800 produced a total of 653 items, though a few of these were undated items ascribed to 1800 for want of better information.

---

[4] Ibid., p. 405.
[5] Pollard, *Trade in Books*, pp. 139–44.
[6] Ibid., p. 145.
[7] *Journal of the House of Commons of Ireland* XVI, pp. 193–94.
[8] *Dublin Evening Post* 24 February 1795.
[9] Royal Irish Academy, MS 4.b.2, 'Reports on trades and manufactures [in] Dublin 1834', p. 184.

THE IMPACT OF THE COPYRIGHT ACT 1801

The Act of Union which came into effect on 1 January 1801 was followed a few months later by a Copyright Act, which came into effect on 2 July 1801. Ostensibly intended to put the publication of books in Ireland and Britain on an equal footing so far as the law was concerned, it had the effect of entirely undermining the basis on which the Irish trade had developed in the preceding century. The surviving publishing business was over the succeeding forty years the repeated object of dismissive comments which deplored both its lack of variety and its quality.

Writing towards the end of the second decade, R. Walsh observed that:

besides the injury the trade has sustained, great numbers who formerly were in the habit of reading are by this Act interdicted from doing so, as the books which once, by their comparative cheapness, were within their means of purchasing, cannot be procured. The printing business is therefore confined to devotional and moral tracts, which are paid for by charitable societies for gratuitous distribution — to printing hand-bills and playbills — to some half dozen newspapers, which are by no means remarkable, and to one or two middling magazines, which can scarcely maintain an ephemeral existence.[10]

He attributed some of the blame to the trade itself:

it is true, there is no encouragement for literary exertion in the Irish metropolis, because the cautious Dublin bookseller will run no risk in publishing an original work, however great its merit. It must first appear in London, or not at all.[11]

The post-Union timidity of Dublin publishers was already noted by S. Burdy in the advertisement to his poem *Ardglass*, which he published in Dublin in 1802. He remarked that:

as the little encouragement given (possibly for good reasons) by the booksellers here to Irish literature obliged him to publish his poems by subscription, he finds some satisfaction in reflecting, that the generality of subscribers were so kind as to offer themselves, without any solicitation, at least on his part, which made their favours still more acceptable.

The 266 subscribers took a total of 282 copies; Graisberry and Campbell printed 625 copies for him.[12]

STANDARDS OF DUBLIN PRINTING AND EDITION SIZES

On 13 October 1821 the Commissioners of Inquiry into the Collection and Management of the Revenue arising in Ireland interviewed William Wakeman, wholesale

---

[10] J. Warburton, J. Whitelaw, R. Walsh, *History of the City of Dublin*, London, 1818, v. 2, p. 1158.
[11] Ibid., pp. 1162–63.
[12] Graisberry and Campbell, Ledger 1797–1806, opening 44.

agent in Dublin for the London publishing house of Baldwin, Cradock and Joy, and also a bookseller in his own right. His comments are revealing:

Do you know anything of the printing of books here? — It is comparatively nothing in Ireland, except a description of Catholic books of a very cheap sort, which are sold at so low a rate, that they could not be printed in England for the same money, and also a few schoolbooks used exclusively in Ireland.

Is it increased or diminished? — Since the Act of Union it is almost annihilated; it was on the same footing as America previous to that time, and every book was reprinted here; but since the Copyright Act has been extended, that cannot now be done openly.[13]

In 1825 the journeymen printers complained in an open letter to the public on the state of the trade that:

the art of printing in this country, at no time prosperous, has been, for many years rapidly decaying under the withering influence of English monopoly. Before the extension of the Copyright Act to Ireland, the re-printing here, of works of a classical character, and of an acknowledged excellence immediately after their publication in London, was very considerable; and thus, an impetus was given to our trade and a tolerable fair price obtained for our labour; but since the introduction of that fatal measure, no Work of sterling merit has ever issued from the Press of Ireland — the brilliant productions of the prolific genius of her Sons have been executed by English capital and English Workmen; so that nothing is left for the degraded Press of this Country but Newspapers, Hand-bills, and such ephemeral Pamphlets as are only adapted to the opinion of the day and the circumstances of the place, and can be of no interest anywhere else.[14]

By 1842 a shift in perceptions can be seen in Carleton's preface to a new edition of his *Traits and Stories of the Irish Peasantry*; there is a sense there that a corner had been turned. Reflecting on the success of his work and regarding himself in terms of Irish publishing as a pioneer author, he wrote:

In truth until within the last ten or twelve years an Irish author never thought of publishing in his own country, and the consequence was that our literary men followed the example of our great landlords; they became absentees, and drained the country of its intellectual wealth precisely as the others exhausted it of its rents. Thus did Ireland stand in the singular anomaly of adding some of the most distinguished names to the literature of Great Britain, whilst she herself remained incapable of presenting anything to the world beyond a schoolbook or pamphlet.[15]

---

[13] *Third Report of the Commissioners of Inquiry into the Collection and Management of the Revenue arising in Ireland* (U.K. Parliamentary Papers 822. XIII. p. 1219), p. 15.

[14] *Saunders's Newsletter*, 2 April 1825.

[15] W. Carleton, *Traits and Stories of the Irish Peasantry*, Dublin, 1842, vol. 1, p. v.

The Dublin journeyman printers had, it seems, a high regard for Carleton's contribution. On the occasion of a theatre benefit night being organised for him in May 1841, a meeting of the Dublin Typographical Provident Society resolved:

that to our knowledge Mr. Carleton has been studiously anxious to print and publish in his own country, and that he has uniformly abided by that resolution all his various works having been invariably printed and published in our own capital; that the great success of Mr. Carleton's works has wiped a stain off the taste and judgement of the country, by showing that works of genius can be equally well printed at home as abroad, and also be highly appreciated by Irishmen, and that he has consequently conferred great advantage upon all those who are employed in the useful mechanical arts, by the aid of which such works are brought out … that we feel ourselves called upon to support him in his coming benefit.[16]

The complaint about the standards of production, mentioned by Preston and implied in the resolutions of the journeymen printers mentioned above, persisted through the whole period. The London publishers were also dismissive. Darton and Harvey wrote to Mary Leadbeater on 5 January 1809 about a proposed publication which she contemplated having printed in Dublin, saying that they would take twenty-five copies of it unseen, 'but in general the form and manner of printing books in Ireland are not calculated for the meridian of London', and suggested that she sell them the rights to print for the English market.[17] Longman and Co. wrote to Richard Milliken offering the option of a share in Henry Grattan's *Speeches* which were being edited by his son, 'Mr. G. wishes to have the work printed in Dublin, stating that it will not be in his power to arrange so as to have the printing carried on in London. We need not tell you that it is almost impossible to have a handsome book printed in Dublin either as to paper or type: at least we have never seen such'.[18] Even as late as 1850 the *Irishman* newspaper carried an article decrying the 'importations from England, which are in the habit of being palmed off upon an unsophisticated public, by Anglo-Irish booksellers, as specimens of Irish manufacture.' According to the article the pretext for this was a complaint that Irish booksellers 'were unable to produce standard works of value, in a style worthy of the patronage of the public'; in fact, the writer asserts, 'Irishmen are willing to encourage native talent, but they require to be guarded against the petty chicanery and money grubbing practices of the aforesaid Anglo-Irish booksellers.' He then goes on to praise the typographic excellence, accuracy and general manner of getting up of two books published by James Duffy.[19]

---

[16] *Freeman's Journal,* 13 May 1841.
[17] NLI MSS 19,082.
[18] Longman Archive I, 101, no. 44, Reading University Library.
[19] *The Irishman,* 16 Feb 1850.

Wakeman and Carleton were broadly correct in their assertions. Publishing did decline in quantity and in the first thirty years was heavily slanted in the direction of religious controversy and education, with some local politics and minor verse thrown in. In fact, an auspicious start to the century had been made with the publication of the Dublin Society's series of county surveys. In 1801 the surveys of Queen's County, King's County, Wicklow, Monaghan and Dublin were each printed in an edition of 150 copies, with a further 100 copies of the Dublin survey being printed later.[20] The evident success of these is reflected in the edition size of 250 copies for the surveys of Leitrim, Down, Cavan, Mayo, Donegal and Sligo in 1802.[21] An improvement in the market is suggested by an order for 750 copies for the Armagh survey in 1804.[22]

Graisberry and Campbell's ledger shows continuing strong demand for books after 1801. One of their chief customers, Patrick Wogan, commissioned works mainly in the educational, religious and literary fields. Between 1801 and 1806 Graisberry and Campbell produced fifty-one titles for him. His sales of mathematical books must have been very steady, for he commissioned an edition of 4,000 copies of E. Voster, *Arithmetic* in 1799, a further edition of 5,000 copies in 1802, and in 1806 an edition of 2,000 copies of a *Key to Gough's Practical Arithmetic*.[23] Geometry was understandably less in demand than arithmetic, but an edition of 1,500 copies was completed in 1803.[24] Latin language primers were still in heavy demand, and his edition of W. Lily, *Rules Construed* was of 6,000 copies.[25] French was less popular, although 2,000 copies of French tables were needed in 1801, and 3,000 of M. A. Porny, *Grammatical Exercises* in 1803.[26]

One courtesy book, *Principles of Politeness*, did well. An edition of 5,000 in 1802 was followed by another of 3,500 in 1805.[27] Religious works were particularly good business. An order of 6,000 copies of a *Catechism* in 1799 was followed by an order for a *General Catechism* in 8,000 copies in 1801, and an order for 10,000 copies of Mr Reilly's *Catechism* in 1802.[28] He commissioned 4000 copies of the *New Testament* (Douai Version) in 1803 and 1,500 Missals in 1804.[29]

---

[20] Graisberry and Campbell Ledger 1797–1806 opening 58.
[21] Ibid., opening 60.
[22] Ibid., opening 107.
[23] Ibid., openings 10, 70, 131.
[24] Ibid., opening 93.
[25] Ibid., opening 131.
[26] Ibid., openings 4, 71.
[27] Ibid., openings 70, 130.
[28] Ibid., opening 10.
[29] Ibid., openings 71, 93.

Wogan also had a market in literature. What is noticeable in Graisberry and Campbell's ledger is the comparative rarity of novel and play printing after 1801 compared with the earlier years. Between 1801 and 1806 Wogan only commissioned one play, R. B. Sheridan, *The Rivals* in a substantial edition of 1,500 copies.[30] In fiction he ordered 1,000 copies of T. Holcroft, *Tales of the Castle* in 1801, and 500 copies of *Amosina* in April 1803, the latter apparently the first edition.[31] Milton appears twice in his list with 1,250 copies of *Paradise Lost* in 1802 and 5,000 copies of *Comus* in 1806.[32] Other substantial editions of poetry were M. G. Lewis, *Tales of Wonder* in 750 copies, and W. Cowper, *Poems* in 1,000 copies, both in 1805.[33]

Graisberry and Campbell were the printers of the official account of Emmet's rising, being commissioned to produce 6,000 copies of H. B. Code, *The Insurrection of 1803*, while Sir Richard Musgrave ordered 1,000 copies of his *Observations on the Remonstrance of the Rev. Peter O' Neill, P.P. of Ballymacoda in the County of Cork.*[34] The trials following Emmet's rising resulted in more business. The firm loyalist John Exshaw commissioned editions of 750 copies of the separate trials of three of Emmet's associates John Begg, Henry Howley, and Dennis Lambert Redmond.[35] These figures, though reasonably large, are insignificant compared with those for a civil case heard in Ennis Crown Court on 27 July 1804. The Marquess of Headfort was sued by the Rev. Charles Massy for the heinous crime of criminal conversation with Mrs Massy. The cuckolded husband sought £40,000 for his injuries; the fact was proved and he was awarded £10,000. By 20 August an edition of 1,000 copies of *An Account of the Trial* was printed off for Matthew Neary Mahon. It was quickly exhausted and a second edition of 1000 copies was completed on 1 September. There was a charge of £2 15s 1½d to pay six men for working on it by candle light, presumably through the night. Five days later a third edition of 1,000 copies was produced.[36]

The publishing output of another contemporary press, the Dublin University Press, was tiny by comparison. During R. E. Mercier's tenancy of the press from 1801 to May 1807 no more than six books were published.[37] His successors, Graisberry and Campbell, who were tenants until 1820, produced thirty-one works in that period — of which over 80 per cent were text books for students.[38] The Dublin University Press published comparatively little in the early years of Ruth Graisberry's

---

[30] Ibid., opening 70.
[31] Ibid., openings 57, 71.
[32] Ibid., openings 79, 131.
[33] Ibid., opening 130.
[34] Ibid., openings 100, 101.
[35] Ibid., opening 101.
[36] Ibid., opening 111.
[37] V. Kinane, *A History of the Dublin University Press 1734–1976*, Dublin, 1994,. pp. 79, 83.
[38] Ibid., p. 89.

tenancy from 1822 to 1842, but in 1827 one of her journeymen M. H. Gill bought a half share in the business, paying £219 19s 1½d for the printing equipment and £138 for his share in the printed stock. In 1837 he bought out the remainder of her share for £362 0s 10½d and an annuity of £100 per annum for the goodwill.[39] Under Gill's direction the Dublin University Press became much more active, publishing twelve books between 1827 and 1831. Following Ruth Graisberry's death in 1842 Gill became printer to the University. Although primarily a printer he moved into publishing with the acquisition of James McGlashan's interests in 1856.

His entrepreneurial spirit was in evidence soon after he became a partner of Ruth Graisberry. He made a proposal to Trinity College to print 10,000 copies of *The Book of Common Prayer* in 32mo.[40] His letter to C. R. Elrington cited the example of other universities printing prayer books and deplored the lost commercial opportunities. He urged that the trade in the book be open to all booksellers. He had sounded out various city booksellers of whom one, W. Curry, Jun. and Co., had at once ordered 2000 copies, and he had in hand orders for one third of the proposed edition. A postscript announced the order by Westley and Tyrrell of another 2000 copies. All that was wanting was the courage to take the initiative and a proper distribution network. Nothing came of the proposal. The lack of a distribution network had greatly hindered earlier publication. The College policy of dealing only with one bookseller — and not on standard trade terms — was castigated in the *Christian Examiner* in 1828.[41]

EDUCATIONAL AND RELIGIOUS PUBLISHING

The business of education publishing became of great importance from the second decade of the century when charitable societies interested themselves in distribution. The foremost of these, the Society for Promoting the Education of the Poor of Ireland (Kildare Place Society) began to issue moral works in 1816 and more directly didactic ones in 1822. A first edition of 10,000 copies of their *Dublin Reading Book* was exhausted by 1823 when a second edition of 50,000 copies was ordered.[42] When Charles Bardin, literary assistant to the Society was examined by the Commissioners on Education in Ireland on 2 December 1824 he claimed sales of 65,000 copies of *Elizabeth* (abridged from Cottin) since 1817; 60,000 copies of Aesop's *Fables* since April 1817; 30,000 copies of Captain Cook's *Voyages* produced since April 1820. He

---

[39] Ibid., p. 103.
[40] TCD MUN/P/1/1581–1582, cited in V. Kinane, op. cit., p. 105.
[41] *The Christian Examiner* VI (1828), pp. 420–23.
[42] *First Report of Commissioners of Inquiry on Education in Ireland* (UK Parliamentary Papers 1825. XII. p. 581), p. 465.

also claimed that there was a huge demand from the public for sensational literature, *The Shipwrecks of the Alceste and the Medusa* being among the most popular.[43] The figures for sales from the Society's Repository in Kildare Street (which opened in November 1817) were enormous. In the first six months until 4 May 1818 they sold 50,311 cheap books.[44] Between 4 May 1818 and 4 January 1819 a further 42,611 and in the twelve months ending 4 January 1820 an enormous 123,753.[45] But these were, designedly, cheap books. The receipts from the sales were quite small. Sales of cheap books and school books brought in £418 0s 2½d by May 1818; £517 17s 7d by January 1819; £958 8s 9½d by January 1820.[46] The Society continued to flourish as a major school book publisher until the early 1830s.[47]

While the success in sales terms of the Society's works is indisputable, their final destination was not always the intended one. By 1819 there were reports of the books being given new title leaves by booksellers who bought in sheets, and also of their being sold in Scotland.[48] Their success may have been due in part to the strenuous efforts made to avoid religious controversy. The books emphasise the merit of good behaviour, thrift, sobriety and hard work.[49]

Societies distributing Testaments and other religious works were prominent. With the assistance of the Association for Discountenancing Vice, Whitley Stokes published a parallel Irish and English text of the Gospel of St Luke and the Acts of the Apostles in an edition of two thousand copies in 1799.[50] It was not a huge success being advertised seven years later in his *Observations on the Necessity of Publishing the Scriptures in the Irish Language*, a work in which Stokes made the claim that an edition of 3000 copies of the Catechism in Irish had been printed in Dundalk. The Hibernian Baptist Corresponding Society, founded in 1814, decided to establish schools for teaching exclusively through the Irish language and it published an Irish and English spelling book in an edition of 2000 copies at 3½d a copy.[51] The Hibernian Bible Society distributed free 1927 Bibles, 14,912 Testaments, 20,680 *Spelling Books* no.1 and 19,295 *Spelling Books* no.2 between 1809 and 1815. In the same

[43] Ibid. (pp. 580–81), pp. 464–65.

[44] Society for the Promotion of the Education of the Poor of Ireland, *Sixth Report*. Dublin, 1818, p. 22.

[45] Society for the Promotion of the Education of the Poor of Ireland, *Seventh Report*. Dublin, 1819. p. 26; *Eighth Report*. Dublin, 1820, p. 26.

[46] Society for the Promotion of the Education of the Poor of Ireland, *Sixth Report*. Dublin, 1818, p. 28; *Seventh Report*. Dublin, 1819. p. 30; *Eighth Report*. Dublin, 1820, p. 26.

[47] H. Hislop, 'The Kildare Place Society 1811–1831: An Irish experiment in popular education', Trinity College Dublin Ph.D. thesis 1990. pp. 854–64; 883–917.

[48] Kildare Place Society Book Sub-Committee, no. 12, 52.

[49] For a discussion of these tracts see N. Ó Ciosáin, *Print and Popular Culture in Ireland, 1750–1850*. London, 1997, pp. 142–45.

[50] W. Stokes, *Observations on the Necessity of Publishing the Scriptures in the Irish Language*, Dublin, 1806, p. 6.

[51] Warburton et al., *Dublin*, 1818, pp. 876–78.

period it sold at reduced prices 55 Bibles, 885 Testaments, 8,812 *Spelling Books* no. 1 and 8,220 *Spelling Books* no. 2.[52]

The most active society at the beginning of the century was the Association for Discountenancing Vice, and Promoting the Knowledge and Practice of the Christian Religion. Between its foundation in 1792 and 1816 it distributed 'at very reduced prices, nearly 50,000 Bibles, 200,000 Testaments and prayer books, and one million of other religious and moral books and tracts, at an expense of almost £25,000'.[53] The Association's bookseller in 1825, William Watson, grandson of one of the founders and the third generation to enjoy a good living from it, gave evidence to the Commissioners on Education in Ireland that not all the works were produced in Dublin, that the Association was obliged to order Bibles, Prayer books and Testaments from the King's Printer in England and (principally) Scotland, but that the tracts were printed locally.[54] At an earlier date the Association is recorded as having commissioned two editions of the Bible in Dublin in 1801 and 1809 of 15,000 copies each.[55] Why the supply should have failed later is unclear, for in mid-June 1816 the King's Printers in Dublin, G. Grierson and J. R. Power, advertised that they had an edition of 20,000 copies of an octavo Bible and 10,000 copies of an 18mo Prayer book in the press.[56] The last main Protestant society, the Hibernian Bible Society, seems only to have acted as a distribution agent for English published Bibles and Testaments, of which 160,000 were distributed between 1809 and 1816.[57]

The Roman Catholics were slow to enter the field. It was not until 1820 that the Society for circulating the Roman Catholic version of the New Testament entered an agreement with Richard Coyne for the printing of 20,000 copies of the New Testament.[58] W. J. Battersby wrote to C. D. Bellew on 26 October 1825 sending him a few books and his catalogue, and commented: 'I agree with you that the Biblicals are industrious in disseminating their pestiferous tracts and the Catholics are grossly negligent in counteracting their efforts. I have at my own personal risk published the works you see marked in the catalogue'.[59] In 1827 the Catholic Society for the Diffusion of Useful Knowledge throughout Ireland (The Catholic Book Society) invited tenders for printing 30,000 Roman Catholic catechisms, and 10,000 of Bishop Richard Challoner, *Grounds of the Catholic Doctrine*.[60] The Society,

---

[52] Ibid., p. 879.
[53] Ibid., p. 893.
[54] *First Report of the Commissioners of Inquiry on Education in Ireland* (U.K. Parl. Papers 1825. XII. p. 498), p. 382.
[55] Warburton et al., *Dublin*, 1818, p. 894.
[56] *Saunders's Newsletter*, 19 June 1816.
[57] Warburton et al., *Dublin*, 1818, p. 897.
[58] *Saunders's Newsletter*, 7 January 1820.
[59] Bellew Papers, NLI MSS 31993 (5).
[60] *Dublin Morning Post*, 23 May 1827.

established in March 1827, had a management committee of twenty-one clergymen who rapidly recognised their incapacity in business and employed W. J. Battersby as their agent.[61] Within a year 100,000 copies of religious books had been distributed. These included works clearly aimed at adults including R. Manning, *The Shortest Way to End Disputes about Religion*, J. N. Grou, *Exposition of The Lord's Prayer*, and W. Gahan, *History of the Old and New Testaments*; their stock in hand included 10,000 *Spelling Books* in four parts and sets of spelling and reading tablets.[62] By the end of 1835 the Society claimed to have printed or published about 5 million books which circulated in Ireland, Great Britain, America and the British settlements.[63] By the end of 1837 it boasted a figure of 6 million.[64] These are certainly impressive figures, but the cash turnover was comparatively small; sales from March 1827 to June 1829 were £3,288 0s 8d. and from June 1829 to 23 November 1838, £17,740 2s 1d.[65]

Its prime objective was 'to procure and circulate books containing a clear exposition of the doctrine and discipline of the Roman Catholic Church, with satisfactory refutations of the errors of the time', but it also proposed that 'in order to give additional facilities to the education of the poor, books of elementary instruction are to be provided for the use of schools'.[66] In the early years of the national school system, a number of the Society's books were, with minor modifications, approved for use by the Commissioners of National Education.[67] A substantial list of the books was published in 1841.[68] The assets of the Society were transferred to Battersby in 1845, and he continued business until the 1850s.[69]

The Catholic Book Society of Ireland for the Gratuitous Distribution of Religious Books, founded in 1835 had a briefer existence; W. J. Battersby was its honorary secretary. In the year 13 December 1835 to 13 December 1836 it distributed 8,631 books to the value of £170 19s 10d and in 1837 10,064 books to the value of £296 3s 7d.[70] Its existence is not recorded after 1840. Another society, The Catholic Society of Ireland, for Promoting the Dissemination of Moral and Religious Books amongst the Humbler Classes of Catholics, based at 17 Arran Quay, published by subscription in 1840 a second edition of J. Reeve, *Practical Discourses on the Perfections and*

---

[61] S. Griffin, 'The Catholic Book Society and its role in the emerging system of national education 1824–1834', *Irish Educational Studies*, 11 (1992), 85, 87.

[62] *First Report of the Catholic Book Society*, Dublin, 1828, pp. 12–13.

[63] W. J. Battersby, ed., *A Complete Catholic Registry, Directory ... for ... 1836*, Dublin, [1835], p. 52.

[64] W. J. Battersby, ed., *A Complete Catholic Directory ... for ... 1838*, Dublin, [1837], p. 305.

[65] W. J. Battersby, ed., *A Complete Catholic Registry, directory ... for ... 1840*, Dublin, [1839], pp. 268–70.

[66] Printed leaflet announcing the Society's aims quoted in S. Griffin, 'The Catholic Book Society', p. 86.

[67] Ibid., pp. 89–90.

[68] W. J. Battersby, ed., *A Complete Catholic Directory ... for ... 1842*, Dublin, [1841], pp. 433–44.

[69] W. J. Battersby, ed., *A Complete Catholic Registry, Directory ... for ... 1846*, Dublin, [1845], p. 543.

[70] W. J. Battersby, ed., *A Complete Catholic Registry, Directory ... for ... 1837*, Dublin, [1836], pp. 176–77; W. J. Battersby, ed., *A Complete Catholic Registry, Directory ... for ... 1838*, Dublin, [1837], p. 460.

Wonderful Works of God, with 643 subscribers for 1,177 copies. The list includes comparatively few of the humbler classes — apart from 47 privates, corporals and sergeants of the 58th Regiment.

The real success in school book publishing was in the series produced under the direction of the Commissioners of National Education in Ireland. Their task upon formation in 1831 was to select and publish a series of elementary works acceptable to all denominations.[71] As late as 1851 they continued to sanction for use in their schools books published by private enterprise as well as the ones they commissioned.[72] From 1838 the Commissioners' books were printed following public tenders for the work.[73] The schoolbooks were soon a success on the export market. Writing to Edward Bulwer on 3 July 1835 Owen Rees, of Longman and Co. noted he had raised the matter of the imports with Mr Powlett Thomson 'as one of the Ministry'; Rees implied that the books were being sold under cost.[74] By 1850 these Irish books had achieved a major export market to England, supplying 25 per cent of the books used by the English Council on Education.[75]

The system of competitive tender for printing kept educational book prices down. The contract which Grierson took in 1850 was over 60 per cent lower than the previous one.[76] This was only made possible by special arrangements made by Grierson with the DTPS permitting him to have eight apprentices; that members of the Dublin Typographical Provident Society would work overtime 'on urgent occasions' at the ordinary rate of 6d per hour; that members could be placed on the establishment for a single day [the norm being a week]; that blank pages were to go to the credit of the house not the men; and that proofing could be done by men on the establishment.[77] The employment involved was considerable and the DTPS had a vested interest in seeing an employer like Grierson who employed union labour being able to undercut the previous holder of the contract, Alexander Thom, who did not. It was claimed in November 1850 that thirty men were on average employed by Grierson, mostly on the establishment.[78]

---

[71] *Statement of the Commissioners of National Education in Ireland, Relative to the Compilation, Printing, Publication, and Sale of National School Books*, cited in J. Goldstrom, 'The correspondence between Lord John Russell and the publishing trade', *Publishing History*, xx (1986), pp. 5–59.

[72] Ibid., p. 18.

[73] Ibid., p. 21.

[74] Longman Archive 1/102 no. 213 N. [draft].

[75] Ibid., p. 11.

[76] Ibid., p. 47.

[77] DTPS Committee Minutes, 16 January 1850.

[78] DTPS General Meeting, 2 November 1850.

SUBSCRIPTION PUBLISHING

The practice of publishing by subscription, well established in the eighteenth century, continued to be used, although it diminished in importance after 1820. As a method of publication it had the merit of testing the size of the market and of providing working capital by the requirement of advance payment of part of the price. A total of 180 subscription lists for 178 books have been identified in the period.

TABLE 1.1: DUBLIN PRINTED SUBSCRIPTION
LISTS IN FIVE-YEAR PERIODS

1801–1805	28
1806–1810	26
1811–1815	32
1816–1820	17
1821–1825	14
1826–1830	12
1831–1835	16
1836–1840	14
1841–1845	15
1846–1850	6

TABLE 1.2: SUBSCRIPTION LISTS BY SUBJECT

Horse racing	50	Music	4
Poetry	30	School books	4
Roman Catholic literature	28	Architecture/building	2
History	18	French language/literature	2
Church of Ireland literature	9	Military	2
Travel, geography	5	Plays	2
Business	4	Periodicals	2
Fiction	5	Biblical theology	1
Law	4	Irish language	1
Miscellaneous literature	4	Medicine	1
Miscellaneous	1	Science	1

The two surprising features of the subject matter of these books are the number concerned with horse racing and the number of Roman Catholic books. The horse racing is easily explained. The annual *Irish Racing Calendar* had a subscription list for each year which in 1810 ran to 1561 names.[79] Roman Catholic literature is more interesting. Of the twenty-eight Roman Catholic books, nineteen were published in the period 1801–1815, making 22 per cent of the total of eighty-five books published by subscription in this period. Although there was not a concerted programme of Roman Catholic publication at this time, this strong showing in subscribers' lists may indicate a growing confidence among Catholic clergy and laity. Of these books, however, only three appear to be original publications: J. C. Keenan, *The Standard of Christianity* published in 1805; an elegy on the Rev. Arthur O'Leary; and B. Murphy, *Sermons for Every Sunday*, published in 1808, in addition to the translation of J. N. Grou, *The School of Christ* published in 1801. In scale these subscription publications vary enormously. At one end is A. Butler, *The Lives of the Fathers*, Dublin, 1802 in six volumes 8°, and B. Murphy, *Sermons for Every Sunday*, Dublin, 1808 in two volumes 8°. At the other extreme is A. Butler, *The Life of the Illustrious Doctor of the Church, Saint Augustin*, Dublin, 1813 which is little better than a chapbook.

Most of these Catholic books show strong clerical support from all around the country, there being particularly heavy subscriptions for A. Butler, *The Lives of the Fathers* (Dublin, 1802), with 529 subscribers for 1065 copies including also strong trade support, Hugh Fitzpatrick the printer of the work taking 200 sets, J. Haly in Cork 100 sets and the exiled Patrick Byrne in Philadelphia 25 sets; B. Murphy, *Sermons for Every Sunday* was an even better seller with 1918 subscribers for 2035 copies. This list shows evidence of considerable organisation as subscribers are listed alphabetically under the centres where the subscriptions were taken up. At the lower end of the scale only 144 subscribers paid for 207 copies of J. N. Grou, *The School of Christ* and only 90 subscribers came forward for King Henry VIII, *Defence of the Seven Sacraments* paying for 245 copies. The three Catholic booksellers most concerned in these publications were H. Fitzpatrick, R. Coyne and J. Coyne. Among the Roman Catholic books, one Mrs West's *Select Translation of the Beauties of [J. B.] Massillon* (Dublin, 1812) was not published primarily as a religious work. It attracted 161 subscribers for 181 copies and, significantly, it carried an advertisement for Mrs West's school for young ladies which had just opened.

The number of subscribers in volumes of poetry and fiction seems to have depended very much upon the exertions of the author and his/her friends. M. Leadbeater received nationwide support for her *Poems* (Dublin, 1808) but she had the advantage of strong Quaker support. The 659 subscribers for Patrick Donnelly, *Love of Britain* (Dublin, 1824) came almost entirely from a twelve-mile radius of his home village of Athboy in Co. Meath. J. Mackey, *Compositions in Verse* (Dublin, 1819) had very heavy Limerick and Clare representation among the 387 subscribers. The most

---

[79] F. A. D'Arcy, *Horses, Lords and Racing Men the Turf Club 1790–1990*, Dublin, 1991, p. 40.

successful of M. Archdeacon's novels, *Everard: an Irish Tale of the Nineteenth Century* attracted 538 subscribers of whom no fewer than 449 came from west of the Shannon, predominantly Co. Sligo.

The four books on commercial arithmetic published by subscription all met with strong support. The most narrowly focussed one, P. J. Hodgson, *The Commercial Revenue Guide for Transacting Business in the Port of Dublin*, Dublin, 1801 had 453 subscribers for 510 copies; W. Jennings, *Jenning's Book-Keeping, Adapted to Modern Practice*, Dublin, 1802 had 517 subscribers for 630 copies; P. Deighan, *A Complete Treatise of Arithmetic*, Dublin, 1804, 949 subscribers for 996 copies including strong schoolmaster support; and P. Comins, *The Science of Commerce*, Dublin, 1814, 1,307 subscribers for 1423 copies. The latter sold at a guinea a copy and must have been a most rewarding undertaking.

One publisher who saw the potential for subscription publishing was John Jones who published at least six works in this way between 1802 and 1816. He had shown a sound commercial sense in reprinting in 1801 J. Antes, *Observations on the Manners and Customs of the Egyptians*, which had been first published in London in 1800. He updated it to include an account of the Battle of the Nile and details of the British Expedition to Egypt in 1801, illustrating it with engravings. In 1802 he published J. Brown, *A Historical, Geographical, Chronological, Etymological, and Critical Dictionary of the Holy Bible*, with 664 subscribers for 1,065 copies, and in it advertised for subscribers for a proposed edition of J. Bunyan, *Pilgrim's Progress* which was published in 1802. He drew attention in his preface to his carefulness, both bibliographical and theological, having:

after the most sedulous industry, collected a variety of former editions of this work, for the express purpose of offering to the Irish nation, a book, calculated in all respects to ensure public patronage: nor would he be sufficiently candid, did he not here avow, that in this undertaking, he has carefully attended to the most seasonable and salutary counsel of several divines.

Two years later he published E. Ledwich, *The Antiquities of Ireland* with distribution arrangements made with named booksellers in London, Bath, Bristol and Liverpool. It was also a commercial success with 527 subscribers for 849 copies in a list that reflected strong trade support. He included in it advertisements for four other works to be published by subscription. He claimed to be well advanced in preparations for producing W. Smellie's translation of Buffon's *Natural History*, to be published in six volumes 8°, at half a guinea a volume in boards on superfine wove paper with over 300 copper plates. Nearly one hundred of these had been completed and could be inspected at his shop. He intended to print it as soon as he procured 500 names and was prepared to publish it in shilling numbers, parts, volumes or sets as required by the readers. P. Deighan's *Treatise on Arithmetic* was to have slightly less lavish production, to be printed on good paper, and type for 11s 4½d, in boards.

Potential subscribers were offered two inducements: if they paid the entire price in advance the book would be supplied handsomely bound in calf and lettered, and the subscribers' names and addresses were to be printed as 'encouragers to an Irish author', and the book delivered on 1 June 1804; all subscribers would be given an *Abstract System of Bookkeeping*, also *A Complete System of Algebra*, free as an appendix to the book which would cost non-subscribers 6s 6d. The 'free gift' sounds remarkably like dead stock in the warehouse.

The third proposed work, E. Teap, *Il Precettore, or the Complete Assistant and Constant Monitor of Juvenile Performers on the Piano-forte*, again required 500 subscribers before publication. It was to consist of more than 24 folio pages of text and 17 plates of examples. The price of half a guinea was, unusually, not to be paid in advance but upon delivery and subscriptions were being taken up by most booksellers and music shops in the United Kingdom. The last work advertised was for a two-volume continuation of Gordon, *Terraquea*, called for because of popular demand for the first four volumes. The price to subscribers for the whole six volumes would amount to £1 11s 6d, and to non-subscribers £2 2s, with subscriptions being taken in at Jones's shop and other booksellers in Dublin. These advertisements were typical of the conditions on which subscription publication was promoted, the usual means of promotion being a publicity sheet showing the quality of the proposed book and newspaper advertising. Jones's advertisement at the foot of his stocklist in Ledwich's book emphasised his confidence in his ability to produce work as good as that done in England, to which end he had ordered new type and prepared an apparatus for hot-pressing the sheets when printed. Jones was also the promoter of subscriptions to J. Gordon, *A New History of Ireland*. This was, at the time of advertisement, being printed in London but the author wished 'to accommodate his country men with a cheap edition' to be available on a very fine paper at £1 2s 9d and on less fine paper at 17s 4d. The author had undertaken to stay in Dublin to correct the proofs.[80]

When P. Deighan, *A Complete Treatise on Arithmetic*, appeared it included proposals for subscription publishing of two further works. *A Treatise on Bookkeeping* was to be on superfine paper in large octavo at 10s 6d; those paying the price in advance would receive their copies bound; those paying on delivery would receive it in boards. Subscribers' names were to be printed 'as encouragers of literary merit, and friends to their country'. The second work proposed, *A General Treatise on Algebra and Fluxions* was to require 600 subscribers and was to be brought out in fortnightly parts at 1s 1d each. A particularly smarmy appeal to the public claimed it

---

[80] *Hibernian Journal*, 18 June 1804.

contained many matters 'absolutely necessary for every lover of learning and the useful arts' and that the subscriber 'may hold the book when the detached sheets are bound together, as a great acquisition to himself and posterity'.

Although subscription publication is insignificant in the total scale of works published, the best produced of them gave an opportunity to printers to display their talent for design and quality of typography. While many of the lists are admitted to be defective, and some works published by subscription never had lists, the names given provide the basis for construction of a database of the reading public with money to spend.[81]

There is little sense of sustained large-scale publishing enterprise in the first thirty years of the century. *Saunders's Newsletter* on 10 March 1824 carried a report that a Joint-Stock Company had been formed 'within the last week' to print and publish books. The principals were respectable booksellers who planned to create a £50,000 company in shares of £50 preferably owned by active members of the book trade. According to a later report several meetings were held but the design came to nothing.[82]

An attempt of similar kind was organised by S. J. Machen in 1849. The proposal was to publish a 'series of improved Dublin trade editions of standard works to be published and sold by such of the trade as have taken shares in the work'.[83] The proposed first publication was Euripides, *Hecuba* with English notes, prologomena, and examination questions by G. B. Wheeler, a work which would have had an assured but small sale — certainly not calculated to make anyone's fortune. A week previously Machen had called a meeting of interested trade parties.[84]

The group of journalists associated with the *Comet* tried in 1831 to interest the public in a Political Tract Society.[85] They intended to combine this with the production of a weekly Sunday newspaper edited on 'principles of complete independence'. Their object was to instruct the people of Ireland in the elements of political knowledge to give them moral 'force' in relation to those who had an interest in keeping them in subjection. They proposed to reinforce the message of the fights and privileges of the people as the real foundation of the other orders of the constitution. The enterprise foundered.

---

[81] Frank Robinson of Avero Publication and the University of Newcastle-upon-Tyne is constructing a database including Irish subscription lists.
[82] *Freeman's Journal*, 14 October 1826.
[83] *Saunders's Newsletter*, 6 December 1849.
[84] Ibid., 29 November 1849.
[85] [T. Browne], *The Parson's Hornbook*, Dublin, 1831. Advertisement leaves bound with copy TCD Library OLS L-2-112 no. 4.

PUBLISHING IN THE 1840S

A project which had much more success was 'The Library of Ireland'. The impetus for the production of the series came from the Young Ireland party arising from a proposal by Charles Gavan Duffy.[86] The Young Irelanders had already had a conspicuous success with the *Nation* newspaper. The series was announced in an advertisement in the *Nation* 7 June 1845 as a means of supplying a 'National literature', to consist of monthly volumes at one shilling each. The publisher James Duffy noted that the series would 'require an immense circulation to enable the publisher to continue it', and urged all persons interested in Irish education and nationality to support it. Successive advertisements in the *Nation* continued in the weeks up to 1 July, the launching date for the first volume, T. McNevin, *The History of the Volunteers of 1782*. A triumphant note was added to the advertisement on 5 July: 'the whole edition of this volume was sold off in a few hours, but a new edition is now ready'. By 19 July the advertisement in the *Nation* claimed that the third edition was ready for delivery. The second volume in the series, *The Ballad Poetry of Ireland* edited by Charles Gavan Duffy, was an instant success. Published at the beginning of August 1845, the whole edition of several thousand copies was gone by 9 August, and the second edition was exhausted by 30 August.[87] Further volumes were produced over the succeeding eighteen months.

Figure 2. The distinctive typeface used for the mast-head of the hugely influential weekly *The Nation* since it was launched in 1842. Its first readers were informed that 'for the convenience of reading and binding THE NATION has been made up in a FOLIO shape, which looks small to eyes unfamiliar to it, but the public are requested to measure the sheet, before it is cut, with the largest of the Dublin weekly journals, to convince themselves that it is THE LARGEST PAPER EVER PUBLISHED IN IRELAND', and by 1845 its circulation was also breaking all records : *The Nation* (4 Oct. 1845). *Courtesy of the Royal Irish Academy Library.*

---

[86] C. G. Duffy, *Young Ireland*, London, 1880, p. 666; *The Nation*, 9 August 1845.
[87] Ibid., 30 August 1845.

Besides cashing in on the growing popular market for distinctly Irish literature, James Duffy became one of the foremost Catholic publishers in the city. His advertisement in the *Nation* on 4 October 1845 listing standard Catholic works and books relating to Ireland covered two and a half columns, of which one and a half were devoted to Catholic literature. Much of this consists of old favourites from the eighteenth century such as George Hay's *Sincere Christian*, works by Alban Butler, Richard Challoner and Robert Manning, and also many popular devotional manuals and a sprinkling of contemporary authors such as Nicholas Wiseman. He had distribution agents in London, Birmingham, Manchester, Liverpool and Glasgow, all cities with substantial Irish Catholic communities. Duffy went on to become after 1850 the major Irish publisher with this successful blend of nationalism and Catholicism.

If the writers associated with the *Nation* caught the contemporary mood to great profit, the way had been in some respects paved for them by some earlier writers, notably Charles Lever. His *Confessions of Harry Lorrequer* was a success in 1839 for the Dublin publishers W. Curry, Jun. and Co., to the extent that three prominent London publishers, Bentley, Colburn and Lardner, separately asked him for another novel in the same style.[88] He remained with Curry and Co. but was able to make a contract for his next book to be published in 12 to 20 numbers at £50 each. This was *Charles O'Malley, the Irish Dragoon*, also successful, which drew a renewed approach from Bentley offering £1000 for a new book in 12 numbers.[89] Curry and Co. outbid Bentley and contracted for a trilogy of novels, *Our Mess* providing for the payment to Lever of £100 for each monthly part, with Curry and Co. being entitled to the profit on the first 11,000 copies and equal sharing of any profits made on copies sold in excess of that number. Nearly 14,000 copies of the first part of the trilogy, *Jack Hinton*, were sold, issued between December 1841 and December 1842 in thirteen monthly numbers. As late as the spring of 1844 Routledge contracted to purchase 2000, though he only took 1500. The second work, *Tom Burke of Ours*, was produced in 22 numbers from early 1843 to the end of 1844. The contract was revised for the third part, *The O'Donohoe*, to provide for profit sharing to begin at 10,000 copies.

Sales for Lever's works slumped in November 1844 and shortly afterwards Curry and Co. went into bankruptcy.[90] The success of Lever's novels and the competence of Curry and Co. in publishing are amply proved by the approaches of the London publishers to Lever. Curry and Co. were also the publishers of *The Dublin University Magazine* which in the early 1840s was selling 4000 copies a month.[91] Downey notes

---

[88] E. Downey, *Charles Lever*, London, 1906. vol 1, p. 132.
[89] Ibid., p. 142.
[90] *Irish Equity Reports* XII (1850), pp. 382–92; Downey, *Lever*, 1906, pp. 196–241.
[91] Downey, *Lever*, 1906. vol. 1, p. 186.

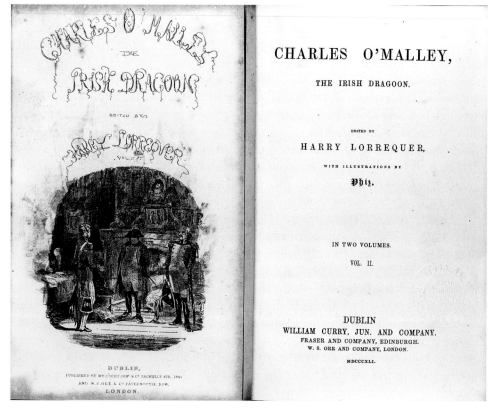

Figure 3. Frontispiece and title-page of the first edition of Charles Lever's classic *Charles O'Malley ...* (1841/2), published in Dublin by William Curry, leader of the revival in Irish book publishing in the 1830s. Publication here was hampered by loss of part of the manuscript in a fire at the printers. *Courtesy of the Royal Irish Academy Library.*

that Lever was repeatedly attacked in the *Nation* and it seems likely that his brand of fiction was a casualty of the changing sentiments in nationalist politics.[92] And this in turn may have dragged Curry down too.

Throughout this period there was a continual if small amount of scientific publication. The learned societies, the Dublin Society and the Royal Irish Academy, published their *Transactions*, the Dublin Society commissioning 250 copies and ceasing in 1810, the Royal Irish Academy commissioning 500 copies.[93] In medicine there were some long lived periodicals. The earliest of the medical periodicals, *The Dublin Medical and Physical Essays* was short lived, lasting only from March 1807 to June 1808 but *The Dublin Hospital Reports* were published between 1817 and 1830;

---

[92] Ibid., pp. 184–86.
[93] Graisberry and Campbell, Ledger 1797–1806, openings 45, 75.

The Dublin Journal of Medical and Chemical Science was founded in 1832 and lasted, with various changes of name, into the twentieth century. *The Dublin Medical Press* began in 1839 and continued until 1923, and *The Dublin Hospital Gazette* began in 1845 and finished in 1863.

Besides these periodicals there were individual works which also attracted an export market. John Murray wrote to Gilbert and Hodges on 6 January 1804: 'as there are no doubt many medical works published in Ireland, I should be very much obliged if you would avail yourself of the earliest opportunity of forwarding them to me'.[94] On 18 February 1804 he was enquiring about the cost of a supply of 100 copies of books (unidentified) by Lind and Arthur Clarke.[95] On 21 January 1806 he acknowledged receipt of 100 copies of R. Carmichael, *An Essay on the Effects of Carbonate of Iron upon Cancer*, of which he had already disposed of 35 copies. These are respectable sales, but the clear bestseller was R. Harrison, *The Dublin Dissector*, first published in 1827 which reached a fourth edition in 1835 (though the title page is dated 1836). Longman and Co. were offered, and had been on the point of ordering, 1000 copies of the work when they discovered it to be already on sale in Edinburgh while they still had stock of the third edition.[96]

There is no doubt that the Dublin publishing trade had recovered considerable vitality by the 1830s. While the literary output was comparatively limited, some of their authors, notably Lever and Lover enjoyed real success, but had their reputations in Ireland successfully damned by nationalist writers. The output of the latter, particularly in the 1840s, was a distinct commercial success. But behind the literary swings of fashion there was a steadily growing amount of publishing in education, law, science, and theology.

JOBBING PRINTING

While books are the most obvious printed products to survive from the past, a major part of printing was jobbing work — notices, circulars, leases and other forms. The Dublin printing houses were either primarily jobbing houses, or newspaper offices, the latter doing little if any other work. The jobbing houses were versatile. When J. and J. Carrick moved from Bedford Row to 29 Bachelor's Walk in 1804, they claimed to have spared no expense:

to render their press a general, complete and expeditious medium of mercantile and public intelligence. They have imported likewise a quantity of new and beautiful type from the first foundry in England, and laid in a stock of fine papers for such publications as may require elegance of typography and ornament ... Advertisements, cards, auction and

---

[94] John Murray Archive, Letter book 1803–1823, p. 27.
[95] Ibid., p. 31.
[96] Longman Archive, 1/102 no.215 N [draft].

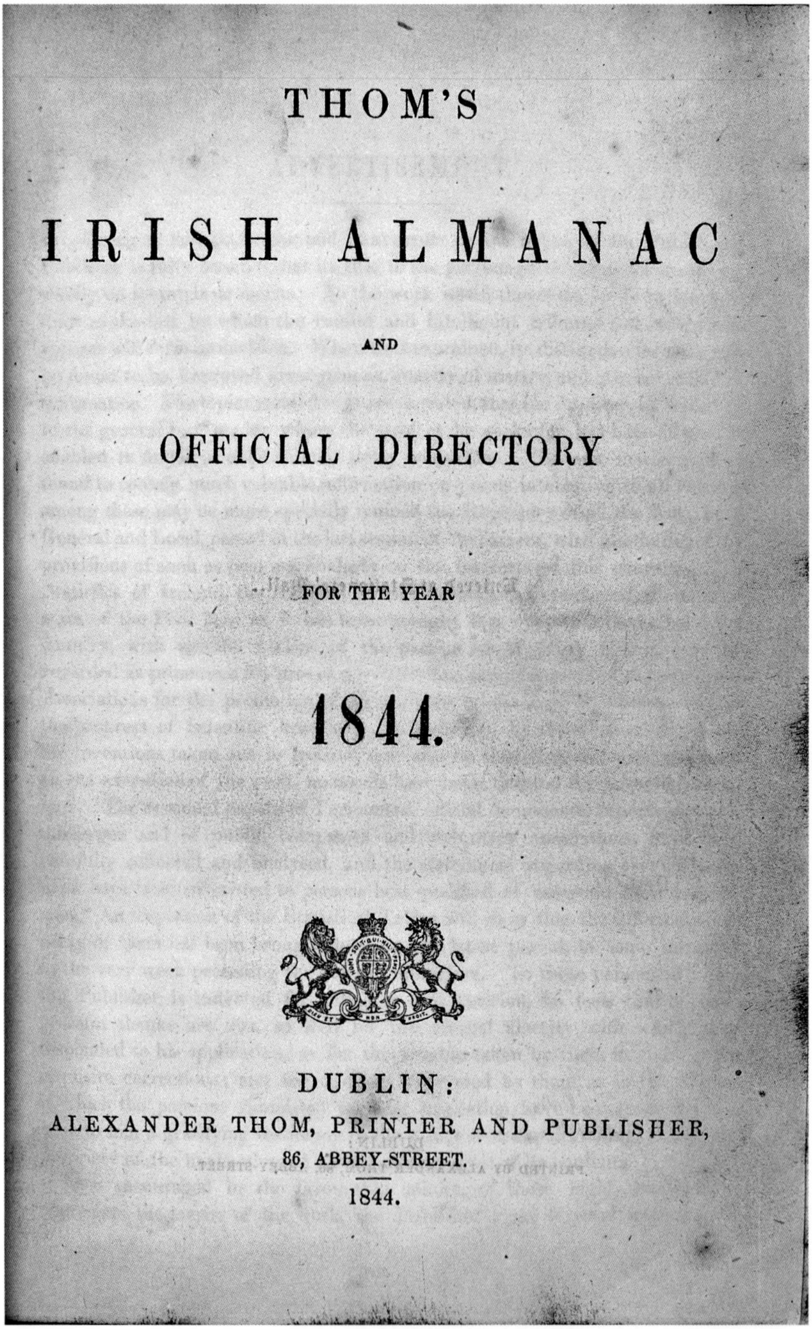

THOM'S

IRISH ALMANAC

AND

OFFICIAL DIRECTORY

FOR THE YEAR

1844.

DUBLIN:

ALEXANDER THOM, PRINTER AND PUBLISHER,
86, ABBEY-STREET.
1844.

Figure 4. Title-page of the most successful and enduring *Irish Almanac* on its first appearance in 1844, with the immigrant Scot Alexander Thom in Abbey St its long-time printer, publisher and principal compiler.
Courtesy of the Royal Irish Academy Library.

handbills, large posting bills, etc. worked off in a few hours without disappointment. Circular letters, mercantile receipts, shop bills, catalogues, &c, leases, rent rolls, ejectments, and legal, military and naval forms of every description executed with expedition and correctness on the same moderate terms as have rendered their office so remarkable.[97]

Such a range is reflected in the work done by Graisberry and Campbell for Matthew Neary Mahon in January 1805, which included

> 1000 copies of the sixth edition of *Intercepted Letter* [by J. W. Croker]
>
> 250 bills for the Wickham cruizer 8°
>
> 250 bills for the Buckingham cruizer 8°
>
> 200 Letters ruled for the Lawyers' Corps 4°
>
> 100 Bills for the sale of whiskey
>
> 250 *Observations on the Habeas Corpus Act*
>
> 1000 *Familiar epistles to Frederick E. Jones* 12° [by J. W. Croker]
>
> 1000 *Cutchacutoo* 12° [by J. W. Croker].[98]

Graisberry and Campbell's range of work went from the substantial volume of Sir Charles Coote, *General View of the Agriculture and Manufactures of the Queen's County* printed in July 1801, to producing 20 pairs of leases for A. B. King in January 1802, to printing 10,000 shop bills for Mr Andrews in February 1803.[99]

Most of the businesses were operating on a small scale with only a few presses. R. Power of Anglesea St advertised the contents of a printing office in 1821 consisting of two good presses fit for newspaper work with twelve pairs of cases for type.[100] J. and M. Woodmason had three presses when they were sold up by direction of the sheriffs in 1826.[101] George Folds of St Andrew St had three presses in 1843.[102] P. D. Hardy was operating on a much larger scale. The illustrations of his office in the *Dublin Penny Journal* 10 May 1834 show at least twelve composing frames, five hand presses and a machine press. He claimed that in 1835 he had employed 15 men regularly and given casual employment to a further 15 to 20 as well as having 7 or 9 apprentices.[103] J. S. Folds who was employed on a lot of educational printing in the late 1830s was thought to be employing 12 to 14 journeymen to work off forms of standing type.[104] In 1841 he gave evidence in the Court of Queen's Bench that in June

---

[97] *Hibernian Journal*, 14 November 1804.
[98] Graisberry and Campbell, Ledger 1797–1806, opening 123.
[99] Ibid., openings 58, 56, 40.
[100] *Saunders's Newsletter*, 24 September 1821.
[101] Ibid., 18 April 1826.
[102] Ibid., 20 July 1843.
[103] *Second Report from the Select Committee on Combinations of Workmen* (UK Parliamentary Papers 1837–1838. VIII. p. 363), p. 43.
[104] Ibid. (p. 418), p. 98.

1840 he had 24 journeymen and 5 apprentices working for him, and had intended to increase the number of apprentices.[105] At the time of his bankruptcy in 1845 he employed 25 journeymen.[106]

In November 1847 thirty-five journeymen employed in the Dublin University Press voted on a proposal to re-establish the DTPS as a separate body.[107] The larger employers of journeymen were generally the newspaper offices. In 1838 the *Evening Mail* employed nineteen journeymen and one apprentice.[108] On 1 November 1847 in the DTPS vote 29 members voted from the *Saunders's Newsletter* office, 22 from the *Evening Mail* office, 11 from the *Nation* and 11 from the *Evening Packet*.[109]

CHANGES IN PRINTING TECHNOLOGY

At the start of the nineteenth century the only available presses were wooden ones. The wooden common press had undergone little technical development in the previous four centuries beyond the substitution of a metal screw for a wooden one for raising and lowering the platen, a metal lever to turn the screw, and an improved method using a crank and straps for running the bed of the press in and out. The press was normally worked by a team of two men who took turns at beating i.e. inking the types, and pulling.[110] Because of the elasticity of the wooden structure and the fact that the head of the press was 'often packed up with elastic substances, such as pasteboard, or even cork', it was impossible to produce an even pressure over a large platen.[111] The necessarily small size of the platen ranged from 45–49 × 29–32 cm, and this required the pressman to make two pulls to a large forme.[112] Despite this it was accepted that the rate of output was 250 impressions per hour.[113]

About the year 1800 the first successful press to be made entirely of iron was devised by Earl Stanhope.[114] It incorporated a much larger platen to enable large formes to be printed with one pull.[115] It was, however, no faster than the old wooden presses. Owen Rees was emphatic on this point in his evidence to the Select Committee on Copyright in 1818: 'if the question refers to Lord Stanhope's press, the art

[105] *Saunders's Newsletter*, 16 April 1841.
[106] Ibid., 7 June 1845.
[107] DTPS Committee Meeting Minutes, 1 November 1847.
[108] *Second Report from the Select Committee on Combinations of Workmen* (UK Parliamentary Papers 1837–1838. VIII p. 418), p. 98.
[109] DTPS Committee Meeting Minutes, 1 November 1847.
[110] J. Moxon, *Mechanick Exercises on the Whole Art of Printing*, London, 1683–1684. reprinted London, 1962, p. 292.
[111] T. C. Hansard, *Typographia*, London, 1825, p. 424.
[112] P. Gaskell, *A New Introduction to Bibliography*, Oxford, 1974, p. 121.
[113] J. Moxon, op cit., p. 29.
[114] J. Moran, *Printing Presses*, London, 1973, pp. 49–51.
[115] For a full description see A. Rees, *The Cyclopaedia*, London, 1819–20, vol. XXVIII, article on printing. Plates, London, 1820, vol. 4.

of printing is not made more rapid by these presses being used than by the presses before in use'.[116] T. C. Hansard observed in 1825: 'The advantages of the iron presses in working are very considerable, both in saving labour and time … in the Stanhope press, the whole surface is printed at once, with far less power upon the lever than the old press, when printing but half the surface. This arises not only from the levers, but from the iron framing of the press, which will not admit of any yielding … The iron has little elasticity, and those who use such presses find it advantageous to diminish the thickness of the blankets in the tympan to one very thin piece of fine cloth; the lever has then very little tendency to return, and the pull is easy in the extreme'.[117] The saving in time was on make-ready.

The earliest Stanhope presses were made by Walker in London in collaboration with the inventor. A structural defect that was apparent in early models was a tendency to fracture in the staple (the cast iron upright part of the frame), which would require repair at a cost of 18 to 20 guineas. After 1806 the problem was overcome by constructing staples with strengthened checks.[118] The earliest models at 90 guineas, were considerably more expensive than a wooden press, which in 1775 cost 16 guineas.[119] As Stanhope did not patent his invention rival manufacturers were quickly into the market. In 1808 C. Stower listed the London prices of various presses:

Common-size printing press [i.e. wooden]	£31 10s
Foolscap ditto	£21
Stanhope ditto by Walker	£73 10s
Brooke's ditto	£42 13s[120]

Brooke's press was an attempt to apply Stanhope's innovations in the bar and spindle to the common press, but wooden frames were unable to resist the increased power generated. Stower reckoned such presses could manage good impressions 'from light formes set in leaded long primer and upwards'.[121]

There was no significant development in manually operated presses until 1816 when George Clymer of Philadelphia designed the Columbian press. His great innovation was the development of a lever and counterbalance system for lowering and raising the platen. Clymer moved to London in 1817 and, having patented his invention, began production there.[122] The presses were made in sizes between Super Royal at £100 and Double Royal at £125. Any size in between cost £112 10 0.[123] His

---

[116] *Report from the Select Committee on copyright* (UK Parliamentary Papers 1818. IX. p. 11), p. 267.
[117] Hansard, *Typographia*, p. 424.
[118] Moran, *Printing Presses*, p. 51.
[119] Ibid., p. 52; J. Nichols, *Literary Anecdotes*, London, 1812–1815. vol. 8, p. 364.
[120] C. Stower, *The Printer's Grammar*, London, 1808, p. 516.
[121] Ibid., p. 506.
[122] *Printing Patents. Abridgements of Patent Specifications Relating to Printing 1617–1857*, London, 1969, p. 137.
[123] G. Clymer, *The Patent Columbian Printing Press*, London, 1818, p. 16.

publicity pamphlet of July 1818 laid great stress on the 'superabundant power, and mechanical precision of impression: and considerably less injury to the types' and the 'much greater facility in working the largest forms, and less injury to the human frame'.[124] He published a further puff in January 1820 announcing a temporary reduction in prices, the Super Royal dropping to £75, the Double Royal to £95 and sizes in between £85 'in consequence of the extreme depression of business, not only in this country but throughout Europe'.[125] He wished to remove any obstacle that might impede the 'speedy and general adoption' of his presses. Columbian presses continued to be manufactured until the first decade of the twentieth century.[126] The Columbian soon had an indigenous English rival, the Albion press invented by R. W. Cope of London and it was in manufacture by 1822, and still available in 1940.[127]

It does not appear that iron presses were very widespread even in the London trade much before 1808. Stower hailed the lower prices charged by Stanhope and Walker's rivals: 'This reduction of the great expense of its purchase was received with much satisfaction by the trade, as it tended to do away that evil which has [sic] been thought would preclude its general use'.[128] Prices remained at the 1808 levels for a decade. In November 1818 Trinity College Dublin paid £150 for two Stanhope presses manufactured by Sarah Walker of Dean Street Soho, which were purchased for the use of Graisberry and Campbell, the leasees of the College Printing House.[129] These had the manufacturer's serial numbers 206 and 209 which indicates a comparatively low level of output by the Walker firm over 18 years. Prices for presses declined in the following two decades. The Columbian presses sold in the mid 1830s by Wood and Sharwoods at the following prices: Crown Broadside £35, Demy £55, Royal £60, Super Royal £65, and Double Royal £90.[130] In 1840 John Cumming, newly appointed as sole Irish agent for Clymer and Dixon, advertised their full range for the Dublin trade at similar prices: Foolscap or Crown Broadside £40, Demy £55, Royal £60, Super Royal £65, Double Crown £70, Double Demy £80, Double Royal £90, Extra Double Royal £100.[131]

The Dublin market for iron presses developed towards the end of the second decade of the century. In August 1820 Thomas Holmes advertised 'a Royal printing press, one pull. With extra power, on Lord Stanhope's principle, complete; considerably below its value; made by Mr. Wm. Richards (who has lately sailed for London)

---

124 Ibid., p. 2.
125 G. Clymer, *Additional Testimonials Respecting the Patent Columbian Printing-Press*, London, 1820, p. 8.
126 Moran, *Printing Presses*, p. 8.
127 R. Stone, 'The Albion press', in *Journal of the Printing Historical Society* no. 2 (1966) pp. 58–73, refs, pp. 64, 73.
128 Stower, *The Printer's Grammar*, p. 499.
129 TCD Muniments Series P4. Bursar's vouchers folder 174 no. 49, 49a.
130 J. Moran, 'The Columbian press' in *Journal of the Printing Historical Society*, no. 5 (1969), 1–23, p. 12.
131 *Saunders's Newsletter*, 19 March 1840.

and who was the only Royal Press Manufacturer in this Kingdom'.[132] Within three years the Dublin market was sufficiently attractive to induce the Birmingham firm of Beilby and Knotts, the sole agents for W. Hope of Jedburgh, to establish a branch headed by R. Beilby. The firm advertised 'Hope's improved Stanhope printing press, having a threefold increase in power over the ordinary Stanhope; remarkable for its power, quickness and truth, warranted to work, without patching with a single blanket. It combines the advantages of the Stanhope form, with the fullest power that belongs to any press now in use. It is so easily worked, that a boy of fourteen years of age can bring off the heaviest impression; and being made of wrought iron, it is secure from breaking by the exercise of its utmost power. In addition to these advantages, its cheapness will secure a preference'.[133] The presses carried a two year warranty. Beilby and Knotts also advertised Hope's portable printing press, which came in two sizes, full sheet foolscap and half sheet foolscap. This they suggested, 'will be found very useful for country printers, booksellers, clergymen, and gentlemen'. The firm only lasted a few years in Dublin being listed in *Wilson's Dublin Directory* for the years 1824–1826.

Mention of iron presses becomes frequent in newspaper advertisements of printers' equipment from the late 1820s, but wooden presses continued to be used, particularly in small businesses, up to the mid-1840s. When Brett Smith retired from business in 1841 the auction of his equipment included an Aldritt-improved Columbian, a Stanhope and two wooden presses.[134] In 1847 Dowling and Shea of 15 St Andrew Street had a Columbian press as well as an 'excellent' wooden one, and in the same year E. & S. Rorke of 15 Beresford Street were using three wooden presses.[135] Of twenty-one advertisements of equipment in *Saunders's Newsletter* between 1825 and 1846 two businesses had only one press, fourteen had two presses, three had three presses, and two had four presses. Of the fourteen offices with two presses, four had only wooden presses, six had only iron presses, and four had one wooden and iron press. *Saunders's Newsletter* itself advertised three wooden presses in 1832 when it was re-equipping itself.[136] A wide variety of English manufacturers sold machines to Dublin businesses. Advertisements of dispersal sales include an Imperial press by Sherwood and Cope, an Imperial press by Clymer and Dixon, and a Ruthven press.[137]

In 1832 a Dublin engineer, Joseph Aldritt, jun., drew the attention of the Dublin trade to 'his new improvement in the Columbian Press, whereby it is evidently more

---

132 Ibid., 5 August 1820.
133 Ibid., 22 April 1823.
134 Ibid., 17 February 1841.
135 Ibid., 25 January 1847; ibid., 28 July 1847.
136 Ibid., 16 February 1832.
137 Ibid., 28 May 1831; ibid., 18 October 1836; ibid., 16 November 1832.

durable; liability to fracture in the frame prevented, and the whole machine rendered more firm'.[138] He claimed that 'the materials of the whole Press are of a superior description to those usually made — much friction is prevented, and, consequently a smaller quantity of oil required.' An illustrated advertisement for the press was placed in *The Dublin Almanac and General Register of Ireland for ... 1834* and included a number of testimonials from satisfied Dublin customers.[139] Indeed, Pettigrew and Oulton, the publishers of *The Dublin Almanac* used two of them in its production, their printers finding 'that for ease, *expedition*, and *evenness of impression*, they excel any others they have hitherto worked'. Brett Smith of Mary Street was well pleased with the model he purchased in June 1834.

As to beauty of impression and ease in working, I do not think it can be surpassed; while its additional strength and *non-liability to accident*, by means of your late improvements, is a desideratum of the highest importance — In fact I do not hesitate to say, that it is far superior to the English iron presses, purchased by me at a much higher rate.[140]

Aldritt went on to invent a small jobbing press, the Hibernia Printing Press, with a platen size of 19½ × 14½ inches, whose 'construction is original, the impression being obtained by means of four balls and sockets, with compound levers, which act on the platen in a manner which prevents slurring, and the power is so regulated that a light or heavy form can be worked with equal facility'.[141]

One of these presses was owned by Philip Dixon Hardy, the proprietor of one of the largest Dublin businesses in 1834.[142] His description of his own printing office in 1834 in the *Dublin Penny Journal*, which he owned and edited, is invaluable for the illustration from the life by Benjamin Clayton jun.[143] That of the pressroom shows five presses and Hardy in the accompanying text indicated that he owned an Aldritt Hibernian Press, a Stanhope, a Clymer, and a Columbian.[144] Hardy published his account at a significant moment in the development of the Irish trade, that of the introduction of steam powered printing machinery to Ireland. Irish printers had lagged far behind English ones in using this technology. *The Times* in London had been printed on a steam press as early as 28 November 1814.[145] The first two steam powered presses erected in Dublin were designed by Robert Gunn, of Edinburgh and manufactured by Claud Girdwood & Co. of Glasgow for P. D. Hardy and the

---

[138] Ibid., 30 May 1832.
[139] *The Dublin Almanac, and General Register of Ireland for ... 1834*, Dublin [1834]. p. [1] of advertisements.
[140] *The Dublin Almanac and General Register of Ireland, for ... 1835*, Dublin [1835]. p. [28] of advertisements.
[141] *Saunders's Newsletter*, 26 November 1834.
[142] *Second Report from the Select Committee on Combinations of Workmen* (U.K. Parl Papers. 1837–1838. VIII. p. 390), p. 70.
[143] *The Dublin Penny Journal*, Vol. II no. 97, 10 May 1834, p. 353–60.
[144] Ibid. p. 358.
[145] M. Plant, *The English Book Trade*, Third edition, London, 1974, p. 274.

JOSEPH ALLDRITT, JUN.

20, STAFFORD-STREET,

Lathe, Tool, Steam=engine, Patent Axle=tree Maker,

AND

PRINTERS' ARTIST,

MOST respectfully solicits the attention of the Trade to his newly improved PRINTING PRESS, the following Testimonials, in favor of which, he has the honor to submit :—

36, *Dame-street, December*, 1833.

SIR,—WE feel pleasure in thus publicly acknowledging the superiority of your improved Printing Presses, Two of which have assisted in the execution of the DUBLIN ALMANAC AND DIRECTORY. The persons employed at them state, that for *ease, expedition,* and *evenness of impression,* they excel any others they have hitherto worked.
PETTIGREW AND OULTON.

MR. JOSEPH ALLDRITT, JUN.
  Stafford-street.

45, *Capel-street,* 21*st December,* 1833.

SIR,—IT affords us great pleasure to say, that the Improved Columbian Printing Press we got from you, nearly two years since, has given us every satisfaction, and we think it only requires to be generally known, that so excellent a Press can be manufactured in this country, for you to obtain from the Trade very considerable patronage, which we sincerely wish you.
RICHARD GRACE AND SON.

MR. JOSEPH ALLDRITT, JUN.
  Stafford-street.

23, *Wellington-quay, Dublin,* 21*st December,* 1833.

SIR,—THE Medium Columbian Press which you made for me has fully answered my expectations. It has been in use now nearly Eighteen Months and performs to the entire satisfaction of myself and the persons who work it. In every instance where you have deviated from the original Columbian Press, I consider you have introduced a decided improvement.
I am, &c.
WILLIAM HOLDEN.

MR. J. ALLDRITT, JUN.

J. A. having made arrangements for the manufacture of every article in his line, used in the Printing Office, will engage to execute all orders he may be favored with, on the shortest possible notice.

Chases, Iron Foot and Side-sticks, Brass Galleys, &c· made according to Order, with the greatest accuracy.

January, 1834.
  a

Figure 5. Advertisement promoting the Columbian printing press then being manufactured in Dublin: [Pettigrew & Oulton], *Dublin Almanac and General Register of Ireland … 1834* (Dublin, 1834). *Courtesy of the Royal Irish Academy Library.*

PRINTING MACHINE.

Figure 6. Benjamin Clayton's remarkable wood engravings (possibly based on drawings by George Petrie) provide an invaluable insight into Philip Dixon Hardy's printing works in Cecilia St, which were published in Hardy's own *Dublin Penny Journal*. Here his new steam-powered press, manufactured in Glasgow by Girdwood & Son, is shown in operation; it was stated to make 3,000 impressions an hour: *D.P.J.* (Dublin, 1834). *Courtesy of the Royal Irish Academy Library.*

THE CASE ROOM.

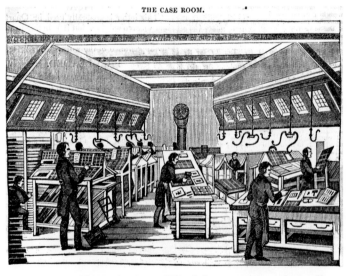

Figure 7. Clayton's view of Hardy's case room, where all typesetters appear to be young men: *D.P.J.* (Dublin, 1834). *Courtesy of the Royal Irish Academy Library.*

THE PRESS-ROOM.

Figure 8. Clayton's view of Hardy's press room with, it seems, five presses at work: *D.P.J.* (Dublin, 1834). *Courtesy of the Royal Irish Academy Library.*

STEREOTYPE FOUNDRY, AND STEAM-ENGINE.

Dublin: Printed by F. D. Hardy, 3, Cecilia-street.

Figure 9. Clayton's depiction of Hardy's type foundry and of part of the steam engine powering the new Girdwood press: *D.P.J.* (Dublin, 1834), *Courtesy of the Royal Irish Academy Library.*

Dublin Evening Mail in 1833.[146] Hardy's press, as illustrated, was a double cylinder perfecting machine. To begin with there were delays in erecting the press as a result of which 'a workman who came over from Scotland to instruct one of our workmen how to manage it, had to return without imparting the requisite information; then, there was a further delay of several months before he could find a man competent to stereotype the wood engravings; finally he had to remove the machine from the upper storey of the building to the ground floor because it was shaking the whole house when in operation.[147] When working at full capacity the machine could produce 3000 impressions per hour.[148] Hardy noted that due to the great length of time required to make ready even formes of moveable type, let alone stereotype formes, that 'it would not be worthwhile printing any number under two thousand on it'.[149] The machinery and its installation cost £500 and the weekly running expenses of 'steam power and persons necessary to attend the machine' were £4 10s 0d.[150]

The contemporary machine at the *Dublin Evening Mail* was reported to run at up to 2,300 impressions per hour. Its impending introduction to service was made the occasion of lengthy self-congratulation in the editorial columns. On 3 January 1834 the paper announced: 'We have at an immense expense, had machinery upon the most improved formation, specially constructed at one of the first manufactories in the empire, for the purpose of printing the journal; and as the machine will be impelled by steam, and worked with amazing rapidity, several hours will be saved in the time heretofore necessary for putting the machine to press'. The opportunity would be taken to increase the size of the paper to 'twenty four columns of the largest dimensions'. On 3 February 1834 the paper appeared in the heralded larger size and in new type and with editorial excuses for any defects:

the difficulty of working new and complicated machinery with effect for the first time — the labour and confusion consequent upon the transfer of a newspaper establishment such as this, from one building to another — the novelty of its mode of operation, and the inexperience of those, by whom it is worked, will we hope be accepted as an excuse for any faults that may be apparent.

During the 1840s an increasing number of steam presses were brought into operation, principally in the newspaper business, but also for book printing. By November 1847 *Saunders's Newsletter* was upgrading its machinery and advertised a double cylinder newspaper printing machine made by Napier of London, and

---

[146] Moran. *Printing Presses*, p. 133.
[147] *The Dublin Penny Journal*, Vol. ii no. 97, 10 May 1834, p. 360.
[148] Ibid., p. 358.
[149] Ibid., p. 358.
[150] Ibid., p. 359.

capable of printing two thousand sheets per hour, 'the proprietor being obliged to part with it to make room for large machinery'.[151] The Napier Double Imperial had been first developed in the 1820s but continued in production until the 1840s. It printed on one side of the sheet only, but with the two cylinders the forme printed when travelling in each direction.[152] When J. S. Folds was printing the *Dublin Times* he used a double cylinder perfecting machine worked by hand which was capable of producing 1,000 perfected sheets per hour.[153] Book printers were slower to invest in steam presses, probably as a reflection of the relatively small edition sizes of most works, but by early 1845 Richard Grace, a large-scale publisher of Catholic devotional works, advertised 'printing work, by steam-press, done in the neatest manner'.[154] Alexander Thom was one of the largest users of steam powered presses in the 1840s having eight machines driven by two steam presses in place by February 1845.[155]

---

[151] *Saunders's Newsletter*, 8 November 1847.
[152] C. Wilson and W. Reader, *Men and Machines: A History of D. Napier & Sons, Engineers, Ltd. 1808–1958*, London, 1958, p. 23.
[153] *Saunders's Newsletter*, 27 April 1846.
[154] *The Nation*, 19 April 1845.
[155] NTA. Western District, Dublin Branch Committee, 17 February 1845.

Chapter Two: Bookselling

THE NATURE OF BOOKSELLING in Dublin is the focus of this chapter. It changed abruptly in 1801 from a reliance on locally produced books to a trade heavily dependent on imports. The growth of these and the mechanics of the trade in the importation, advertising and selling of books are considered as well as problems of individual firms' cash flow and credit. The period saw the emergence of wholesale booksellers as well as the growth of charitable and religious societies as large scale distributors of books and tracts.

Dublin booksellers before the Act of Union were principally dealing with domestically produced books. Many of these were published by congers, large or small numbers of booksellers subscribing for shares in a particular book.[1] The Dublin reprints of British publications were able to supply much of the domestic demand for literature, law, agriculture and theatre. Where they could not compete was in grand books, such as architectural and travel books with large numbers of engravings. There was towards the end of the century a growing importation of books from Great Britain.[2]

After the Copyright Act came into force on 2 July 1801 the Dublin reprinting of current publications was virtually stopped and for much of their stock the booksellers had to look to London and Edinburgh for supplies. This had considerable implications for their requirements for capital. English books were more expensive than Dublin imprints. Not only that but even after the Union the two exchequers had a separate existence until 1824. A system of countervailing duties and drawbacks was in place until then.[3] Wholesale commerce between Britain and Ireland remained expensive and slow, tying up the booksellers' money for long periods.

---

[1] Sometimes very large numbers were involved; e.g., W. Robertson, *History of America*, Dublin: printed for Messrs Price, Whitestone [and 44 others], 1777.

[2] M. Pollard, *Dublin's Trade in Books 1550–1800*, Oxford, 1989, p. 154.

[3] Repealed in 1824 by 'An Act to repeal the duties on all articles the manufacture of Great Britain and Ireland respectively on their importation into either country from the other' 5 Geo IV.c.22.

THE GROWTH OF IMPORTS

Book imports into Ireland from Great Britain were valued at £7,000 in 1799.[4] The importation figures from the Custom House ledgers are divided into figures for bound and unbound books.[5] For bound books only a value is given, and for unbound books the weight. From 1730 unbound books were valued at £10 a cwt for Customs purposes. The accuracy of the ledgers in relation to the volume of trade was doubted by Lord Sheffield in 1785: 'Many books have been very well printed in Ireland; still a considerable quantity must be imported, and more than would be supposed from the following account — Indeed the mode of rating unbound books, viz. at 10l. per cwt is not very satisfactory. A great number of books are carried into Ireland without being entered.'[6]

For the first eighteen years of the nineteenth century it is possible to compare annual figures from the Customs ledgers. The figures for bound books are kept separately from the unbound ones. In 1801 unbound books to a weight of 560 cwt and a customs value of £5,600 were imported into Dublin from Great Britain while bound books were valued at £337 11s 4d. By 1808 the figure for unbound books had doubled to 1,192 cwt valued at £11,920, while bound books were valued at £1 18s 7d. The importation of unbound books peaked in 1813 at 2021 cwt valued at £20,210 while bound books reached £711. Importation declined to 1,354 cwt valued at £13,540 in 1817 with bound books valued at £377 8s 2d that year. The downturn reflects in some respects the economic slowdown in the aftermath of the Napoleonic wars.

The graph of the combined figures of unbound books imported from England and Scotland in figure 10 shows the scale of growth in the trade during the first fourteen years of the century and the decline during the depression following the end of the Napoleonic Wars. The dominance of Dublin in the trade is apparent as the figures for the next two significant trading towns, Belfast and Cork, are included. Neither experienced the same rate of growth in the book trade that Dublin enjoyed although Belfast had overtaken Cork as a bookselling centre by the end of 1818. Figures 11 and 12, compiled on differing scales, show the relative importance of English and Scottish sources of supply to each destination.

Compared to the trade in unbound books the level of business in bound books is very small and irregular. In Cork it hit a peak of £1,499 in 1807 but was nil in Dublin in that year; the peak in Dublin was at £1,240 in 1816 when the business in Cork was valued at £224. Figure 13 shows the pattern of importation of bound books to Dublin, Belfast and Cork from Great Britain. Figures 14 and 15, compiled necessarily on

---

[4] Pollard, *Trade in Books*, p. 154.
[5] TNA, CUST 15/105–128.
[6] J. Holroyd, Lord Sheffield, *Observations on the Manufacture, Trade and Present State of Ireland*. 3rd ed. London, 1785, pp. 252–53.

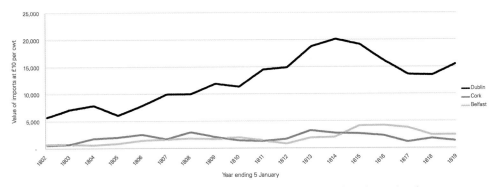

Figure 10. Value of unbound books imported from England and Scotland, 1801–1818.
Source: TNA, CUST 15/105–122.

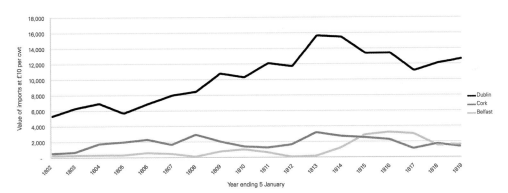

Figure 11. Value of unbound books imported from England, 1801–1818.
Source: TNA, CUST 15/105–122.

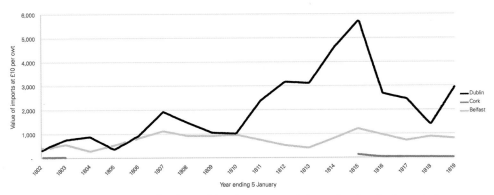

Figure 12. Value of unbound books imported from Scotland, 1801–1818.
Source: TNA, CUST 15/105–122.

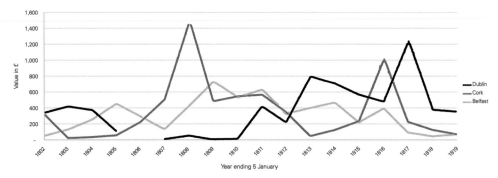

Figure 13. Value of bound books imported from England and Scotland, 1801–1818.
Source: TNA, CUST 15/105–122.

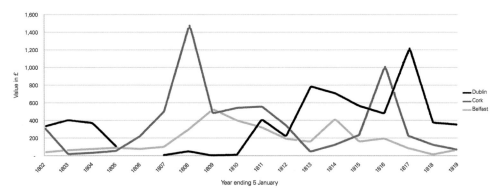

Figure 14. Value of bound books imported from England, 1801–1818.
Source: TNA, CUST 15/105–122.

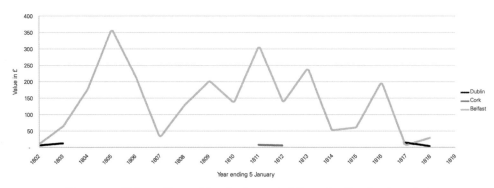

Figure 15. Value of bound books imported from Scotland, 1801–1818.
Source: TNA, CUST 15/105–122.

differing scales, show the patterns of imports from England and Scotland. Although the values of Scottish imports are very modest it is significant that the trade is almost entirely with Belfast.

PROBLEMS OF CASH FLOW

On the face of it the figures for imports represent a prosperous trade but the correspondence of booksellers with one of the great collectors, Christopher Dillon Bellew, underlines continual problems in cash flow. Christopher Dillon Bellew (1762–1826), inherited a large estate at Mountbellew in the 1790s where he developed extensive milling interests besides sheep and cattle grazing. His income was large; in 1793 he was spoken of as heir to £5,000.[7] For the first couple of decades in the nineteenth century he collected books on an heroic scale. His custom was much prized by Dublin booksellers and some 250 letters survive in the Bellew papers.[8]

One of his chief correspondents, John Archer wrote to him on 10 July 1799, 'Pressing demands on me for money by the booksellers in London with whom I must settle in a few days, compels me to trouble you concerning your account — be assured it is far from being my wish to entreat your attention to it — if it is not entirely convenient'.[9] On 25 June 1804 he acknowledged two drafts of £100 each, 'nothing could be more timely than your recollection of me — for during the whole of my life, I never was so much in want of money'[10] On 6 June 1807 he reflected 'there is very little novel in the Book way & Business can not be worse', and in July that year he announced his intention of going to London to close accounts: 'Business is so very bad I am completely discounting'.[11] By 4 December 1807 acknowledging a draft for £280 he wrote 'this money is a very timely supply. The London booksellers had drained me of my last shilling … to be candid, I never had more occasion for your assistance'.[12]

Another bookseller, C. P. Archer, wrote to Bellew on 3 August 1814 enclosing his invoice for £456 3s 9d expressing the greatest reluctance for troubling Bellew 'at this very critical time, when there is the greatest difficulty imaginable in getting in money', having overstretched himself in expenditure on a new house and extra stock. 'Protested bills are constantly returned on me which I was obliged to provide for to keep up my credit, which once lost I might never be able to retrieve — at this moment I have several hundred pounds of protested Bills in my desk for which I

---

[7] W. T. Tone, *The Life of Theodore Wolfe Tone*, Washington, 1826, vol. 1, p. 231.
[8] Bellew Papers NLI MSS 27,293–27,311. Bellew's collection of novels is discussed in M. Sadleir, *XIX Century Fiction*, London, 1951. v. 1, pp. xx–xxi.
[9] Bellew Papers NLI MSS 27,293 (2).
[10] Ibid., NLI MSS 27,293 (5).
[11] Ibid., NLI MSS 27,293 (6); ibid., NLI MSS 27,293 (7).
[12] Ibid., NLI MSS 27,293 (6).

cannot get one shilling'.[13] Two years later on 27 August 1816, acknowledging a payment he was grateful 'particularly at this time when there is scarcely a possibility of getting any money — I have never known anything equal to the present distress'.[14] On 22 January 1820 the refrain was the same; sending his bill, Archer complained of protested bills having come back amounting to about £600, 'never have I known money so scarce, or difficult to be got … as to my engagements in London I cannot possibly meet them next week, unless my kind friends will assist me'.[15] Returning thanks for Bellew's prompt response, Archer noted that all people in trade were complaining about the difficulty of getting cash.[16]

This may, of course, merely be a matter of two individuals in the trade over extending themselves, but the difficulties seem to have been widespread. A bill for £200 sent by Gilbert and Hodges to Longmans was protested in 1812.[17] On 1 June 1812 Longman and Co. wrote firmly to Mr Jones in Dublin expressing surprise that they did not receive payment for bills drawn on him and requested him to return the bills accepted or their amount in cash 'which will prevent further trouble to both parties'.[18] On 19 June 1814 they were alarmed at not receiving money to liquidate Gilbert and Hodges' account, then standing at over £1,100, and declined further orders until the account was settled. The alarm was justified. Gilbert and Hodges went bankrupt shortly afterwards and the outcome was unfavourable to the creditors. The first payment on the debts was 6s 8d in the pound in October 1815 and the second of 1s in the pound was to be paid on 9 and 10 August 1816.[19]

Stock selection was made in a number of ways through commercial travellers, visits of Dublin booksellers to other centres, or from trade catalogues. There appears to have been a considerable growth in the numbers of commercial travellers in the early nineteenth century. T. F. Dibdin believed that the number being sent out had doubled in recent years concluding that as a result 'three orders are now received where one formerly was scarcely given'.[20] Owen Rees, partner of T. Longman, was a regular traveller to Ireland taking in both Dublin and Cork. In addition to promoting new publications he was also able to check on the creditworthiness of booksellers. He was in Dublin in 1811 when he caught some unpleasant rumours about W. Figgis, and on his return to London the company wrote to Figgis saying that Rees was sorry 'to observe that he did not find you so regularly in your shop as he had formerly the pleasure of seeing you', and that he had heard such unpleasant reports that the

13 Ibid., NLI MSS 27,301 (6).
14 Ibid., NLI MSS 27,301 (6).
15 Ibid., NLI MSS 27,301 (15).
16 Ibid., NLI MSS 27,301 (15).
17 Longman Archive I, 97 no. 282.
18 Ibid., I, 97 no. 326.
19 *Freeman's Journal*, 31 Oct. 1815; Carrick's *Morning Post*, 8 August 1816.
20 T. F. Dibdin, *The Library Companion*, London, 1824, p. xxii.

company declined to fill Figgis's order.[21] Rees expected to be in Dublin in July and August 1817 and anticipated being over in 1821 and again in 1827.[22]

The Edinburgh firm of Oliver and Boyd had a traveller who visited Dublin regularly between 1825 and 1827.[23] G. B. Whitaker of London in 1838 employed two travellers who visited the leading towns of England and Wales and the great towns in Ireland (presumably Belfast, Cork, and Dublin) twice a year.[24] Adam Black, the Edinburgh publisher of the *Encyclopaedia Brittanica*, toured Ireland in 1830 finding few shops outside Dublin and Cork worth visiting and relating that in some towns few books other than Roman Catholic prayer books were sold. He disapproved of the style in which his Dublin wholesaler, John Cumming, lived, recording that he had two carriages, a town and country house, and that he frequently gave sumptuous dinners 'for which his creditors had to suffer in due time'.[25]

After the Union some London publishers saw particular opportunities in Dublin. John Cook, brother-in-law of Joseph Butterworth the law publisher, set up business in Dublin in April 1802, arriving with law books, and continued there until 1826.[26] Baldwin, Cradock and Joy employed William Wakeman as their resident agent, and he also traded on his own account.[27]

Some Dublin booksellers travelled extensively in search of books. John Archer was in London in July 1799 and intended going on to the continent to build up his stock.[28] He advertised in *Saunders's Newsletter* on 25 April 1802 that he intended to visit France and Germany and sought commissions. He bought extensively there during the short peace, but much of his stock (to the value of £700) was caught up in the resumption of hostilities.[29] One Dublin bookseller, Zachariah Jackson, became a prisoner of war when fighting broke out in 1803 and was still confined in 1806.[30] He was not, however, a principal in business in 1803. In August 1814 Jane Fitzpatrick, minding the business while her husband Hugh Fitzpatrick languished in jail, told Bellew that her son was going to Paris to buy French theological works and miscellaneous books.[31] Richard Milliken travelled regularly to London, being there early in 1821 and again in 1831.[32]

[21] Longman Archive I, 97 no. 154.
[22] Longman Archive I, 100 no. 87, 97, 197; Longman Archive I, 101 no. 153; Longman Archive I, 102 no. 47B.
[23] Oliver and Boyd Travellers Logbook, National Library of Scotland Acc. 5000.1109.
[24] *First Report from the Select Committee on Postage* (UK Parliamentary Papers 1837–1838. XX. p. 265), p. 261.
[25] A. Black, *Memoirs*, Edinburgh, 1885, pp. 74–75.
[26] *Dublin Journal*, 13 April 1802; *Freeman's Journal* 7 June 1826.
[27] *Third Report of the Commissioners of Inquiry into the Collection and Management of the Revenue arising in Ireland* (UK Parliamentary Papers 1822. XIII. p. 1217), p. 13. Appendix no. 2.
[28] Bellew Papers NLI MSS 27,293 (3).
[29] Ibid., NLI MSS 27,293 (4).
[30] *Freeman's Journal*, 1 Sept. 1806.
[31] Bellew Papers, NLI MSS 27,300 (1).
[32] Longman Archive I, 101 no. 119; Longman Archive I, 102 no. 175A.

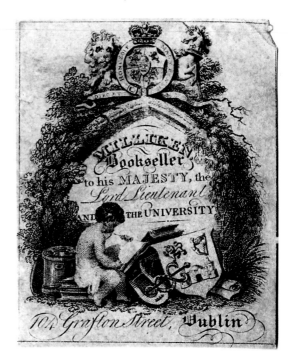

Figure 16. A curious juxtaposition in Milliken's trade card, mixing the image of the studious young child with references to its status as bookseller to Trinity College and Dublin Castle. *Courtesy of the Royal Irish Academy Library.*

ADVERTISING

Two trade catalogues were published during the half century. *Bent's Monthly Literary Advertiser* was first produced in 1802 and the *Publishers' Circular* in 1837. As Simon Eliot has pointed out, both of these were unrepresentative in character being much more likely to have coverage of expensive books than cheap pamplets.[33] Publishers' lists were regularly produced and circulated, and were aimed as much at the retail buyer as at booksellers. As John Murray wrote to Gilbert and Hodges on 2 November 1804, advising them not to omit any 'opportunity of advertising your own publications at the end of every book or pamphlet that you print — the additional expense is a mere trifle and the advantages that continually flow from this are very great indeed'.[34] John Coyne included a three-page list of his publications at the end of P. J. Carew, *An Ecclesiastical History of Ireland*, Dublin, 1835.

Separate publishers' lists and prospectuses were regularly inserted in books and magazines at the time of boarding up. Most were subsequently discarded during binding but several examples survive in books in boards in TCD, as Longman, Hurst, Rees, Orme and Brown's sixteen page catalogue of *Modern Publications, and New*

[33] Simon Eliot, *Some Patterns and Trends in British Publishing 1800–1919*, London, 1994, p. 60.
[34] Murray Archives, Letterbook 1803–1823, p. 44.

Editions of Valuable Standard Works corrected to March 1813, bound with G. Colman, *Vagaries Vindicated*, London, 1813, and their *Modern Publications, and new Editions of Valuable Standard works* corrected to March 1814 bound in R. Reece, *The Medical Guide*, London, 1814. John Murray's sixteen-page catalogue *Mr. Murray Has the Following Works Very Nearly Ready for Publication* in 1828 is stabbed with W. Grenville's *Essay … on a Sinking Fund* which Murray published that year. An Irish example is *Mr McGlashan's List of New Publications* dated December 1847 bound with W. H. Maxwell, *Rambling Recollections*, Dublin, 1848.

Such inclusions were clearly effective. At the height of the success of Sir Walter Scott's Waverley novels in 1831, when a volume a month was being published, the Dublin wholesale bookseller John Cumming wrote to John Murray in London thanking him for being given the management of a new edition of Lord Byron's *Works* for the Irish market:

it would be of great advantage, if I could have 2500 Prospectuses without covers sent off by return of coach as I may have them in time to paste into the December volume of the Waverley novels and standard novels where they will be sure to meet the view of the very persons who will be the most likely to subscribe.

He promised to delay the issue of the Waverley novels for a day or two, regarding it as more important to have the prospectuses inserted.[35] The strategy paid off. Two years later Cumming wrote to Murray enclosing a statement of the expenses in Ireland of publishing Byron's *Works*; these were £95 for advertising and £88 for carriage, set against a sales return to Murray of £5,000.[36]

The covers of journals and inserts in them were effective means of advertising to retail customers, though generally discarded on binding into volumes. Two examples from TCD Library are an issue of the *Monthly Review* for May 1821, and the *Dublin Review* for June 1847. The first is stabbed in blue paper wrappers which consist of eight pages of advertisements from a range of publishers including Longman, Hurst, Rees, Orme and Brown; John Murray; Rudolf Ackermann; Lackington, Hughes, Mavor and Lepard; Henry Colburn and Co.; Archibald Constable and Hurst, Robinson and Co. The second example also contains the *Dublin Review Advertiser* for June 1847 which is a 28-page catalogue including four pages of foreign theological books sold by Miss Dowling at Essex Bridge; advertisements for Gerald Bellew, the bookseller and bookbinder for Richard Grace's Irish Metropolitan Catholic book school and stationery warehouse. It is followed by four pages of advertisements for George Willis of Covent-Garden, bookseller; by David Nutt, *A List of Old Books, 1st June 1847* in sixteen pages; Thomas Richardson and Son, *Catalogue of the Derby*

---

[35] Murray Archives, Miscellaneous correspondence, 1820–1840.
[36] Ibid.

Reprints and New Catholic Works in thirty-six pages. Sundry small advertisements in the *Dublin Review Advertiser* include ones for P. Noonan's Catholic Repository, Liverpool and for R. Lynch, Catholic bookseller, Manchester.

The use of newspaper advertising, popular in the eighteenth century, was considerably diminished in the early nineteenth century by the severity of the tax on it. The tax introduced in 1774 at 2d an advertisement rose to 6d in 1780, and in 1785 to 1s for the first ten lines and 1s for every further ten lines.[37] Proclamations and government advertisements were exempt.[38] Simultaneously the stamp duty on every copy was raised to 1d. The stamp duty was further raised to 2d in 1798.[39] That increase coupled with extra duties on paper forced the price of newspapers up to 4d. The doubling of the advertisement tax in 1810 forced a further rise in the price of newspapers to 5d and depressed the circulation. It clearly diminished the amount of advertising. The doubling of duty, instead of producing £30,000 as officially anticipated, brought in a mere extra £2000.[40] In fact, the revenue from advertisements declined from £21,000 in 1813 to below £15,000 in 1829.[41] Advertisements for books were depressed as much as those for other commodities. In 1833 the duty on advertisements, by then standing at 2s 6d for ten lines was reduced to 1s for ten lines and this medium revived as a means of promoting books.

There was no regular pattern for promoting individual works; everything depended on the publisher's judgement and willingness to spend. On 6 January 1804 John Murray wrote to Gilbert and Hodges in Dublin about his hopes for the sale of *The Revolutionary Plutarch*, saying that 'a recent occurrence in Dublin respecting a too favourable account of Buonaparte has led me to suppose that the volumes of The Revolutionary Plutarch will meet with a favourable reception'. He had doubled the number ordered by Gilbert and Hodges hoping to save carriage expenses if there should be a good demand and priced them low to encourage Gilbert and Hodges to promote them. Murray wished them to be advertised twice in each of the best morning and evening papers.[42]

He was also disappointed to find out in August 1805 that the sales were sluggish, not having heard of their progress before then. He had already sold 500 copies of a new edition and regretted the lost sales of the copies lying in Dublin, for the work had been two months out of print. He gave specific instructions for re-advertising the book:

---

[37] Pollard, *Trade in Books*, p. 131.

[38] B. Inglis, *The Freedom of the Press in Ireland*, London, 1954, p. 45.

[39] B. Inglis, op. cit., p. 110–11.

[40] *An Account of the Amount of the Produce on Advertisements in Ireland* (UK Parliamentary Papers 1810–1811. VI, p. 1093).

[41] *Stamp Duties on Newspapers Ireland* (UK Parliamentary Papers 1830 XXXV, p. 363).

[42] Murray Archive, Letter Book 1803–1823, p. 27.

As to advertising whenever I send a book to your management it is my intention & wish that you should manage it in this and other respects as if it were your own publication … the book was stated to you at the lowest Sale Price — I know very well that a work will not sell without being advertised, & therefore I wish this to be done liberally, & indeed if I remember I noticed this to you at the time when I sent the book, upon which occasion I enclosed an advertisement. You will therefore … do me the favour to advertise the Plutarch immediately to the amt of £10-0-0 — associating if you think proper the name of Archer with your own — & likewise that of your friend Mr. Bull of Waterford & of any of your correspondents in other parts of Ireland.

Advertisements were to be placed in newspapers published around the country and *The Female Plutarch*, which had nearly sold out in London, was to be advertised to the amount of £5.[43] The two parties were still disputing the lack of success of the book in 1807, when Murray was defending his treatment of Gilbert and Hodges' publications, one of which had not done well: 'they received all the care of my own books & if the sale of them was not sufficient to cover the expenses of the Advertisements, this was the fault of the Book & not of me, who by advertising them adopted the best & only way of making a book sell if it be good for anything'.[44]

One of his successful ventures in 1808 was M. Rundell, *Domestic Cookery* of which he had high hopes for a good Irish sale, confident of disposing of 500 copies with proper advertising.[45] Thanking Wogan and Cumming on 2 December 1808 for advertising it in Belfast, he urged them to advertise in all the principal towns sending them a second batch of 250 copies and offering as an inducement to greater effort an additional discount of 2.5 per cent on sales.[46] These went sufficiently well for Murray to promise to put Wogan and Cumming's names on the title page of a new edition which he was preparing.[47] When he was preparing to launch his new *Quarterly Review* in the spring of 1809 he asked Wogan and Cumming to advertise it six times in the best newspapers and proposed to send 50 or 100 copies on publication.

Before the development of prefabricated easel bindings in the 1820s and 1830s, the way in which books arrived to the bookseller was unbound in quires. Boarding of books was done at the point of sale, as was binding in leather. The practice of supplying books in unbound sheets seems to have been general in London and Dublin. Longman and Co. rebuked an English printer in 1821, instructing him on no account to continue to sew a book of *Biblical Anecdotes* in boards:

[43] Ibid., pp. 58–59.
[44] Ibid., p. 130.
[45] Ibid., p. 197.
[46] Ibid., p. 227.
[47] Ibid., p. 249.

For God's sake how came you to think of putting these in boards so contrary to every custom? The London publishers invariably have all their works delivered to them by their printers made up in perfect books in quires of from 15 to 20 sheets each ... The reasons for this are various: in the first place they wish to incur no more expence that [i.e. than] necessary, in the next that the books may always have a fresh appearance, they have them done up only as they are required to meet the sale ...

And if the book failed to sell the remainders would be less valuable in boards than in sheets.[48] John Murray instructed Wogan and Cumming in April 1809 to have copies of *Gil Blas* and *Don Quixote* done up with peculiar neatness in extra boards to be put into the principal retail shops, confident that they would 'sell out of the window'.[49] When he was negotiating with John Archer over the possibility of Archer selling M. Rundell's *Domestic Cookery*, boarding up was to be a charge on the wholesaler.[50] By contrast when Longman and Co. were dealing with Edward O'Reilly offering them two titles, neither of which promised good sales, they suggested that the copies be sent in boards.[51]

Costs of importation

In the early part of the century the discount from London publishers to booksellers seems to have been in the range of 20 to 33.3 per cent. In 1821 Longman and Co. quoted the trade price of a volume retailing at 12s in boards as 8s in sheets.[52] Evidence was given to the Select Committee on the Copyright Acts in 1818 of the trade price being 'about 25 per cent below the retail selling price; from 20 to 25 per cent according to the books'.[53] A further discount was given in the custom of charging for twenty-five copies as twenty-four and in some cases thirteen copies as twelve. The retailer's margin was diminished by the cost of boarding up. By mid-century the standard discount was 25 per cent, but from the early eighteenth century there had been trade sales in London at which the bookseller could contract to purchase new titles at prices which by the 1840s were in the range of 10 to 15 per cent below the trade price. Remainders were also offered on these sales at a heavy discount or by auction.[54]

Individual deals could be very favourable. When John Murray was negotiating with John Archer over the wholesaling rights for Ireland of M. Rundell, *Domestic*

---

48 Longman Archive I, 101 no. 42.
49 Murray Archive, Letter Book 1803–1823, p. 249.
50 Longman Archive I, 101 no. 89.
51 Ibid., I, 100 no. 188.
52 Ibid., I, 97 no. 47.
53 *Report of the Select Committee on the Copyright Acts* (UK Parliamentary Papers 1818. ix.), p. 5.
54 J. Chapman, *Cheap Books and How to Get Them*, London, 1852, p. 20.

Cookery he proposed to send over 500 copies. The retail price was 7s 6d in boards, and he would charge Archer 4s 10d in quires, a discount of just over 35 per cent. He would allow a further 5 per cent on actual sales and allow Archer the drawback of duty. Murray would bear the advertising costs, but not the carriage unless sales failed to reach 250 copies, nor, as mentioned earlier, would he pay for boarding up.[55] In 1831 Longman and Co. had a share amounting to 79 copies in Baron, *Abridgement*, which was to be in eight volumes and to retail at £12 in boards with the trade price of £8 in sheets. The work was offered to Milliken at a further discount of 16s off £8 in sheets, the same relative discount that Milliken had enjoyed on 26 sets of J. Comyns, *Digest of the Laws of England*; the invoice was to be settled by an acceptance at twelve months from the date of shipping.[56] Owen Rees was of opinion that the books should be sent in boards.[57]

Credit terms improved as a business became established. Longman and Co. would offer eight months credit when dealing with a beginner in trade, although expecting ready money for at least half of the first order.[58] To an established country bookseller they offered nine months credit or 7.5 per cent discount for ready money, the same rate charged to their other clients in Ireland.[59] By 1831 they were giving an average credit of twelve months to Hodges and Smith.[60]

Longman's practice when wholesaling a book on commission for an individual was to make up the accounts at the end of June and to pay by bills at four and six months dated 1 August and giving the regular trade terms to retailers; the alternative, if the retailers were not to have the regular trade terms, was that they would be compelled to make the booksellers pay ready money which deterred them from holding stock.[61] If the book was a ready money book, they would account for it half yearly and settle accounts at a month's notice.[62] It is likely that similar conditions were followed in Dublin.

Credit given by retailers to customers was equally long or longer. Much of the evidence that follows is taken from dealings of Dublin booksellers with C. D. Bellew, who was an exceptional customer. Generalisations drawn from his case may be misleading. He was purchasing on an enormous scale and the temptation to extend his credit was present. George Mullen, the bookseller and bookbinder, wrote to Bellew on 28 October 1822, 'I should feel both proud and happy by your commencing a regular yearly account with me to any amount [for books] … I should also feel

---

[55] Murray Archive, Letter Book 1803–1823, p. 197.
[56] Longman Archive I, 102 no. 175A.
[57] Ibid., I, 102 no. 176A.
[58] Ibid., I, 97 no. 83.
[59] Ibid., I, 98 no. 21.
[60] Ibid., I, 102 no. 159 [draft].
[61] Ibid., I, 97 no. 108.
[62] Ibid., I, 97 no. 116.

most happy to open a yearly acct with you for that part of my business [book-binding]'; he suggested that he should visit Mountbellew at his own expense to confer about binding and would send his account for books every Christmas, and for bookbinding every Midsummer.[63] John Cumming furnished his bill for books bought for the period 15 November 1814 to 18 September 1815 amounting to £402 1s 4d. writing that a bill at four months would be an exact average of twelve months credit.[64]

Early in 1815 Bellew decided to settle his account with M. N. Mahon which had been running since 22 May 1813. Enclosing his bill for £1,358 17s 3d he observed that a year and nine months had elapsed since the start of the account. Bellew's proposed schedule of payment was August and October 1815 and August and October 1816 which would make the range of credit between two years and three months and nearly three and a half years. Mahon hoped he was not being unreasonable in asking for five per cent interest on the bills postponed to 1816.[65] Cumming was also prepared to stretch the credit line. Sending two French catalogues which he had just received on 16 September 1816 he hoped to be favoured with a large order and if Bellew required a 'longer extent of credit than the arrangements at present existing betwixt us I shall comply with great pleasure'.[66]

There were serious hindrances to the development of the trade in the early part of the century. In the first place until the exchequers of Britain and Ireland were united in 1824 a system of countervailing duties and drawbacks was operated. In 1800 the duty on unbound books was set at 3d per pound weight.[67] Not only was there duty but extensive administrative costs were involved. William Wakeman explained the working of the provisions to the Commissioners of Inquiry in 1821:

When importing large parcels entered for drawback by Liverpool, and by long sea, that is, from London direct, we have to enter into bond, the expense of which is 1l. 2s. 6d. British; the cost of entry at the Custom house here 5s. 6d. British; and the expenses after we have got a certificate of landing, in getting the drawback from the broker on the other side, that is double postage both ways. The expense of forwarding the certificate to the broker, and receiving money from him, that is 4s. 6d.[68]

Charles Palmer Archer in evidence to the same body found every importation attended by 'a certain degree of inconvenience, expense, annoyance and unpleasant-ness; for instance, if I pay 50l. duty here on an importation, perhaps it is six or twelve

---

[63] Bellew Papers, NLI MSS 27,314 (1).

[64] Ibid., NLI MSS 31,933 (4).

[65] Ibid., NLI MSS 27,298 (6).

[66] Ibid., NLI MSS 27,306 (1).

[67] 40 Geo.3 c.4. Ireland. Schedule A.

[68] *Third Report of the Commissioners of Inquiry into the Collection and Management of the Revenue arising in Ireland* (UK Parliamentary Papers. 1822 XIII. p. 1217), p. 13.

months before I get that back again'.[69] Such was the scale of the administrative costs that it was not worthwhile entering any quantity of books weighing less than 160 pounds for draw back.[70]

Both Wakeman and Archer considered the trade inhibited by the existence of these duties. Wakeman's London employer, Baldwin, Cradock and Joy, found it uneconomic to send copies of new books on approval, for if the books were not taken there was the double loss of duty paid on importation into Ireland and on returning them to England. The firm's custom in England was to send books on approval; it benefited the trade in enabling it to see a book soon after publication which they would not see at their own risk.[71]

Archer believed that the system made both London and Dublin booksellers wary. In his own case, 'if I have orders for twenty five copies of a work, perhaps I would not get thirty, I would not like to risk the chance of sale, there is no profit, there is nothing to induce us to import them'. The difficulty and cost of returning books was such that London publishers 'will not send books latterly on sale or return, except in very few circumstances; they do not wish to do it; if they send a hundred copies of a work to Dublin on the chance of sale, and they do not sell, the expenses on getting them back are so very great, that it deters them from attempting it, except in very few cases'.[72] Longman and Co. had apparently given up the practice about 1815 except for their Edinburgh connections, they 'found it a ruinous plan of doing business'. Archer said that he had in his possession several hundred pounds worth of books accumulated over a dozen years, including about 500 pounds of Longman's stock, which the London publishers would have been anxious to get back for the duty.[74]

As for periodicals, Archer maintained that importing them was a profitless exercise. For the sake of speed the booksellers were obliged to transport them from London by coach, and across the Irish sea by mail packet and that this left little or any profit, the discount from the London publisher being almost swallowed up in the expenses.[75] John Murray had written to the Commissioners of Customs in Dublin asking them to permit the *Quarterly Review* to be transported on the regular Government packets from Holyhead to Dublin as the *Review* was in its way a perishable commodity.[76]

---

[69] Ibid., p. 17.
[70] Ibid., p. 14.
[71] Ibid., p. 14.
[72] Ibid., p. 16–17.
[73] Longman Archive I, 102 no.159 [draft].
[74] *Third Report of the Commissioners of Inquiry into the Collection and Management of the Revenue arising in Ireland* (UK Parliamentary Papers. 1822 XIII. pp. 1220–21), pp. 16–17.
[75] Ibid., (p. 1220), p. 16.
[76] Murray Archive, Letter Book 1803–1823, p. 399.

The expense of postage was also widely regarded as a hindrance to the development of trade on both sides of the Irish sea. Several booksellers were interviewed by the Select Committee on Postage in 1838. Most of these would have sent out a lot of circulars; one, L. Fenwick de Porquet, had done such marketing exercises since the stamp duty was reduced, purchasing 500 to 1,000 copies of a newspaper in which he had placed an advertisement and circulating copies to everybody he traded with, schoolmasters as well as booksellers. He found the results satisfactory, his business increasing by more than one third. If postage were cheap he would send out more. The cost of letters was such that orders were delayed and sent in batches. He had received such an order which contained orders for three other publishers in London. The letter had cost him 1s 3½d. He was expected to cut it into four and to distribute the other parts. High postage costs limited small orders: it was not worthwhile for a bookseller to send an order for one or two copies of a book on which Fenwick de Porquet had to pay 7d or 10d postage.[77]

STOCK SIZES

The sizes of the stocks held by the booksellers were not in most cases particularly large. The available sources are catalogues and information on booksellers going out of business. In the case of catalogues what is listed is unlikely to represent all of the stock in the shop; in the case of liquidation of business or *post-mortem* sales there was always the possibility of extra stock belonging to others being off-loaded at the same time.[78] It can be accepted that catalogues of current stock were being put out by the more enterprising and better capitalised booksellers. Many of the titles indicate a mixed new, secondhand and antiquarian business. Harriot Colbert's *Catalogue of Ancient and Modern Books* issued *c.* 1802 listed 2,844 items with solid representation of literature especially fiction. Gilbert and Hodges issued a more substantial catalogue of 7,146 books in 1811; while M. N. Mahon's *Catalogue of Books in Various Languages and Classes* contained 6,199 works.

The enterprising firm of Grant and Bolton published a series of catalogues from the late 1820s. Their *General Catalogue of Cheap Second Hand Books* published in 1833, listing 4,415 items, had a neatly bound unattributed copy of *Sense and Sensibility* with a note indicating that it would sell at £1 3s in London. Grant and Bolton only wanted eight shillings for it. Their *Catalogue of Second Hand Books, in Every Branch of Literature* in 1836, listing 8,987 items, included a copy of Shakespeare, *Comedies, Histories and Tragedies* which they priced at six guineas assuring the bargain hunter

---

[77] *First Report from the Select Committee on Postage* (UK Parliamentary Papers. 1837–1838. XX. pp. 278–83), pp. 274–79.
[78] A time-honoured practice at country house auctions in Ireland.

Figure 17. Grant & Bolton's trade card, a reminder that even the most fashionable booksellers in Dame St dealt in second-hand as well as new books. *Courtesy of the Royal Irish Academy Library.*

that it would retail for three times as much in London. Two years later they issued a 7,928-title *Catalogue of an Extensive Collection of Second Hand Books* which contained fourteen volumes of Reformation tracts. These were bought by the missionary priest William Ullathorne who was in Dublin and in his leisure time picked up in the bookshops what he thought might be useful in Australia.[79]

These catalogues and the surviving catalogues of book auctions point to the existence of an active market in second hand and antiquarian books.[80] This impression is reinforced on the one hand by evidence of competition at auctions and on the other by book purchasing from irregular sellers. So far as auctions were concerned T. Jones, bookseller and auctioneer, was on at least two occasions unable to secure Bellew's commissions. Writing on 6 January 1812 after F. Fortescue's auction he remarked 'such as I did not get were either not fit for you from their condition, or that sold extravagantly high, at least far beyond what I thought their value'.[81] Again, on 6 August 1814, after I. A. Eccles's sale he wrote 'such articles as I did not buy were either faulty or *enormously* dear'.[82] At the other end of the scale were people

---

[79] W. Ullathorne, *The Autobiography*, London, 1891–1892, vol. 1, p. 136.

[80] W. G. Wheeler identified 710 extant catalogues in his *Libraries in Ireland before 1855* (Unpublished Diploma in Librarianship thesis, University of London, 1957); the annotated copy in the Department of Early Printed Books in TCD lists a further five for the period.

[81] Bellew Papers NLI MSS 27,296 (3).

[82] Ibid.

like Patrick Martin, a shoemaker who had a library of five or six hundred books. He had been buying for several years from James Reilly who kept a bookstall, and only bought religious works. He provided character evidence for Reilly who was accused of highway robbery.[83]

Catalogues of stocks of booksellers retiring from business or already dead show extreme variations in size. Richard Harman, whose career as a bookseller lasted less than eighteen months, listed about 1200 items in his retiring *Catalogue of Modern Books Now Selling at Unusually Low Prices* in 1830. The advertisement for George Mansfield's retiring sale in 1829 mentioned a stock of over 2,000 books while T. Bowes had 3,000 in 1837.[84] The more prominent booksellers had considerably larger stocks. M. N. Mahon in 1831, A. & W. Watson in 1832 and R. M. Tims in 1848 advertised respectively 15,000; about 13,000; and above 10,000 books.[85] These were dwarfed by the immense amount of 60,000 volumes of stock auctioned at a series of sales two years after Bennett Dugdale's death in 1826.[86]

Besides individual purchases there were a growing number of institutional and commercial libraries in the city which required supply. Among the former were the Dublin Society, whose regulations on admission to the library were gradually eased by the 1840s to allow non-members limited access, and the Dublin Library Society which had about 20,100 volumes in 1850.[87] The Dublin Mechanics' Institute founded in 1837 had 4,000 volumes in 1850.[88] But the really extensive purchasers of books were the commercial circulating libraries, some of which were very substantial. The largest of these was Gerrard Tyrrell's in Sackville St which advertised a total of 40,000 volumes in 1846.[89] As early as 1829 he published a catalogue of over 500 popular French and Italian books for lending.[90] J. Kempston had a thriving library of 8,000 volumes, including 600 in French, in 1816 and by March 1817 had 10,000 volumes.[91] On a much smaller scale H. Bourke had only 600 volumes when he tried to sell his library in 1826.[92] A number of circulating libraries developed as adjuncts of churches such as the Roman Catholic Andrean Library in Townsend Street which in 1831 subscribed for two copies of A. Rodriguez, *The Practice of Christian Perfection*, published by J. Christie that year, or the Society of St John the Evangelist recorded

---

[83] The support was unavailing. Reilly was convicted and sentenced to death. *Saunders's Newsletter* 3, 7 January 1828.

[84] *Saunders's Newsletter*, 7 March 1829; *Saunders's Newsletter*, 18 March 1837.

[85] *Saunders's Newsletter*, 19 October 1831; 5 December 1832; 20 April 1848.

[86] *Saunders's Newsletter*, 11 March; 28 March 1828.

[87] J. W. Hudson, *The History of Adult Education*, London, 1851, p. 236.

[88] Ibid., p. 236.

[89] *The Nation*, 17 October 1846.

[90] *Saunders's Newsletter*, 26 November 1829.

[91] *Saunders's Newsletter*, 7 December 1816.

[92] *Saunders's Newsletter*, 21 March 1817.

in Smock Alley (later Essex St West) and afterwards at North King St between 1835 and 1850.[93] This had a branch at the Catholic Church in Phibsborough from 1836 to 1850.[94]

The figure of the wholesaling bookseller becomes more defined in the second decade of the century. Clearly the subscription by booksellers for large numbers of 100 or more books implies the function, but the earliest clear mention that I have found is the description of W. Pickering and Co. as wholesale booksellers in the subscription list of N. Caussin, *The Holy Court*, published 1815–1816. The person who emerges as the chief wholesaler is John Cumming who combined publishing and wholesale and retail bookselling. In publishing he had a strong line in school and college text books with a countrywide distribution. During the late 1830s a string of announcements in *Saunders's Newsletter* testify his growing importance in the trade and a change in the way the trade is organised. An advertisement in the *Freeman's Journal* on 1 January 1836 lists him as the Irish agent for Fisher, Son and Co.; in *Saunders's Newsletter* on 28 June 1836 is news of him as Henry Colburn's Irish agent; then sole Irish agent for E. Moxon in *Saunders's Newsletter* on 14 February 1837; the same for C. Tilt on 24 April 1837; the same for Effingham Wilson on 2 May 1837; and Irish agent for How and Parsons on 25 March 1841. One agency he did not obtain was that for Samuel Bagster's Bibles. R. M. Tims announced this agency in *Saunders's Newsletter* on 20 July 1836, but then his son had married Bagster's daughter a month before.

In the mid-1840s Cumming's business was for a while very profitable. Early in 1846 when Cumming was negotiating with one of his assistants Clement Ferguson about going into partnership the profits were estimated at £2,500 a year. Ferguson was offered a half share in the assets and profit for £5,000. The only asset excluded was Cumming's house and twelve acres at Roebuck on which Cumming was supposed to have spent £3000. Ferguson became a partner, having been a clerk at £150 a year and between March 1846 and July 1847 drew £900 out of the business; Cumming drew £2017 8s 10d. The turnover was reckoned to be £20,000 a year and the value of stock on 1 June 1847 over £15,000. The firm crashed in July 1847, brought down by losses incurred when other firms went out of business; the claims against Cumming and Ferguson were for over £17,000.[95]

The desirability of being associated with a charitable society is well marked in the evidence of William Watson to the Commissioners of Education in Ireland on 24 January 1825. The family had been booksellers to the Association for Discountenancing Vice since 1792 when his grandfather had been a co-founder. Distributing as

---

[93] *Saunders's Newsletter*, 26 February 1826.
[94] Pettigrew and Oulton's *Directory*, 1836–1848, Thom's *Almanack and Directory*, 1849–1851.
[95] *Saunders's Newsletter*, 27 July 1848.

they did large numbers of tracts meant a comfortable living for the Watsons. Up to 1822 they had operated on a 25 per cent gross margin when selling the Association's wares. They ordered Bibles, Testaments and Prayer books from Great Britain, principally in Scotland, and had tracts printed locally in Dublin.[96] In 1821 the gross profit on selling the Association's goods was £1,906.[97] Such had been the amount of sales that in 1822 the gross profit margin on sales had been cut to 20 per cent and the Watsons had since seen sales decline.[98]

At the start of the century Dublin booksellers had generally added ten or twelve per cent to the price of books imported from Great Britain to cover the expenses of duty and importation.[99] This practice had, however, almost ceased by 1821. Even in the early years there were booksellers who endeavoured to increase their market share by offering discounts. John Archer advertised in *Saunders's Newsletter* on 25 April 1802 that because of reductions in the rates of insurance and freight charges consequent on the signing of the Treaty of Amiens, he would, in future, sell books imported from Great Britain at the original British prices. A few years later, although hostilities with France had been resumed, T. Henshall advertised that he was expecting a stock of novels which he would sell at London prices.[100] In the second decade of the century Christoper Dillon Bellew was being offered even more favourable terms than a reduction to London prices. In 1817 Matthew Neary Mahon offered him a fifteen per cent discount and two years' credit on items listed in his catalogue.[101] C. P. Archer offered him a five per cent discount on items in his catalogue in 1820 claiming at the same time that the books in the catalogue were already listed at lower prices than other Dublin booksellers would charge.[102]

Developments in binding practices and the advent of publishers' cloth bindings made standardised pricing possible and led to systematic undercutting of prices.[103] In London in 1829 a number of publishers and booksellers established a permanent Booksellers Committee which drew up regulations to protect their trade interests.[104] The aim was to establish retail price maintenance, the means of enforcing it commercial blackmail. No bookseller was to sell new books or reprints below the established price; if he did so, publishers would refuse to supply him with their books at trade or wholesale prices: the only discounts permitted were ten per cent to

---

[96] *First Report of the Commissioners of Education in Ireland* (UK Parliamentary Papers. 1825. XII. p. 382), p. 382.
[97] Ibid., p. 385.
[98] Ibid., p. 384.
[99] *Third Report of the Commissioners of Inquiry into the Collection and Management of the Revenue arising in Ireland* (UK Parliamentary Papers 1822. XIII. p. 1220), p. 16.
[100] *Dublin Evening Post*, 12 Nov 1807.
[101] Bellew Papers, NLI MSS 27298 (3).
[102] Bellew Papers, NLI MSS 27310 (3).
[103] J. J. Barnes, *Free Trade in Books*, Oxford, 1964, pp. 5–6.
[104] Ibid., p. 6.

customers for cash and fifteen per cent for book clubs.[105] The economic power of the Booksellers Committee, which by 1832 contained representatives from Longman and Co., John Murray, Simpkin, Marshall and Co., J. G. and F. Rivington, J. and A. Arch, Baldwin and Co. among others, was such that within a year of the formulation of the *Regulations* some 650 booksellers had undertaken to cooperate.[106]

THE DUBLIN BOOKSELLERS' SOCIETY

The regulations in London came into effect in January 1830. That same month a Dublin Booksellers' Society was founded with the objectives of regulating the bookselling trade and organising shared publications.[107] The criteria for membership were the serving of apprenticeship to a bookseller or having practiced the trade for a year. Those who had served an apprenticeship were admitted by ballot; those who had become booksellers without serving an apprenticeship were admitted on a fee of ten guineas; the annual subscription was set at one guinea. At its second meeting on 18 February 1830 it was agreed to undertake the shared publication of two unspecified standard works in editions of 1,500 and 1,000 copies, it being urged that no further reprinting take place until all the copies were sold.[108] It does not appear from O'Kelly's account that the publication programme ever amounted to very much as the only firm decision to publish was taken on 27 January 1831 when it was determined to reprint Thomas Nugent's French dictionary at an estimated price of £315.[109] The editor was to be paid £100 and it was to be financed by 21 shares of £15 each.

The principal focus of the Society was the same as the object of the London one, namely the prevention of undercutting of prices. At the outset the members agreed that there should not be any more than ten per cent discount given and then only on sales worth 15s or more.[110] In May 1830 it was agreed to raise the minimum qualifying limit for discounts to £1 but this proved impossible to maintain and on 16 August 1832 it was reduced to 10s.[111] This reduction was almost certainly due to a failure to recruit booksellers to the Society, it having been noted in May 1830 that twenty booksellers had not joined.[112] The Society's Committee report for 1830 urged that any bookseller offering a discount of more than ten per cent be treated as a

---

[105] Ibid., p. 7.
[106] Ibid., p. 1.
[107] J. J. O'Kelly 'The house of Gill' Appendix B, p. VIII, TCD MSS 10310. O'Kelly saw the Society's Minute Book for 1830–1846; it does not appear to be extant.
[108] Ibid., p. VIII.
[109] Ibid., p. X. No copy of this proposed edition has been traced.
[110] Ibid., p. VIII.
[111] Ibid., p. IX; ibid., p. XI.
[112] Ibid., p. IX.

member of the public and by implication excluded from any trade discounts.[113] The Committee had notified the London Booksellers' Committee of its existence. There was further contact with London in 1833 when the Booksellers' Committee declined to supply the Dublin Society with a copy of its rules on grounds of preserving privacy.[114] A week after this rebuff, the Dublin Society decided on 12 September 1833 that it would be inexpedient to publish its rules.

The question of discounted sales continued to agitate the Society. On 5 September 1833 it received a recommendation from Owen Rees of Longman and Co. that discounts of ten per cent by given on cash sales of 10s and above, of fifteen per cent to book clubs and of two pence in the shilling to schools.[115] The latter discount was close to the fifteen per cent which the Committee agreed to give to the Commissioners of National Education on 25 June 1834.[116] The advent of the London bookseller Thomas Tegg to Dublin caused considerable anxiety. Tegg had made much of his money by specialising in remainders; the Dublin booksellers were upset by his advertising tactics of giving his catalogues to hawkers.[117] When in 1837 W. H. Holbrooke advertised novels and other books at fifteen to twenty per cent discount, and proved obdurate in refusing to fall into line the Committee determined on 13 December to notify the London merchants of his behaviour. It also instructed its Secretary to call on George Young, another bookseller offering excessive discounts.[118] Young seems to have been unimpressed, in 1846 he was offering books from Bohn's Standard Library and Bogue's European Library at 'great reduction' from the published price.[119]

The records of the Dublin Booksellers' Society appear to have been very sketchy in the 1840s but it continued in existence until at least February 1846 when it was urging two of its members to call on booksellers generally to try to induce them to keep to the Society's discount limits.[120] The relative failure to impose standard practices on discounts is attributable to a reason beyond the control of the Dublin Booksellers' Society, namely their inability to control the supply of books from British publishers. If the London Booksellers' Committee had taken an active role in collaboration with Dublin it would have been a distinctly different matter.

[113] Ibid., p. X.
[114] Ibid., p. XII.
[115] Ibid., p. XII.
[116] Ibid., p. XIV.
[117] Ibid., p. XIV.
[118] Ibid., p. XVII.
[119] *Saunders's Newsletter*, 16 December 1846.
[120] J. J. O'Kelly, 'The house of Gill,' Appendix B, p. XVIII.

Chapter Three: The Journeyman Printer

T HE LIFE OF A JOURNEYMAN PRINTER was a precarious one. The responses to the insecurity of work run through this chapter in which the establishment and effectiveness of wage agreements are examined in the light of information on wages paid from actual records. The formation of a trade union society which became a major influence in maintaining wage levels and its alliances with other print unions in the Irish Typographical Union form the theme of the latter part of this section. Financial pressures due to unemployment levels in 1847 led to the secession of the Dublin branch from the National Typographical Association and its re-establishment as an independent society.

PAY SCALES

Printing was one of the best paid trades if work could be obtained, but under-employment was rife, exacerbated all through the half century by an over-abundant supply of apprentices. The printing business had a regular annual cycle of activity in the autumn and winter and slackness in late spring and summer. The unpredict-able demand for printed material led to the development of a two tier system of employment for compositors and pressmen. This was a more marked feature in book and jobbing houses than in newspaper offices where the amount of type to be set each week remained reasonably constant. A fortunate minority of employees were in full-time employment on the establishment, i.e. paid a weekly wage, others were employed on piecework as need arose. Towards the end of the eighteenth century a practice developed of negotiating wage scales in individual cities. The earliest formal agreement known in the British Isles was for the London trade. This was signed in 1785, modified in 1793, and replaced by further agreements in 1805 and 1810, the latter being modified in 1816.[1] Five agreements are known for the Dublin trade in the nineteenth century, the first of which, modelled on the London one, came into force on 1 January 1800.[2] The second started on 1 July 1808; the third, in 1822, is only

---

[1] E. Howe, *The London Compositor*, London, 1947, pp. 171, 188–90.
[2] *Prices of Printing Work, agreed upon by the Employers and Journeymen of the City of Dublin, commencing January 1, 1800* [Dublin, 1799]. (Copy in St Bride's Printing Historical Library, London).

known about from evidence given much later to the Select Committee on Combinations of Workmen; the fourth dates from early 1829 and was in force until 1870; the last was adopted in March of that year.[3] There was a widespread development of similar scales in other cities of the United Kingdom; separate ones, derived in many cases from the London ones, were in force in Edinburgh in 1805, Manchester in 1810, Glasgow in 1815 and Leeds in 1826.[4]

The Dublin scales deal separately with the rates for compositors and pressmen, and are entirely concerned with piecework. No mention is made of establishment wages. Under the terms of the 1800 agreement the basic rate for compositors setting bookwork in typesizes between English and Brevier was fourpence halfpenny per thousand ens, while the smaller sizes of Minion and Nonpareil were to be paid at fivepence halfpenny, and the smallest, Pearl, at sixpence per thousand ens. Head and direction lines were included in the casting up of the work. This last provision had only been conceded in London in 1793.[5] Matters that called for detailed regulation include the use of small type in side, bottom, uncut and cross notes, setting in foreign languages and dictionaries. Article XI of the compositors' scale stipulates:

that jobs of every description, not otherwise provided for, be entitled to an increase of three pence in each shilling, according to the rules which govern bookwork: — and that all extra work at the stone be paid sixpence per hour; where the time spent at the stone may not amount to an hour, less than sixpence per form shall not be paid for each time of laying up.[6]

The scale which came into operation in 1808 shows an increase in most rates for the compositors with the basic setting rate for bookwork rising from fourpence halfpenny to fivepence per thousand ens. The stipulation that manuscript copy be paid at the rate of one halfpenny per thousand in addition to the rules that governed bookwork appears here for the first time. This presumably reflects the changed conditions in the Dublin booktrade following the Copyright Act of 1801 when the reprinting of books published elsewhere ceased to be the staple of the trade. There are no details known about the 1822 agreement though Matthew Ryan stated to the

---

[3] *Prices of Printing Work agreed upon by the Employers and Journeymen of the City of Dublin, commencing July the first, 1808* [Dublin, 1808]; *Second Report from the Select Committee on Combinations of Workmen* (UK Parliamentary Papers 1837–1838, VIII, p. 425) p.105; *A Scale of Prices for Compositors and Pressmen, agreed upon by the Employers and Journeymen Printers of the City of Dublin, February 9, 1829*, Dublin, 1842 (a later edition printed in Dublin in 1853 has explanatory notes showing the general practice of the trade); *Compositors' Scale of Prices. Revised and adopted, March, 1870*, Dublin, 1877.

[4] E. Howe, *The London Compositor*, London, 1947, pp. 247–53.

[5] Ibid., p. 76.

[6] 'Anything which printed does not exceed a sheet is termed a Job, and is paid for extra to the compositor, because there is no return of furniture or of letter; he has generally to put up fresh cases, and has some additional trouble in getting the fight letter, and in making up the furniture.' W. Savage, *A Dictionary of the Art of Printing*, London, 1841, p. 428.

Select Committee on Combinations of Workmen that 'the men consented to a reduction in wages on particular works that were considered too highly paid before, and on which they [the employers] could not employ any but apprentices; and consequently, in order that the workmen might get the benefit of those works, they [the journeymen] reduced the prices'.[7] He also stated that in 1829 'there was another arrangement subsequently made, in which they reduced their weekly payments a second time, for the purpose of being able to get that work which the masters complained of as being too dear, and that they could not employ journeymen upon it'.[8] Though the 1829 scale retained the basic rate of fivepence per thousand for bookwork, and the extra halfpenny per thousand for manuscript copy, most of the other rates show a reduction on the 1808 scale. The principal features of the 1800, 1808 and 1829 scales are shown in Table 3.1.

There is very little information about the actual wages paid during the first quarter of the century; there is no extant wage-book. It is known that establishment wages for compositors reached their highest levels during the Napoleonic wars. Newspaper offices paid higher wages than book and jobbing offices; and morning newspapers paid more than evening ones because of the night work involved. In his evidence to the Select Committee on Combinations of Workmen in 1838 Michael Staunton recalled that 'before the termination of the war, 40s a week was the wages at the morning press of Dublin'.[9] In line with price reductions in the formal agreements between master printers and employees there was a gradual decline in compositors pay during the 1820s until in 1829 their pay in morning papers was only £1 10s a week. Before the adjustment of the Irish currency to par with the British one in 1826, the *Dublin Evening Post* had paid £1 16s. Efforts by the Dublin Typographical Provident Society to have this rate paid in the new money were so successfully resisted by management that by 1838 the paper only paid £1 1s and was a non-union house.[10] An attempt in March 1829 by the DTPS to enforce payment at the rate of £1 17s per week on morning papers and £1 12s 6d on evening papers led to a long dispute in which the DTPS was heavily defeated. By November 1829 the DTPS was recommending acceptance of £1 12s on morning papers and by February 1830 would accept £1 10s.[11]

The impact of the fall in wage rates was to some extent alleviated by a fall in commodity prices. There was a very considerable fall in the prices of potatoes, oats

---

[7] *Second Report from the Select Committee on Combinations of Workmen* (UK Parliamentary Papers 1837–1838, VIII, p. 425), p. 105.

[8] Ibid. (p. 426), p. 106.

[9] Ibid. (p. 367), p. 47.

[10] Ibid. (p. 388), p. 68.

[11] Dublin Typographical Provident Society, Committee minutes 14 November 1829; Dublin Typographical Provident Society, Council minutes 13 February 1830.

TABLE 3.1: COMPOSITOR'S RATES, 1800–1829

DATE OF SCALE	1800	1808	1829
Common matter, in type size of English to Brevier per 1000 ens	4½d	5d	5d
ditto, Minion/Nonpareil	5½d	6½d	5½d
Manuscript copy per 1000 ens	—	½d extra on bookwork	
Undersized work per sheet			
English or larger type	7s	8s	7s
Pica	9s	10s	8s 6d [Octavos and under 9s.]
Small Pica	11s	12s	11s
Long Primer	13s	15s	14s
Bourgeois	16s	18s	17s
Brevier	19s	21s	20s
Side notes per half page in a sheet	1s	1s	1s
Foreign work			
per sheet regular size	1s	5½d common type per 1000 ens	5½d common type per 1000 ens
per sheet above regular size	2s		6d minion 6¾d nonpareil 7¾d pearl
Shared work between houses extra per sheet	1s	1s	1s 6d
Ruled sale catalogues	Bookwork + 50%	Bookwork + 50%	—
sale catalogues	—	—	5½d per 1000 ens
English dictionaries per 1000 ens	5d	5½d	5½d
Correcting	6d	6d	6d

and wheat after 1815–1817. While prices of both fluctuated in the pre-famine decades, oats being somewhat higher than their levels in the 1790s and wheat at approximately the same levels as the early 1790s. Potatoes fell at times to levels lower than them. Price rises in the famine years were more marked in potatoes and oats than in wheat.[12]

There was only a slight improvement in wages during the 1830s. In 1838 the rate at the *Daily Morning Register* and two other morning papers was £1 12s 6d, a rate also paid by the evening papers; the best pay of all, £1 16s 11d per week, was on *Saunders's Newsletter*.[13] Gunn and Cameron, proprietors of the *General Advertiser*, who paid wages of £1 12s 6d a week in 1838, thought the costs of setting very expensive in Dublin. This was due to a limitation on the number of lines a compositor would set to 840 a week. This, they believed, could be done in 48 hours and reckoned it as equivalent to paying eightpence per 1000 ens compared to fivepence-halfpenny for the same work in Edinburgh.[14] It is difficult to draw absolutely direct comparisons without knowing the size of the letter involved, but the rate per 1000 ens compared favourably with those paid in 1835 in London on *The Times* where matter set in nonpareil was paid at a rate equivalent to eightpence-farthing per 1000 and where the news compositors, working 6 p.m. to 5 a.m., were on establishment wages of £2 8s a week.[15] By 1849 compositors on the *Freeman's Journal* were earning £1 14s 7½d per week.[16] Employees acting in a supervisory capacity were, of course, better paid. Michael Staunton paid his foreman at the *Daily Morning Register* 'about' £3 a week and provided him with rent-free accommodation.[17]

The earliest wage-book extant for a jobbing firm is that for Richard Webb's office [later Webb and Chapman] which was established in Great Brunswick Street in 1828.[18] It illustrates the precarious nature of employment for printers and suggests that local office arrangements ran contrary to the tidy regulations on work practices of the Dublin Typographical Provident Society. Webb's first journeyman, after earning 15s in his first week ending on 29 November 1828 was then put on establishment wages of £1 10s until early June 1829. Wages, however, were very variable for men working on piecework. M. Servant became an employee on piecework late in

[12] L. Kennedy and M.W. Dowling, 'Prices and wages in Ireland, 1700–1850', *Irish Economic and Social History*, XXIV (1997), pp. 62–104.
[13] *Second Report from the Select Committee on Combinations of Workmen* (UK Parliamentary Papers 1837–1838. VIII, p. 420), p. 100.
[14] Ibid. (p. 389), p. 69.
[15] *Report from the Trade Council of the London Union of Compositors, preparatory to a Special General Meeting to be held on Tuesday, the 15th September* [London, 1835] reprinted in E. Howe, *The London Compositor*, London, 1947, pp. 406–07, 414.
[16] DTPS Minutes of Committee meeting, 31 December 1849.
[17] *Second Report from the Select Committee on Combinations of Workmen* (UK Parliamentary Papers 1837–1838. VIII. p. 388), p. 68.
[18] NLI MS 139.

January 1829 and continued in employment until 9 May. His weekly earnings in that time ranged from 6s 1d to £1 3s 10d. In the sixteen weeks he earned more than £1 on four occasions and less than 11s on eight occasions. In March 1836 Patrick Garvey, who had served his apprenticeship to Webb, re-entered his employment as a journeyman. In the succeeding thirteen weeks his weekly wages ranged between a low of 15s and a high of £1 10s 6d, and only in seven weeks did he earn more than £1 4s. In a truly exceptional week ending 12 August 1848 one employee William Kite, earned £3 6s which comprised £1 10s for establishment wages, £1 10s for night work, and 6s for overtime.[19]

Although establishment wages in book-houses remained at £1 10s from the 1820s until at least 1870, in some cases larger wages were paid. Philip Dixon Hardy paid his best workman £1 12s 6d a week over a period of eight years, and then advanced his wages to £2 a week.[20] Hardy, who in the mid 1830s was one of the largest employers in the printing trade in Dublin, did 'not think 30s a week is over the fair price which a man, having served seven years, and having got a good education, or an education fitting him to be a compositor, in that department of printing should receive.'[21] Both Webb and Hardy employed some compositors on the establishment and others on piecework. Hardy considered that on very good work a good compositor could earn as much as £3 in a week but that 'it would take a good workman very nearly the same time to earn 30s. upon inferior work as a bad one'.[22] Although the bye-laws of the *Constitution* of the DTPS as revised in 1842 ordain that 'no member shall accept of employment, to be paid for the same on the establishment, for a shorter period than a fortnight' and Article II of the Appendix to the *Scale of prices* reprinted in 1853 explains that 'this rule strictly prohibits any member, although employed in the house, from doing work of any kind on time, except correcting, as provided by Article XXVI of the Scale, or making-up matter, by Article I of the Appendix.' There is abundant evidence in the employee's bill book of R. D. Webb's of employees working part of the week on time and part on piecework.[23] In the week ending 28 October 1848 William Kite spent one hour on Monday, and two on Thursday on time, two days on the establishment, and also set 772 pages of Connolly's catalogue at piecework rates.[24]

---

[19] R. D. Webb./Webb and Chapman bill book f. 92v.

[20] *Second Report from the Select Committee on Combinations of Workmen* (UK Parliamentary Papers 1837–1838. VIII. p.350), p. 30.

[21] Ibid. (p. 357), p. 37.

[22] Ibid. (p. 358), p. 38.

[23] *Constitution of the Dublin Typographical Provident Society*, Dublin, 1842, p. 29; *Scale of Prices for Compositors and Pressmen, agreed upon by the Employers and Journeymen Printers of the City of Dublin, February 9, 1829*, Dublin, 1853, p. 31.

[24] NLI Ms 141 £102.

The establishment wage of compositors in bookhouses placed them among the elite of the working classes in Dublin. The table of 'the full regulated pay for the best men in their respective trades' in Dublin in 1845 given by Thomas Willis in *Facts Connected with the Social and Sanitary Condition of the Working Classes in the City of Dublin*, Dublin, 1845, has printers, hatters, ironfounders and tailors at the top with £1 10s per week followed by slators, plumbers and housepainters at £1 8s. Few skilled occupations were rated below £1 6s per week. The gap between these levels and the pay of unskilled workers was large; shop porters and bricklayers' labourers earned only 10s a week. The wages for compositors in Dublin outstripped those paid elsewhere in Ireland, for compositors in Belfast earned between £1 1s and £1 5s; in Derry between £1 1s and £1 4s; in Cork £1 1s.[25] Wages in book houses in Great Britain ranged from £1 13s in London, to £1 5s in Glasgow.[26]

The regulations governing pressmens' pay increased in complexity with the successive agreements between the master-printers and the journeymen. The agreement which came into force on 1 January 1800 began by establishing the standard sizes, the width of line and number of lines of an octavo, duodecimo and octavo-decimo formats, and the price to be paid per hour for presswork on such forms when they were set in the standard letter size of Long Primer, or a larger typesize.[27] This rate, 4d per hour, applied where an edition size of 1000 or more was being worked off. The basic rate was increased to fourpence halfpenny per hour under the 1808 agreement, and remained at that level until 1870.[28] In the 1829 agreement the pressmen made a concession on the width of a line of octavo, from 21 to 24 Pica ens.[29] Any variation from the standard limits in the number of lines, width of the page, or size of the type was subject to a surcharge. It is a measure of the unambitious nature of the printing work being done in Dublin at the start of the century that no separate scale for folio or quarto work occurred until the 1829 agreement.

It was, wrote Caleb Stower in 1808 'the general custom to print of every work what is called an even number, either 250, 500, 750, 1000, etc. These quantities are set out for the wetter in tokens: viz. for 250 (sheets) one token containing 10 quires 18 sheets.'[30] The norm for reckoning costs was one token printed on one side per hour,

---

[25] *Second Report from the Select Committee on Combinations of Workmen* (UK Parliamentary Papers 1837–1838. VIII. p. 426), p. 106.
[26] [C. Knight]. *The Printer*, London, [1847], p. 37; *Second Report from the Select Committee on Combinations of Workmen* (UK Parliamentary Papers. 1837–1838. VIII. p. 347), p. 27.
[27] *Prices of Printing Work, agreed upon by the Employees and Journeymen of the City of Dublin, commencing January 1, 1800* [Dublin, 1799].
[28] *Prices of Printing Work, agreed upon by the Employees and Journeymen of the City of Dublin, commencing July the first, 1808* [Dublin, 1808].
[29] *A Scale of Prices for Compositors and Pressmen, agreed upon by the Employers and Journeymen Printers of the City of Dublin, February 9, 1829*, Dublin, 1842, p. 13.
[30] C. Stower, *The Printer's Grammar*, London, 1808, p. 403.

the eight extra sheets being 'allowed for tympan-sheets, register sheets, and other incidents, such as bad sheets, faults committed in beating, pulling, bad register, &c'.[31] The surcharge on printing a lesser number than 1000 grew heavier as the edition size shrank. For octavos where only 750 copies were to be printed an extra halfpenny was charged per hour's work; if only 500 copies, an extra penny per hour; if 250 copies, then an extra penny-halfpenny per hour. These surcharges for octavos set in Long Primer remained constant in all the agreements, but beginning with the 1829 agreement matter set in type of sizes smaller than Long Primer carried an increased surcharge of a halfpenny an hour for Bourgeois and Brevier, and a penny an hour for Nonpareil. Charges for duodecimos and octodecimos in Long Primer ran at the same level as for octavos until 1829 when the surcharge for an edition size of 250 became twopence-halfpenny on the basic rate of fourpence-halfpenny and further charges for small typefaces. The surcharge reflected the unavoidable fixed costs of make-ready, i.e. the time involved in cutting the frisket, ensuring that the register was correct, and any packing of the tympan necessary to secure a good impression. Under the 1800 and 1808 agreements all works exceeding the standard length of line by an em were 'to be paid at the rate of one halfpenny [extra] per hour, and for every additional *m*, one farthing per hour'.[32] The 1829 agreement provided for charging a halfpenny per hour for extra width, unless the edition size was 250 copies, in which case an extra penny per hour was required.[33] Further provisions in each agreement provided rates for all sorts of jobbing work; variables included the size and quality of paper other than common printing paper, such as super royal or superfine thick post, work to be done on parchment, or with coloured ink.

By 1828 the Dublin Typographical Provident Society had to take account of the rising importance of new technology, stereotype plates, the use of which required an extra skill from the pressman, both in laying the plates, often done by the compositor, and in bringing up the forme. Writing in 1825 T. C. Hansard explained 'to place, or lay down those plates, a compositor alone can be possessed of adequate skill, and his time must be valued — a proof must be pulled, folded, and followed — batters and other accidents looked after and repaired, if the printer is to have any regard to the appearance of the work'.[34] As for the actual printing he wrote, 'the trouble of preparation, to the pressmen, of even the best-cast and most accurately-dressed plates, is considerable; and in very open works, from the height of the field

---

[31] Ibid., p. 404.

[32] *Prices of Printing Work, commencing January 1 1800*, Dublin, 1799. Article VII of the pressmen's scale.

[33] *A Scale of Prices for Compositors and Pressmen, February 9, 1829*, 1842, p. 13.

[34] T. C. Hansard, *Typographia*, London, 1825, p. 831.

of the plates, a frisket of the greatest accuracy, must be cut for each forme.'[35] On 20 August 1828 the DTPS committee resolved that pressmen should be paid an allowance above normal rates on a sliding scale related to the number of sheets to be printed. This scale called for threepence per hour extra where 1000 or fewer were to be worked, twopence for 1000 to 1500 copies, a penny halfpenny for 1500 to 3000, a penny for 3,000 to 10,000 copies; and a halfpenny for numbers above 10,000. In the 1829 agreement this scale was consolidated into lump sum payments: for laying plates in octavo or duodecimo whether by compositor or pressman, sixpence; in the case of eighteens or twenty fours, ninepence; and a payment of sixpence to the pressman for bringing-up the forme.[36]

Pressmen's wages were generally lower than those of compositors, and the work, though requiring more physical strength, was less demanding intellectually. Press-men were generally employed on piecework, although in newspaper offices some had jobs on the establishment. In the course of the settlement of a dispute with the proprietor of the *Daily Morning Register*, the Committee of the DTPS resolved that 'the sum of £1 10s each be the salary for the three pressmen employed there'.[37] The employee whom P. D. Hardy trained as a machine printer in the mid 1830s 'had been a common pressman, earning not more than a guinea or 25s a week, or 30s, at the utmost'.[38]

The only records for the Dublin booktrade which allow a study of the relationship between work done and the wages paid in this period are those for R. D. Webb/Webb & Chapman in Great Brunswick Street. The surviving men's bill book, which lists the work completed by the compositors and pressmen and the amount they charged their employer, covers the period 28 February 1846 to 12 October 1850.[39] The book indicates the complexity of employment practices, with compositors employed for part of the time on the establishment, sometimes employed on a mixture of time and piecework, or entirely on piecework. At the beginning of 1846 the firm was only getting enough work to keep one press fully occupied — operated by Edward Smith and Thomas Brady (succeeded after 5 December 1846 by A. Ferguson). Occasionally, and with increasing frequency, a second press was brought into operation, and one

35 Ibid., p. 831.
36 *A Scale of Prices for Compositors and Pressmen, February 9, 1829*, Dublin, 1842, p. 14.
37 DTPS Minutes of Committee meeting, 14 November 1829.
38 *Second Report from the Select Committee on Combinations of Workmen* (UK Parliamentary Papers 1837–1838 VIII. p. 356), p. 36.
39 R. D. Webb/Webb and Chapman bill book.

of the compositors, M. Byrne, usually formed part of the team for this. This practice of working at case and at press was contrary to the express advice given by the Committee of the Dublin Typographical Provident Society on 18 February 1843, that 'in every house where pressmen are employed, no compositor ought to interfere, or take any work which should be accomplished by them, but that in every instance the pressmen should get the preference.'

The wages earned by the regular team varied widely from one dismal week ending 15 August 1846 when the partnership only earned 15s to a high point of £3 16s 5d in the week ending 13 July 1850. Figures extracted from the wage book of the firm from 28 February 1846 to 28 December 1850 show that in 163 weeks out of 243 the earnings of each pressman exceeded £1 5s, and that in 70 weeks earnings exceeded the establishment rate of £1 10s paid to compositors, as shown in Tables 3.2–3.3.[40]

TABLE 3.2: EARNINGS PATTERN OF SMITH AND PARTNER AT PRESS
FEBRUARY 1846 TO DECEMBER 1850

	1846	1847	1848	1849	1850
No. of weeks earning 15s or more	44	—	—	—	—
No. of weeks earning £1 0s 1d or more	43	—	—	52	—
No. of weeks earning £1 5s 1d or more	43	52	—	51	52
No. of weeks earning £1 10s 1d or more	39	51	53	51	51
No. of weeks earning £1 15s 1d or more	34	50	52	50	50
No. of weeks earning £2 0s 1d or more	32	45	52	49	45
No. of weeks earning £2 5s 1d or more	29	44	45	40	41
No. of weeks earning £2 10s 1d or more	23	38	42	30	30
No. of weeks earning £2 15s 1d or more	18	25	36	25	18
No. of weeks earning £3 0s 1d or more	12	13	26	10	9
No. of pay weeks in period	44	52	53	52	52

[40] R. D. Webb/Webb and Chapman wages book, fols 29v–47v.

TABLE 3.3: EARNINGS PATTERN OF SMITH AND PARTNER AT PRESS
28 FEBRUARY 1846 TO 31 DECEMBER 1850

	1846	1847	1848	1849	1850
No. of weeks earning 10s to 15s	1	—	—	—	—
No. of weeks earning 15s 1d to £1	—	—	—	—	—
No. of weeks earning £1 0s 1d to £1 5s	—	—	—	1	—
No. of weeks earning £1 5s 1d to £1 10s	4	1	—	—	1
No. of weeks earning £1 10s 1d to £1 15s	5	1	1	1	1
No. of weeks earning £1 15s 1d to £2	2	5	—	1	5
No. of weeks earning £2 0s 1d to £2 5s	3	1	7	9	5
No. of weeks earning £2 5s 1d to £2 10s	6	6	3	10	11
No. of weeks earning £2 10s 1d to £2 15s	5	13	6	5	12
No. of weeks earning £2 15s 1d to £3	6	12	10	15	9
No. of weeks earning £3 0s 1d to £3 5s	8	7	19	4	7
No. of weeks earning £3 5s 1d to £3 10s	3	4	5	4	—
No. of weeks earning £3 10s 1d to £3 15s	1	2	2	1	1
No. of weeks earning £3 15s 1d to £4	—	—	—	1	1
No. of pay weeks	44	52	53	52	52

There was a marked contrast between the relatively high earnings of Smith and Ferguson on the first press, and those of M. Byrne who was on piece work and working partly at case and partly at press e.g.

Week ending	Smith/Ferguson partnership	M. Byrne
6 May 1848	£3 2s 4d	10s
13 May 1848	£3 9s	8s 4½d
20 May 1848	£2 0s 10d	5s 4d
27 May 1848	£2 10s 11d	16s
3 June 1848	£3 9s 2d	16s[41]

---

[41] Ibid. f. 37v.

M. Byrne's bill for the last week of the period shows the mixed nature of his work. The reference to Curran is to his companion at press with whom he had worked off 200 handbills for Malone Brothers, and 500 handbills for the Kingstown Jetty.

3⅓ pages of Connolly's catalogue at 3s per page	10s
deduct rec. on a/c	9s
2⅓ pages Methodist Mag[azine] Brev[ier]	4s 8d
Half of Curran's bill 8s 4d	4s 2d
500 Working Kingstown Lying in Hopstl [sic] handbill	1s 8d
Saturday 9 hours on time sundries	4s 6d [42]

A rush of work could push up earnings to a very high level. In August 1848 there was a sudden demand for railway tickets. M. Byrne spent the weeks ending 5 August 1848, and 12 August 1848 working solidly on this job, manning the machine press.

Week ending 5 August 1848 [43]		
Monday 11 hours on time altering & resetting Railway tickets &c	5s 6d	
Tuesday 11 on same & cor sundries	5s 6d	
Tuesday night 12 on Tickets at machine	5s 6d	
Wednesday night 12 same	6s	
Thursday night 12 same	6s	
Friday night 12 same	6s	
4 nights overhours on do		£1
Sat night (from 7 to 12 o'clock) with overhours	4s	
		£2 19s

Week ending 12 August 1848 [44]	
Sunday night 7 hours (12 to 7 o'clock) with overtime at machine. Railway tickets	7s
Monday night 12hrs same	6s
Tuesday night 12 hrs same	6s
Wednesday night 12 hrs same	6s
Thursday night 12 hrs same	6s

---

42 R. D. Webb/Webb and Chapman bill book, f. 83v.
43 Ibid., f. 90r.
44 Ibid., f. 91r.

Friday night 12 hrs same		6s
Overtime on five nights	£1	5s
Saturday night 5 hours (7–12) with overtime		4s
	£3	**6s**

The ticket printing was going on all day as well for A. Ferguson earned £1 10s for working it in normal hours.[45] The amount of work done by Smith and Ferguson in their highest paid week (that ending 13 July 1850) was enormous and shows the range from bookwork on Churchill and Larcom to placards and labels.[46]

1500	Churchill 2 half sheets no. 22–23		16s
500	Placards J. H. Webb shirts	9s	2d
200	Placards for Myles McDonald	3s	8d
1000	Engineers Table Book Sig. D	4s	8d
500	Report Captain Larcom Title		2s
500	do. inner forme		2s
500	circular Bewley & Evans		2s
700	Cards for do. Blue ink	4s	8d
100	Copies J -L Naghten Quarto		10d
200	Quarter sheet for Steward	1s	2d
250	Circulars A Lesage Blue ink	1s	7d
500	2 Set Parcels Dockets K. R. Ruled	1s	10d
200	Kingstown Jetty		10d
	23 hours on Murrays labels	£1	6s
Total		**£3 16s**	**5d**

The wage books of R. D. Webb/Webb and Chapman clearly illustrate the volatility of employment. In October 1842 the highest number employed by Webb and Chapman in any week was 19, the lowest 12; in October of the following year the highest number was 28, the lowest 12. In October 1849 the numbers ranged between 20 and 9.[47]

The matters which most concerned the journeymen printers in the early nineteenth century were the two issues which had agitated most skilled trades since time immemorial, namely, the attempt to ensure security of employment by restricting

---

[45] Ibid., f. 92r.

[46] Ibid., f. 163r.

[47] R. D. Webb/Webb and Chapman wages book, fols 7r, 20r, 20v, 43r.

entry to the trade and their determination to maintain their wage levels. Printers had been among the better paid journeymen in the eighteenth century.[48] They continued to be so in the nineteenth century, but the pattern of piecework employment left the journeyman very vulnerable to fluctuations in business activity.[49] Much of the history of the journeymen printers in this period is concerned with their attempts to establish and maintain a strong trade union, capable of negotiating wage rates and hours of work with employers, and capable of ensuring observance of agreements by masters and journeymen. Other trade union concerns were the provision of relief for out-of-work members, and, in the mid-1830s, the impact on jobs posed by the application of steam power to printing.

The number of journeymen printers in Dublin increased considerably during the half century. The amicable society of printers claimed to have 76 members in 1773 and there may have been others outside that body.[50] The membership of the DTPS grew from 258 in 1833 to 347 in 1842, and to 356 by mid-1849.[51] Returns from the census of 1831 for Dublin city and county give a total of 503 printers. The figure includes males of twenty years and upwards working in the trade and so puts masters, journeymen and appropriately aged apprentices in a single category.[52] Returns from the 1841 census were analysed differently and figures were given for male and female workers over and under the age of 15. This brought a larger proportion of apprentices into the higher category. The total in the trade over the age of 15 was 759 (including one female) and 39 under that age.[53] The returns from the 1851 census were analysed in similar fashion to the returns for 1841 and show a further growth in the trade: the total of letterpress printers in the city and county had now reached 903 in the case of workers over the age of 15 and 44 under that age.[54] The expansion in the numbers recorded is evidence of the increased availability of apprenticeship and of a demand for labour at that price level. It is clear that the demand for journeymen labour did not often match its supply. In reply to a question on the level of employment of the 429 printers recorded in the 1831 census Michael Staunton told the Select Committee on Combinations of Workmen that he believed

[48] M. Plant, *The English Book Trade*. 3rd ed. London, 1974, p. 157.

[49] T. Willis, *Facts Connected with the Social and Sanitary Condition of the Working Classes in the City of Dublin*, Dublin, 1845, p. 34.

[50] *Dublin Gazette*, 26 January 1773.

[51] *Constitution of the Dublin Typographical Provident Society*, Dublin, 1833. pp. 17–20; *Constitution of the Dublin Typographical Provident Society*, Dublin, 1842, pp. 31–34; *Typographical Protection Circular* no. 6 (June 1849), p. 21.

[52] *Population of Ireland* (UK Parliamentary Papers. Accounts and Papers. 1833. XXXIX p. 76) p. 14; (p. 86), p. 24.

[53] *Report of the Commissioners appointed to take the Census of Ireland, for the year 1841* (UK Parliamentary Papers. 1843. XXIV, p. 130), 22; (p. 142), p. 34.

[54] *The Census of Ireland for the year 1851*. Part VI. General Report (UK Parliamentary Papers 1856. XXXI. p. 173, 188), pp. 29, 44.

'that not more than half that number of printers are employed'.[55] Thomas Daly thought that only about 140 of the members of the DTPS had permanent employment.[56]

These increases in numbers occurred despite extensive emigration. In the four years 1834 to 1837 the DTPS assisted 120 members to emigrate. The usual reason was 'want of employment; there are cases where men from choice wish to emigrate, but they are very few in number'.[57] In the eleven months following the reinstatement of emigration allowances in 1 May 1848 a total of 29 members received emigration money, 14 to go to England, 5 to America and 10 to provincial destinations.[58] During the summer of 1849 a further 8 members went to America and 1 to Australia.[59] Some of the emigrants returned to Dublin but the majority do not appear to have done so. Unemployment was heavy among those who remained; between 1834 and 1836 the Dublin Typographical Provident Society paid £226 17s 1d, £195 5s 2d, and £190 12s 9d in unemployment benefit.[60] As an unemployed man could draw benefit at the rate of £4 per annum then, the money paid was equivalent to having between 47 and 56 men continuously out of work. Thomas Daly ascribed the level of unemployment among journeymen at the time more to the unchecked growth in the number of apprentices than to a decline in the amount of work commissioned.[61] The numbers claiming benefit in the late 1840s show unemployment ranging up over 25% of the workforce on occasion during the slump of 1847.

APPRENTICES

The simplest way for a master printer to keep his labour costs down was to have apprentices do the bulk of the work. The recognised period of apprenticeship in the trade was seven years both for compositors and pressmen, but an apprentice quickly acquired enough skill to be economically useful to his master. P. D. Hardy remarked to the Select Committee on Combinations of Workmen in 1838 that 'I consider in our business so much may be learned by a lad in six months, as to enable him to come here [i.e. London] and get a situation on a paper, or in Dublin, or in a country

---

[55] *Second Report from the Select Committee on Combinations of Workmen* (UK Parliamentary Papers 1837–1838 VIII p. 379), p. 59.

[56] Ibid., (p. 421–22), p. 102.

[57] Ibid., (p. 417), p. 97.

[58] DTPS Printed Abstract of accounts 1 April 1848 – 31 March 1849 in DTPS Committee Minute Book at April 1849.

[59] Typographical Protection Circular 8 (August 1849), p. 30.

[60] *Second Report from the Select Committee on Combinations of Workmen* (UK Parliamentary Papers 1837–1838. VIII. p. 417), p. 97.

[61] Ibid., (p. 418), p. 98.

town; it is merely setting up types, and therefore many would try it.'[62] The economic advantage, to an employer at that date can readily be seen in the difference between the wages of 10s per week paid to an apprentice in his final year, and the £1 10s per week which a journeyman who had just finished serving his time would earn on establishment wages.[63]

Beginners in the trade were taken as either indoor or outdoor apprentices at various rates of premium. A premium of £100 is said to have been paid when M. H. Gill was apprenticed to Graisberry and Campbell.[64] On removing his business from North Earl Street to 156 Capel Street in 1817, T. Henderson advertised that 'a lad of genteel connexions will be taken as an in-door apprentice with a moderate fee.'[65] In 1830 N. D. Kelly advertised that 'a respectable lad will be taken as an indoor apprentice and treated as one of the family, to the wholesale and retail stationery paper and leather department, and general printing establishment. A fee will be required.'[66] Brett Smith wanted a pressman and a compositor in 1824 and was prepared to give a liberal salary 'to a lad who has served a part of his apprenticeship to the printing business, for the remainder of the term.'[67] Speaking of apprentice compositors in 1838, P. D. Hardy said that 'So far as my apprentices go, I have had 20 l., and two years' diet and lodging; that is, the parents board and lodge them for two years; I never take an in-door apprentice but we allow them 5s, 6s, 7s, 8s, 9s, and 10s a week.'[68]

The progress of a few apprentices can be followed in the wage book for R. D. Webb's jobbing printing office.[69] His first apprentice, Patt Garvey began at 3s a week from the beginning of 1828 to the beginning of December 1829; for the following three years he earned 5s a week, and then in January 1833 was placed on 7s a week. Economic difficulties in the business resulted in a reduction to 6s a week for several months after mid June 1833, but for most of 1834 he earned 7s a week, and this rose in December 1834 to 10s a week for his last year of apprenticeship. Occasionally he was it seems able to earn larger sums for the amount of £1 11s 2d was paid him on 22 March 1834. Webb's last apprentice in this period, G. Perrin, earned 3s a week in his first year, beginning at the end of August 1848, and rose by annual increments of one shilling to earn 8s a week from September 1853 to September 1854, and thereafter was paid 10s a week for his final year.

---

[62] Ibid., (p. 363), p. 43.
[63] Ibid., (p. 353), p. 33.
[64] P. White, 'The printing trade in Dublin', *The Irish Printer*, IV, no. 1 (August 1908), p. 6.
[65] *Saunders's Newsletter* 24 January 1817.
[66] Ibid., 19 July 1830.
[67] Ibid., 10 March 1824.
[68] *Second Report from the Select Committee on Combinations of Workmen* (UK Parliamentary Papers 1837–1838. VIII. p. 353), p. 33.
[69] R. D. Webb/Webb and Chapman wages book, NLI Ms. 139.

Michael Staunton, in running a newspaper office, had a different practice for apprentice compositors:

I never required a fee in any instance, and in my case the apprentice comes very speedily into the enjoyment of wages. In six months I put him in receipt of six shillings a week, and he has an increase of a shilling a week each year, till he is out of his time, and sometimes I even exceed that; I give a volunteer shilling or two in most instances, and with me the apprentice has the advantage of permanent employment when out of his time.[70]

In another newspaper office, that of the *Dublin Monitor*, Patrick Pollard began employment as a boy and worked for a long period as a feeder to a steam printing press for 10s to 12s a week. On becoming an apprentice in September 1843 he was given £1 a week.[71] As far as apprentice pressmen were concerned Hardy considered the work to be 'mere manual labour; they are of an inferior grade; a lad without education will do as well as one with it, if he is a smart lad; and he is paid from the commencement.'[72]

For the journeymen the two dangers in an unrestricted growth of apprentice numbers was the damage to the employment prospects of journeymen, and inadequate levels of training. For the employers who operated fair houses, i.e. who worked in harmony with the DTPS, there was the risk of price undercutting by those establishments which were run mainly on apprentice labour. There is a long international history of disputes between journeymen and masters on the question of excessive numbers of apprentices. In England journeymen printers raised an agitation on the issue in 1666.[73] In Ireland legal limits were placed in the early eighteenth century on the number of apprentices that could be taken at any one time. By mid-century, abuses were such that the Dublin printers advertised in the *Dublin Gazette* of 12 November 1765 that in order 'to suppress the illicit Practice of all and every Person or Persons in the Business, who now have, or continue to take, more Apprentices thereto than each Master is allowed by Law, [they] are unanimously determined, immediately to put in full Force, an Act passed in the Eighth Year of Queen Anne, whereby very considerable Fines are to be levied on all those who, at any time, presume to take and keep above two Apprentices.' They went on to claim that there were more than 116 apprentices and only 70 journeymen in the city. In their petition to the House of Commons in 1780, the journeymen printers complained that they

[70] *Second Report from the Select Committee on Combinations of Workmen* (UK Parliamentary Papers 1837–1838. VIII. p. 373), p. 33.

[71] *Saunders's Newsletter*, 20 April 1844.

[72] *Second Report from the Select Committee on Combinations of Workmen* (UK Parliamentary Papers 1837–1838. VIII. p. 353), p. 53.

[73] Howe, *The London Compositor*, p. 111.

would be brought to 'actual ruin' by the 'Practice of carrying on the Printing Business in the Country Towns of this Kingdom almost entirely by Apprentices, who afterwards pour into *Dublin*, and glut the Business with their Number's to the great Injury and infinite Distress of the Petitioners.'[74] They gave figures of 140 journeymen and 127 apprentices in the country and held that 'scarcely one-third are employed; and except those engaged on Newspapers, that small number are not upon an average, half a year kept at work, from the injurious custom of taking too many apprentices.'

The issue continued to be contentious. In 1838 Matthew Ryan dated the start of serious trouble over apprenticeships to 1810.[75] In April 1825 Michael Farrell, Chief Constable of the police in Dublin, gave evidence to the Select Committee on Combination Laws that 'there is a very serious misunderstanding on the subject of apprentices, particularly in the bookprinting.'[76] The unemployment in Dublin in 1825 was so grave that the journeyman printers issued a statement to the public 'in the hope of preventing unwary parents from becoming the dupes of artful and designing persons.'[77] They felt obliged 'to lay open and expose an iniquitous system of fraud and imposition, practised by petty master printers in this city, and the provincial towns throughout Ireland.' These men 'by representations of the prosperous state of the printing business — of the respectability and intelligence of the members of that Art — of the golden prospects that await a young man completing his Apprenticeship contrive to have apprentices indentured to them with a fee.' The instruction of the apprentice was neglected in the hope that he would ask for his indentures to complete his instruction elsewhere, which request would be readily conceded 'and, thus, room is made for another Boy and *another fee.*'

The journeymen gave their view of the real state of the trade 'in order to dissipate the delusions which these interested individuals have so industriously disseminated, and prevent, as far as we can, the calamitous consequences that, inevitably ensue to the victims of their avarice and peculation'. They believed that 'the art of printing in this country, at no time prosperous, has been for many years rapidly decaying under the withering influence of English monopoly'; that since the introduction of the Copyright Act:

no work of sterling merit has ever issued from the Press of Ireland — the brilliant productions of the prolific genius of her sons have been executed by English capital and English workmen; so that nothing is left for the degraded Press of this country but Newspapers, Hand-bills, and such ephemeral Pamphlets as are only adapted to the

---

[74] *Journals of the House of Commons of Ireland*, vol. X, Dublin, 1796, p. 115.

[75] *Second Report from the Select Committee on Combinations of Workmen* (UK Parliamentary Papers 1837–1838. VIII. p. 425), p. 105.

[76] *Report from the Select Committee on Combination Laws* (UK Parliamentary Papers, 1825. IV. p. 588), p. 20.

[77] *Saunders's Newsletter*, 2 April 1825.

opinions of the day and the circumstances of the place, and can be of no interest anywhere else.

But the number of hands had increased, and wages been so driven down that:

no trade or profession requiring an equal proportion of intelligence is so badly paid as printing. In most of the printing establishments in Dublin, an intense and unremitting application, during sixteen hours in the day, and six days in the week, is requited by a pittance so trifling, as to be insufficient for the comforts of the Applicant himself, independent of his wife and family.

This was, perhaps, overstating the case.

TRADE UNIONISM

The journeymen printers' reaction to the uncertainties of their lives was the formation of friendly societies that were the precursors of trade unions. Other trades in Dublin had similar organisations, carpenters as early as 1764, the builders in the 1780s, and the saddlers in 1791.[78] The Irish Parliament had taken notice of 'unlawful combinations' as early as 1729 and passed an act to prevent their existence.[79] Acts passed later in the century continued the pressure on workers' organisations, and one passed in 1780, *An act to prevent combinations, and for the further encouragement of trade*, removed previous limitations on the taking of apprentices either as to number or creed. The law on combinations in Ireland was brought into conformity with that of England (but with more severe penalties) after the Act of Union, and was eventually repealed in 1824 allowing tradesmens' societies to come into the open.

Trade unions were a considerable force in the craft-based occupations as early as 1820. D'Arcy records twenty unions of skilled labour that year, rising up to forty-five unions by 1850. Some trades had more than one union. Most were comparatively small. Of a sample of sixteen unions examined in the 1830s only three had more than 300 members; some were enormous, like the tailors with over 1,000 members, others, such as the glovers with twelve members, minute. Printers were in the upper range in numbers in the trade at 429 in 1831. The degree of unionisation in the trades varied. In 1836 three trades, cabinet makers, hatters and paintstainers claimed 100% membership. D'Arcy suggests that only 45% of printers belonged to the DTPS in the early 1830s.[80]

---

[78] *Fifth Report from Select Committee on Artizans and Machinery* (UK Parliamentary Papers 1824. v.), pp. 429, 446; J. Gandon, jun. and T. J. Mulvany, *The Life of James Gandon*, Dublin, 1846, pp. 63–64, p. 446.
[79] 3 Geo II. C. 14 (Ireland).
[80] F. D'Arcy, 'Dublin artisan activity, opinion and organisation, 1820–1850'. Unpublished M.A. thesis, N.U.I. 1968.

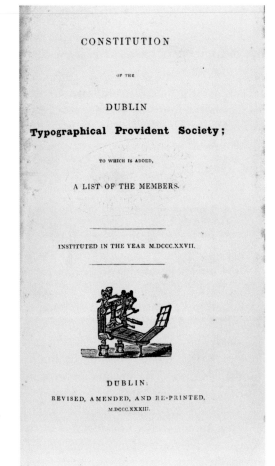

CONSTITUTION

OF THE

DUBLIN

Typographical Provident Society;

TO WHICH IS ADDED,

A LIST OF THE MEMBERS.

INSTITUTED IN THE YEAR M.DCCC.XXVII.

DUBLIN:
REVISED, AMENDED, AND RE-PRINTED,
M.DCCC.XXXIII.

Figures 18 and 19. Title-page and opening preamble of the revised constitution of a key journeyman fraternity in the printing trade (Dublin, 1833). *Haliday Pamphlet Collection: courtesy of the Royal Irish Academy Library.*

   The roots of journeymen printers' organisations in Dublin go back at least to the 1770s. The 'amicable society of printers, being seventy-six in number' publicly repudiated some scurrilous journalism published in the *Monitor* in 1773.[81] In 1795 they petitioned the House of Commons again, this time against a renewal of the importation duties on paper.[82] With the exception of these few public announcements and the printed wage agreements between representatives of the journeymen and masters dating from 1800 and 1808, the existence of the societies remained shadowy due to the penalties enforcible under the combination laws.[83] It can be

[81] *Dublin Gazette*, 26 January 1773.
[82] *Journals of the House of Commons of Ireland*, vol. XVI, Dublin, 1796, p. 193.
[83] For a discussion of this legislation see J. D. Clarkson, *Labour and Nationalism in Ireland*, New York, 1925, p. 33–57.

CONSTITUTION

OF THE

𝔇ublin

TYPOGRAPHICAL PROVIDENT SOCIETY.

ARTICLE I.

Of the Name and Objects of the Society.

THIS Society shall be styled " THE DUBLIN TYPO-
GRAPHICAL PROVIDENT SOCIETY," and shall be composed of the Journeymen Printers of the City of Dublin:

Its Objects shall be, the formation of a permanent Fund
for affording relief to such of its Members as may, from
time to time, be out of employment—assist such as may
wish to Emigrate—settle the price of Labour, by communication, between the Employers and Employed—and
promote the general interests of its Members.

ARTICLE II.

Of the Officers and Boards for conducting the Society.

The Officers shall consist of two Treasurers and a
Secretary; and the business to be conducted by a Council
and Committee.

concluded that some form of society was in operation before 1800 for when the application of Anthony Egan to join the Dublin Typographical Provident Society came before that body's council on 15 May 1830 it was stated on his behalf that he had served his apprenticeship to Hugh Fitzpatrick, that he had been working in London for thirty-one years, and that he had been a member of the former society.[84]

The DTPS (now the Irish Print Union) regards 1809 as its year of origin.[85] However, an unidentified correspondent, D.O., in a letter dated 26 September 1808 and published in the *Freeman's Journal* on 1 October promised to give the editor 'a particular account of the meetings that are held by the Journeymen Printers, of the

---

[84] DTPS Minutes of Council meeting, 15 May 1830.
[85] *The Irish Printer*, v, no. 5 (December 1909), pp. 3–6 recording the centenary banquet.

regulations and laws which they make; in short, of the system of combination which they have adopted.' No details were published. In his evidence to the Select Committee on Combinations of Workmen in 1838 Matthew Ryan, then secretary of the Irish Typographical Union, stated that the society which was in existence in 1818 became extinct in 1825 'in consequence of its inefficiency to support, or be of advantage to, the men'.[86] According to Ryan the DTPS was established in reaction to the very severe unemployment among printers towards the end of 1825 and in 1826. This was so great that the printers appealed in the newspapers for donations and 'they were hurt at being obliged to make a public appeal, that they determined to avoid it in the future; and in consequence they formed the rules of the present Dublin society.'[87]

Despite Ryan's statement on the demise of one body in 1825, some form of amicable society seems to have had a continued existence. The evidence for this is a list of the journeymen who were admitted to membership of the DTPS in 1827. This list gives the names, a description of the journeymen's society affiliation (if any), and records the rate of entrance fee charged. The standard fee was one guinea, but of the forty-eight men who joined in 1827, five who paid only 6d to join were described as 'members of the A.S.'; another who was described as a 'former member of the A.S.' paid the full one guinea fee. Some others who had been variously members of the Carlisle, Glasgow and Limerick societies paid at the concessionary rate of five shillings.[88]

The DTPS had a chequered existence in the years before 1850. It twice amalgamated with other societies, in the Irish Typographical Union from 1836 to 1842, and in the National Typographical Association from 1845 to 1847. Both of these alliances collapsed, the latter as a result of financial difficulties. The DTPS Council minute books, which also record many of the committee decisions, survive for the periods 1827 to 1830 and from 1845 to beyond 1850. The earliest extant rule book is the *Constitution of the Dublin Typographical Provident Society*, Dublin, revised, amended and reprinted 1833.[89] This edition, and one revised in 1842 following the break up of the Irish Typographical Union, provide lists of the members.[90] The objects of the society as listed in 1833 were 'the formation of a permanent fund for affording relief to such of its members as may, from time to time, be out of employment; [to] assist such as may wish to emigrate; [to] settle the price of labour, by communication, between the employers and employed; and [to] promote the general interests of its

---

[86] *Second Report from the Select Committee on Combinations of Workmen* (UK Parliamentary Papers 1837–1838. VIII. p. 425), p. 105.

[87] Ibid. (pp. 425–26) pp. 105–06. The appeal was published in *Saunders's Newsletter*, 19 September 1826.

[88] The list fills the last few pages of the DTPS Council Minute book for 1827–1930.

[89] Copy in the Royal Irish Academy, Haliday Pamphlets vol. 1563.

[90] *Constitution of the Dublin Typographical Provident Society*, Dublin: revised, amended and reprinted, 1842.

members'.[91] It was governed by a council and a committee assisted by a secretary and two treasurers. The council conducted the run-of-the-mill business of the society at its weekly meetings, and was composed of one delegate from each printing house in which three members were employed, a different person being chosen as delegate each month. Where only two members were employed a delegate needed to attend only once a fortnight. The principal duties of the delegates at their Saturday night meetings were to receive subscriptions, to admit new members, and to rule on claims from the funds. There was no regulation as to the frequency of meetings of the committee but the earliest extant minutes from 1845 show that it was meeting regularly each week on Tuesdays. Its main duties were to decide on appeals from the council or individuals, and to negotiate wages with the employers.[92]

Admission to the society was confined to men who had been properly apprenticed and who had served their time for seven years. In the case of applicants from Dublin offices, their indentures had to be produced and the applicant vouched for by two members. If the council accepted these as satisfactory the applicant's name, and details of his apprenticeship were circulated to the printers' chapels in the city and voted upon. The entry fee for a newly elected member was one guinea. A journeyman who came to work in Dublin, having already been a member of a similar society elsewhere, could join at the reduced fee of five shillings upon acceptance by the council of a card issued by his original society. The weekly subscription was 6d and the only concession to low paid workers was that members earning eight shillings or less did not have to pay the weekly subscription provided that the secretary was informed of the level of their earnings. There were penalties for late payment, and if arrears of subscriptions were not paid off within four Saturdays the offending member was expelled.[93]

The rules on qualification were strictly enforced. In 1843 the opinion of the various chapels on the application of a Mr. Rothwell to join the Society was sought by the council. He had certificates to prove his six-year apprenticeship in Edinburgh but the chapel of J. S. Folds's business considered that, despite six years being the acknowledged length of apprenticeship for pressmen there, it would be an infringement of the rules and also 'an injustice to those who must in this country, and in England, serve the full period of seven years'.[94] Rothwell decided to return to Edinburgh before the issue came to a vote.

The benefits payable to those out of work fell into two categories, those available to members, to cope with unemployment, emigration and burial, and those for

---

[91] *Constitution of the Dublin Typographical Provident Society*, Dublin, 1833, p. 33.
[92] Ibid., p. 5.
[93] Ibid., p. 8.
[94] DTPS Council Meeting, 25 February 1843.

'tramps'. Members who came into benefit after paying a subscription for six months were entitled to a total of three months unemployment pay made up of six weeks payment at the rate of seven shillings and sixpence, and seven weeks payment at five shillings. Any money earned casually while drawing benefit was set off against these sums. Unemployed members were obliged to enter their name, address and branch of the trade, whether compositor or pressman, in a book kept by the proprietor of the public house where the Society held its meetings. A failure to register resulted in claims on the fund being unsustainable.[95] Employers seeking casual labour could contact workers through the register. The allowance made to 'tramps' was much more limited. 'Tramps' were unemployed journeymen travelling from town to town in search of employment. The practice was that the society in the home town would issue a tramp card which could be presented to the secretary of any local society. Prior to 1830 the allowance in Dublin had been seven shillings and sixpence, but this was reduced by a resolution of the committee of the DTPS on 17 September 1830 'in order to preserve our funds for the support of those deserving members of our society who may be thrown out of employment'. The reduced rate, as enshrined in the *Constitution* of 1833, provided that tramps 'shall receive (if from a principal city or town) five shillings — if from a minor place, two shillings and sixpence'. The regulations also provided that no individual should be relieved more than once a year.[96]

Other societies, such as Manchester, also operated a differential scale of payment depending upon the origin of the claimant. A. E. Musson notes that societies in small towns could give only tiny allowances, as low as ninepence being known, and this resulted in discrimination against their tramps in the larger towns.[97]

Strict regulations were applied to the issue of emigration allowances because of the relatively large sums of money involved. In order to qualify for a grant of eight pounds, those intending to emigrate to America or Australia had to be fully subscribing members for one year, to produce four sureties, and to intend to remain abroad for eighteen months. If the emigrant returned before the expiry of this period the sureties had to repay the money advanced at the rate of one shilling each week. Commensurate with the smaller grant of four pounds, intending emigrants to Great Britain were only required to be paid up members for six months, to produce two sureties, and to intend to be absent from Ireland for six months. The same penalties for the failure of an emigrant to stay away applied to the sureties in this case as to those supporting American emigrants. In order to protect the sureties it was provided that no member who returned early could be in benefit until the sureties

---

[95] *Constitution of the Dublin Typographical Provident Society*, Dublin, 1833, pp. 9–10.
[96] Ibid., p. 11.
[97] A. E. Musson, *The Typographical Association*, London, 1954, pp. 29–30.

were repaid. Emigration money for travel to the provincial towns of Ireland was limited to one pound ten shillings and the required period of absence was two months. The prospective migrant had to be in benefit, and produce two sureties. Those returning early would be received back as members upon payment of two shillings and sixpence, but would not be back in benefit for two months. The sureties faced similar penalties to the other categories in the case of an early re-appearance of the emigrant. There was only one other benefit available: in appropriate cases the sum of two pounds was payable to offset funeral charges.[98]

It is clear that the DTPS rapidly achieved the predominant support among the journeymen; such solidarity was essential for conducting effective negotiations with the master printers and for building up funds for the payment of benefits to out of work members. Within the second month of its existence delegates to the DTPS council represented eighteen different businesses, including seven newspaper offices.[99] By the fourth month, delegates came from twenty-two businesses, and in October a total of 103 members voted on the admissability of a candidate for membership.[100] By 12 November 1831 a total of 194 journeymen had been admitted in addition to the founding group; most of these remained members although 78 emigration allowances were given in this period.[101]

The founders of the DTPS had to recruit from a demoralised and impoverished work force which had experienced the collapse of one society and which had suffered severe unemployment in the economic crisis of 1826.[102] The problems of recruitment are reflected in the minutes of council. On 19 July 1828 the council resolved to adopt the recommendations of the committee 'with regard to soliciting such persons, whose time can be satisfactorily proved, to join the society'. On 9 August 1828 council endorsed a committee resolution of 2 August urging members to ensure as far as possible that only fellow members be recruited as regular hands or smooters 'from a feeling that it is a species of injustice, to encourage those men who are opposed to us in preference to men who are paying their money weekly'.[103] These measures may have had some success as a notice published to the chapels in late April or early May had a more forceful tone, requiring those eligible for membership to come forward within a month or to risk being declared forever ineligible to join.[104]

---

[98] *Constitution of the Dublin Typographical Provident Society*, Dublin, 1833, pp. 12–13.
[99] DTPS Delegates to council Feb. 1827.
[100] Ibid., Apr. 1827; ibid., 27 Oct. 1827.
[101] Lists of those admitted after the foundation of the DTPS, and lists of emigrants are at the end of the DTPS Council Minute Book 1827–1830.
[102] *Second Report from the Select Committee on Combinations of Workmen* (UK Parliamentary Papers 1837–1838. VIII. pp. 425–26), pp. 105–06.
[103] Copy of the notice pasted into the DTPS Council Minute Book 1827–1830 with minutes of meeting of 9 Aug. 1828.
[104] Copy of the notice pasted into the DTPS Council Minute Book 1827–1830 with minutes of meeting of 2 May 1829.

By the late 1830s the DTPS represented a huge majority of the journeymen printers. Its secretary, Thomas Daly, told the Select Committee on Combinations of Workmen that there were 260 members, twenty to thirty journeymen who were not members and 180 apprentices in Dublin in 1838.[105] It seems to have been able to retain the loyalty of the men in most of the Dublin offices, with the noteworthy exception in the early 1840s of Alex Thom's office where Thom pursued a resolutely anti-union policy. At times a certain pragmatism prevailed. When on 6 May 1845 two delegates of the non-union men employed in the *Dublin Evening Post* approached the committee seeking membership, they indicated the men's willingness to join on the explicit understanding that the system on which the establishment functioned was not interfered with. The committee accepted the condition and the men were accepted into the National Typographical Association.[106] This flexibility attracted the disapproval of the Western District Board of the NTA which wrote to the committee pointing out the impropriety of admitting men of 'unfair' character without a penalty.[107] The rebuke was accepted and in the future 'unfair' men were generally charged a fine over and above the regular admission rates.

While the internal discipline of the DTPS ultimately rested on the feelings of mutual solidarity among members it was buttressed by the availability of three sanctions, the imposition of fines, suspension from benefit and in extreme cases expulsion from the society. The most serious offences were the taking of work in non-union offices without authorisation from the committee; such an action could lead to expulsion as when Mr Mahony went into the *Freeman's Journal* in November 1829, and it was resolved that he could stay there 'as the Business will discard all such persons'.[108] On his application to rejoin the DTPS in January 1830 the council roundly declared that he had totally disqualified himself by his flagrant opposition to the known orders of the society.[109] There was more trouble with the *Freeman's Journal* office in March 1830 when two men, Mills and Anderson, were found guilty of working for less than the union's recognised rates there. They were threatened with expulsion unless they quitted work at once and forfeited any claim for benefit from the DTPS.[110] Nonetheless suspension from benefit was comparatively rare. In the difficult mid-1840s there were a couple of cases of members making false claims for unemployment benefit; Mr Barker was suspended for twenty-six weeks for this in

---

[105] *Second Report from the Select Committee on Combinations of Workmen* (UK Parliamentary Papers 1837–1838. VIII. p. 418), p. 98.
[106] The DTPS had become the Dublin branch of the National Typographical Association 1 January 1845.
[107] 'Unfair' meaning a journeyman who worked, or who had been an apprentice in a non-union house; NTA Western District. Dublin Branch Committee meeting, 24 June 1845.
[108] DTPS Council meeting, 28 Nov. 1829.
[109] Ibid. 16 Jan. 1830.
[110] Ibid. 24 March 1830.

1847 and Mr Palmer for three months also in 1847 for such offences. They were both obliged to return the money thus obtained.[111]

The friendly but informal links which existed to give mutual recognition of tramp cards led to closer contacts with societies in Great Britain. In the late 1820s there was a move in England to establish national unions in several trades, marked by the formation of the National Union of Cotton Spinners in 1829 and the Potters' Union in 1830. The need for greater union among printers was first acted on by the Manchester Society which called a meeting on 13 September 1830, attended by representatives from Liverpool, Preston and Sheffield. The DTPS was also invited to attend. The committee discussed the matter on 21 August 1830 and, although lukewarm about the invitation, 'not deeming the frauds (as stated in the letter) committed by the tramps, of sufficient importance, in itself, to warrant such a proceeding', decided to seek further information. The extra information received in time for the meeting of 2 September 1830 made the committee 'strongly recommend the propriety of sending a delegate' to represent them at the meeting to be held 'for the purpose of forming a plan to check the growth of apprentices in the three kingdoms, and other matters of importance to the profession'.

The meeting drew up the rules for a Northern Typographical Union, which in the mid-1840s merged into the National Typographical Association.[112] The initial reaction of the DTPS committee was enthusiastic and a printed notice was issued requiring the fathers of each chapel to report the number of apprentices employed, and the stage of apprenticeship each was at, and the number of employees who were not members of the society. The notice also contained the committee's resolution:

that we are of opinion that a Union should immediately be formed between the different Societies throughout Ireland, England, and Scotland; and that those of the country parts of Ireland, be likewise requested to forward to our Secretary, like returns, namely, the number of apprentices, and the period of time served, with a view to adopting some course to check the growth of that baneful Apprentice-taking system, without which, all our efforts for the amelioration of our condition, will be altogether fruitless.[113]

However nothing further appears to have come of this resolution and the Northern Typographical Union limited itself to the English provinces where it flourished, and by 1840 had 44 branches and 984 members.[114] Its main constituent society, that in Manchester, led the way in 1834 in limiting the number of apprentices in 'fair' offices to two, unless there were four journeymen regularly employed, in which case three

---

[111] NTA Western District. Dublin Branch Committee meetings 13, 17 May 1847.
[112] Musson, *The Typographical Association*, pp. 33–38.
[113] Printed notice headlined 'Typographical Provident Society. Committee Room 1st October 1830' pasted in DTPS Council Minute Book for 1827–1830 after committee minutes for 17 September 1830.
[114] Musson, *The Typographical Association*, p. 39.

apprentices could be taken. The Northern Typographical Union [NTU] adopted this regulation in 1836.[115]

The example of the NTU was followed in Ireland; in 15 September 1836 a meeting of delegates from all societies was held at the instigation of the DTPS, in Dublin, which agreed the rules for a new umbrella body, the Irish Typographical Union.[116] The DTPS was by far the largest member of the new body; evidence to the Select Committee on Combinations of Workmen in July 1838 showed a total of 280 journeymen and 160 apprentices in Dublin compared to 44 men and 82 apprentices in Belfast, the next largest Irish printing town.[117] Following the example of the NTU, the rules of the Irish Typographical Union allowed individual societies to remain autonomous in matters relating to local conditions.[118] The new organisation, how-ever, legislated from the beginning on the two matters at the heart of conditions in the trade, that is on apprentice limitations, and the conduct of disputes. Rule 10 laid down 'That after the 15 day of September 1836, no office shall employ a greater num-ber of apprentices than the proportion of one to two men permanently employed; two to four, three to six; and where more than six are employed, the number of apprentices may be increased to four; but on no account shall that number be increased. Where more are now under indenture, the introduction of others shall be resisted by all legal means, until the numbers shall be reduced to the prescribed limits.'[119]

The DTPS had been concerned about the problem of apprentices for some years but primarily restrained from taking action on the matter by shortage of funds to finance strikes. For a number of years it had followed a pragmatic line trying to bal-ance the wish to restrain the number of apprentices against risking any actions that might close down businesses. There was a lengthy and ultimately unsuccessful attempt to deal with Michael Staunton, proprietor of the *Morning Register*. On 25 October 1828 the committee of the DTPS resolves 'that it is the opinion of the Committee that the introduction of the apprentice complained of by the compositors of the *Morning Register* cannot be opposed with any probability of success under existing circumstances, but in the event of the proprietor adding to the present number, and disregarding any remonstrance that may be made against such a proceeding, that the members of the society shall not be at liberty to give any assistance in the way of smooting under a fine of half a guinea.'[120] In November 1835

---

[115] Ibid., p. 42.
[116] *Second Report from the Select Committee on Combinations of Workmen* (UK Parliamentary Papers 1837–1838. VIII. p. 421), p. 101.
[117] Ibid. (p. 426), p. 106.
[118] Ibid. (p. 419), p. 99.
[119] Ibid. (p. 426), p. 101.
[120] 'When the business of a house is slack, or, in other words, when work is insufficient to employ fully the workmen regularly employed, and they go to some other house for temporary employment.' Savage, *Art of Printing*, p. 776.

Staunton had a less successful dispute with the DTPS.[121] Having decided to expand the *Morning Register* from sixteen columns to twenty he proposed taking a sixth apprentice to keep the costs of extra composition down. He was forced to give way and the following year was obliged to give up his fifth apprentice.

The Irish Typographical Union's action to limit apprentice numbers was not universally welcomed by the employers. The adoption of the regulation showed a distinct hardening of the attitude of the journeymen compared with their behaviour in 1829 when at a meeting with the master printers they accepted a reduction in payment 'and the master printers pledged themselves not to take the extraordinary number of apprentices they were before in the habit of taking.'[122] Many of the master printers reluctantly acquiesced in observing the limit; P. D. Hardy 'objected from the first instant (though I submitted rather than have a turn-out of the men) to that proposition'.[123] Hardy said,

I felt myself there was some necessity to protect the men in a fair way, if it could be done properly, not to have such a number of apprentices trained as formerly there were. I considered it was hardly fair towards a man who had served his time seven years, to be turned out immediately at the end of his time, and another apprentice taken in his stead.[124]

Hardy acknowledged that there had been abuses:

I believe, from knowing Ireland tolerably well, that in many towns in Ireland, there are offices conducted altogether without a journeyman, where lads are trained as printers; they have come to Dublin, when out of their time, perhaps only half knowing their business, or perhaps not half knowing it; but still they have served seven years, and are printers; and also in Dublin, there are printers who do not employ men at all, but train lads; and if any means could be devised to protect the men in any way, I should say it would be but fair that, men having got a good education, and having served seven years, should not be obliged to hunt the world for employment. I should say it is a reasonable thing, if a respectable man serves his time, that at the end of it there should be a fair hope of his being employed; and really there was not, in the way things were going on.[125]

Michael Staunton, a newspaper proprietor, agreed with Hardy about the number of apprentices:

I knew that latterly the apprentices have been greatly multiplied; I think there has been a growing abuse in that regard. Small printers, speculating on casual works, have taken in apprentices almost without limitation.[126]

---

[121] *Second Report from the Select Committee on Combinations of Workmen* (UK Parliamentary Papers 1837–1838. VIII. pp. 369–70), pp. 49–50.
[122] Ibid. (p. 426), p. 106.
[123] Ibid. (p. 362), p. 42.
[124] Ibid. (p. 344), p. 24.
[125] Ibid. (pp. 346–47), pp. 26–27.
[126] Ibid. (p. 372), p. 52.

The Irish Typographical Union became involved in a number of trade disputes often on account of apprentice limitation. The existence of a central organisation allowed financial support to be made available speedily to branches involved in major strikes. In 1838 a total of £100 was sent to the Belfast society to assist it in a dispute with F. D. Finlay, and £90 to the printers in Newry as assistance in their struggle with James Henderson.[127] The ITU's funds came under great strain in 1840 as a result of two serious disputes in Dublin, both fundamentally over apprentices, which put over forty journeymen out of work. Despite a levy on members of the ITU, the DTPS had to make a direct appeal to printers in England, explaining to the London Union of Compositors that they had spent £400 in six weeks supporting the strikers.[128] The ITU survived this particular battle and claimed that by 1842 its funds were steadily increasing.[129] Despite the fact that their sixth Annual Report was published in June 1843 it seems possible that the ITU had already disintegrated before publication. The printers' society in Cork had resumed an independent existence in 1842.[130] The DTPS agreed a revised constitution on 15 October 1842 which made no mention of affiliation to the ITU.

The revised rules of the society show several changes from the 1833 version. The duties of the various officers, the secretary, the treasurers, auditors, council and committee were minutely laid down. There were extensive changes in the financial regulations, almost certainly in response to the heavy expenses of the dispute with J. S. Folds's, which ended early in 1841, and the long running dispute with Alexander Thom. The procedure for admission to the Society did not change and the entry fee for journeymen who had served their apprenticeship in Dublin continued to be one guinea.[131] The weekly subscription remained at sixpence, although the earning threshold for paying it was raised from eight to ten shillings. Charges for immigrants to Dublin were sharply increased. The entry fee for those who had served all their apprenticeship outside Dublin was raised from one to two guineas. Journeymen who had become members of other accredited societies and then moved to Dublin could, on producing a card from their home society, become members on payment of seventeen shillings and sixpence compared with five shillings in 1827.[132] There was provision made for the imposition of a levy if the funds of the Society fell below £100.[133]

[127] Ibid. (p. 427), p. 107.
[128] London Union of Compositors. Ms. draft summary of the delegate meeting held 19 August 1840 (St Bride's Printing Historical Library no. 29001).
[129] *The Compositor's Chronicle*, 35 (1 June 1843), p. 227.
[130] *Centenary of the Cork Typographical Society 1806–1906*, Cork, 1906, p. 10.
[131] *Constitution of the Dublin Typographical Provident Society*, Dublin, 1842, pp. 14–15.
[132] Ibid., p. 14.
[133] Ibid., pp. 15–16.

The new rules made it harder to claim money from the Society. The change in the rule for qualifying for benefit was substantial: while in 1833 a new member was in benefit after paying six months' subscription, in 1842 the period before qualification was one year. The amount of benefit payable annually remained unaltered.[134] The conditions for claiming emigration benefit became more restrictive. In the 1830s there had been heavy use of this benefit: in the four years 1834–1837 the Society had paid £329 16s 3d in assisting 120 emigrants, which was a considerable drain on its resources.[135] A prospective emigrant to America or Australia now needed to be a member in benefit for two years; someone going to Great Britain had to have been a member in benefit for a year and to intend to stay away for a year. The benefit payable, the number of sureties, and the penalties for unsatisfactory performance remained as they had been in 1833. The provisions for provincial emigration were eased by allowing early returners to be in benefit as soon as the emigration money was cleared off.[136] All tramps were now entitled to one payment of five shillings in a year, no distinction being made between major and minor societies.[137] There was a new provision for an employer to be compensated out of the Society's funds in the case of a member writing 'horse' and leaving his employment without clearing it off.[138] The most interesting additions to the rules were the new bye-laws. These deal with the procedure to be followed in disputes with employers over wages, hours of working and overtime rates, regulations on machine working, double jobbing by members, and tactics for maintaining a closed shop.[139]

By the beginning of 1843 the Society was well on the way to replenishing its funds which had been so heavily depleted during the disputes in 1840. At some point in late 1842 a levy had been imposed, which was still in operation in January 1843 bringing in £19 17s 7d in that month, with a further 12s 2d of arrears coming in February.[140] At the beginning of the year the Society had £149 14s 5½d in hand, and had receipts in the first quarter of £129 9s 5d which comfortably exceeded the expenditure of £55 19s 7½d. It is clear that the level of employment was high, as subscriptions exceeded £30 in each month while the total number of claimants of benefit was small, 41 in both January and February, and 52 in March. By contrast claimants in March 1847 numbered 183.[141]

---

[134] Ibid, pp. 16–17.

[135] *Second Report from the Select Committee on Combinations of Workmen* (U.K. Parl. Papers 1837–1838. VIII. p. 417), p. 97.

[136] *Constitution of the Dublin Typographical Provident Society*, Dublin, 1842, pp. 18–20.

[137] Ibid., p. 20

[138] Ibid., p. 26. 'If any journeyman set down in his bill on Saturday night more work than he has done, that surplusage is called Horseflesh: and he abates it in his next bill'. J. Moxon, *Mechanick Exercises on the Whole Art of Printing*, 2nd ed. London, 1962, p. 344.

[139] *Constitution of the Dublin Typographical Provident Society*, Dublin, 1842, pp. 27–30.

[140] *Abstract of accounts* 1 January – 31 March 1843.

[141] NTA Western District, Dublin Branch/DTPS Account book January 1845 – May 1849, pp. 21–22.

In England there were mounting difficulties in the early 1840s with the provincial societies facing extensive burdens from the number of tramps, and heavy strike pay expenditure. A writer in the *Compositors' Chronicle* in 1841 urged the substitution of local allowances to the unemployed and strikers, and the abolition of the tramp system.[142] By 1842 the Northern Typographical Union had a large deficit. Reorganisation was needed, and this was urged by the NTU's Annual Report for 1843, and by various writers in *The Printer*. A Delegate Meeting was held in Derby from 15 to 19 July 1844 at the end of which plans were agreed for a National Typographical Association which would come into being on 1 January 1845.[143] The Association was divided into five districts of which Ireland was the Western District. The District was governed by a District Board of, initially, seven members (later more), elected by a delegate meeting. Above the District Boards was the executive committee consisting of the members of the District Boards and served by a General Corresponding Secretary. Below the District Board came the branches governed in the case of the Dublin one by the committee and council which had pertained before the amalgamation. The principal powers remaining with local branches were the admission of members, the local negotiation of payrates, the payment of unemployment benefit and strike pay, and the election of local officers. Local branches did not have complete control over the money raised in subscriptions, as surplus cash after the payment of liabilities was held to the credit of the District Board which, in turn, would supply assistance to branches in need, and which could, *in extremis*, itself apply to other District Boards for help via the General Secretary. Under the terms of the amalgamation the liabilities of all the local societies would cease on 30 June 1845 and benefits under the rules of the National Typographical Association would be payable from 1 July.

The District Boards had the duty of investigating proposed strike action, and had to refer such proposals to the Executive, on which each District Board had one vote. District Boards could blacklist jobs. One instance where this occurred was when the secretary of the Dublin branch announced to a delegate meeting on 20 December 1845 that the District Board had issued an order 'That no member of the Association accept an engagement in the city of Londonderry'.[144] The Association made no general regulation on apprentice restriction, wages or hours of work. At the outset it fixed the subscription at 6d per week for those in full employment, and at a proportion of this for those partially employed, while the unemployed paid nothing.

There was an entrance fee of 5s for new members. Casual earnings of up to 8s a week could be made without incurring a liability to subscription. In an attempt to

---

[142] Musson, *Typographical Association*, pp. 57–61.

[143] Ibid., pp. 61–66. The account of the NTA is taken largely from this source and from the *Printer* no. 10 (1 August 1844), pp. 129–31 where the rules agreed at the meeting in Derby were published.

[144] NTA Western District, Dublin Branch, Delegate meeting, 20 December 1845.

abolish the tramp system the Association undertook to provide weekly unemployment and strike payments locally, the latter being at the rate of three quarters of the wages formerly earned for six months, and as out-of-work payments at the rate of 6s a week thereafter.[145] Although the local payment of unemployed members diminished tramping, there was a provision that 'every member desirous of changing his locality may do so, by obtaining a certificate of membership, and a statement of his account, if any, addressed to the secretary of the town to which he is going'.[146] This would entitle him to free membership there, and, furthermore, he could draw his unemployment pay in whatever town he happened to be in on a Saturday night. The latter part of 1844 and early 1845 were times of reasonable prosperity in the printing trade in the United Kingdom. A letter from John Backhouse, secretary to the Liverpool society, read to the committee of the DTPS on 22 January 1845 announced that Liverpool was now in a position to repay the balance of a £50 loan from Dublin.[147] The offer to repay was accepted and the money received by 1 February.[148] Despite a debt of £22 5s owed by the former secretary, Thomas Daly, the funds were large enough for a proposal to be made at a half yearly general meeting on 18 January that the subscription to the local society should cease on 1 February.[149] In the event the question of the subscription was referred to the incoming committee, and continued to be taken up. After the payment of all demands on 30 June there remained a surplus of £105.[150]

The level of business activity ran quite low in the summer of 1845 with consequent impact on the local finances. In July a dispute in the *Dublin Monitor* newspaper came to a head, chiefly over the demand by Mr Coffey, the proprietor, that the compositors should set minion type and charge it as brevier, but with an undercurrent of allegations of partial under-payment of wages, the deficit owing to the men being about £40.[151] Coffey gave notice to six men, and by the end of July had ceased publication of the *Dublin Monitor*.[152] Five of the men, who were being paid 12s 2d strike pay, remained a long term drain on the finances.[153] They claimed respectively for 13, 20, 21, 22, and 22 weeks by the end of the year.[154] In late August and September claims on the branch's funds considerably exceeded the revenue. The number of claimants rose from thirty-five on 23 August claiming £14 7s 2d against income of

---

[145] Musson, *Typographical Association*, p. 65.
[146] *The Printer* no. 10 (1 August 1844) p. 130.
[147] NTA Western District, Dublin Branch Committee meeting, 22 January 1845.
[148] Ibid., 1 February 1845.
[149] NTA Western District, Dublin Branch General meeting, 18 January 1845.
[150] NTA Western District, Dublin Branch Committee meeting, 19 July 1845.
[151] Ibid., 8 July 1845.
[152] Ibid., 29 July 1845.
[153] Ibid., 2 August 1845.
[154] NTA Western District, Dublin Branch/DTPS Account book January 1845 – May 1849, p. 90.

£5 9s 5d, to fifty claimants on 27 September claiming £16 15s 4½d against income of £5 4s 11½d.[155] Thereafter trade improved and on 25 October the outgoing president of the council congratulated the members on the state and prospects of the association generally, and of the branch in particular, observing that the number of claimants was steadily decreasing, while receipts were as steadily on the increase.[156] The number of claimants dwindled to ten on 29 November.[157] Indeed, the chapel at Pettigrew and Oulton's sent in a resolution to council the following week expressing surprise that Zachariah Dowling had claimed from the funds on 29 November 'whilst every man that could work was sought for in every avenue for the last fortnight or three weeks'.[158] The resolution castigated his claim as 'not only unjustifiable but criminal.' In this first half year of benefit paid by the society as a branch of the National Typographical Association 134 members claimed benefit; of these seventy-five members claimed for 4 weeks or less, twenty-nine claiming for just one week. Only eight were out of work for any longer than 19 weeks, and of these four were strike claimants from the *Dublin Monitor* office.[159]

The level of unemployment rose during the early months of 1846: claimants numbered twenty-nine on 7 March, but declined to seven on 25 April. This was the lowest number reached; by 30 May the number had again reached twenty-nine. From then until late in October there was a severe depression in business, and the numbers claiming benefit rose sharply, never fewer than thirty-two in June, forty-two in July, fifty-four in August and forty-six in September. By then the worst was over with the exception of the week ending 17 October when sixty-one members were claimants. By the end of October the numbers had diminished to thirty-eight and continued to fall, there being only sixteen claimants on 26 December. The huge cost of servicing the claims is reflected in the jump in the overall expenditure of the Dublin branch from £185 0s 10d in the six months to 30 June to £388 0s 0½d in the six months ending on 31 December. As early as June the branch was obliged to seek extra funds from the District Board, and received £30 to pay the last benefit week of the half year. This being more than was needed resulted in a surplus of £19 19s 4½d on 30 June. The second half of the year was harder to finance. Between July and September the Dublin branch obtained £145 from the District Treasurer to supplement local subscriptions. In August the committee empowered the Treasurer and Trustees to sell £50 Government stock belonging to the pre-amalgamation funds 'to be applied when necessary as a loan, to meet the demands on the Dublin fund, and

---

155 Ibid., pp. 4–6.
156 NTA Western District, Dublin Branch Committee meeting 25 October 1845.
157 NTA Western District, Dublin Branch/DTPS Account book January 1845 – May 1849, p. 6.
158 NTA Western District, Dublin Branch Committee meeting 6 December 1845.
159 NTA Western District, Dublin Branch/DTPS Account book January 1845 – May 1849. The account of unemployment levels, income and expenditure from 1845–1849 is largely taken from this source.

to be repaid out of the same fund as soon as possible'.[160] The slump was not confined to Dublin: a report in the *Typographical Gazette* of July 1846 observed that:

from a period of great activity we have descended to a time of almost unparalled slackness; and … the present lamentable state of trade in London, and in various other large cities in the provinces, in Scotland, and in Ireland … approximates closely to that which existed in 1841.[161]

The pressure on the funds throughout the Association was such that the Executive felt obliged to double the subscription for three months from October.[162] Despite the consequent increase in income the DTPS ended the year only £6 16s 5½d in credit. The District Boards collectively had £402 in hand. The Executive decided to continue the double subscription for three months in an attempt to put the Association back in a safe financial state. This did not happen largely due to a major strike in Edinburgh which began on 6 February 1847.[163] In essence that strike's roots lay in the efforts of the Edinburgh printers to restrict apprentice numbers. A number of employers combined to defeat this and to resist some other practices of the journeymen. The resulting strike involved over 200 men and the total strike pay cost over £100 a week. The Executive continued the double subscription for a further three months from the end of March, and imposed a further levy of 6d per week for the duration of the strike which was taken up in Dublin on the weeks ending 27 March, 3 and 10 April.

By the middle of March 1847 members of the Dublin branch were apprehensive about the state of affairs locally and the committee decided to call a delegate meeting 'to consider the present state of the Association's funds, and the prospect of paying unemployed members during the coming summer'.[164] By then the number of claimants had jumped rapidly. Up to the end of the first week in March the number never went higher than twenty-seven.[165] On 13 March the figure rose to forty-six, and reached forty-seven by the end of the month. The worst week in April saw seventy-three claimants and by 29 May there were eighty-four. Unemployment continued at that high level until the end of September, monthly peaks being ninety-nine on 10 July, ninety-seven on 14 August, and eighty-eight on 11 September. After a bad start to October when seventy-three claimed in the first week numbers began to fall down to forty-one by 30 October. Although there was a peak of fifty-two on 13 November numbers shrank steadily in December to end the year at nine on benefit

---

160 NTA Western District. Dublin Branch Committee meeting 3 August 1846.
161 Quoted in Musson, *Typographical Association*, 1954, p. 70.
162 Ibid., p. 71.
163 Ibid., pp. 72–73.
164 NTA Western District, Dublin Branch Committee meeting 23 March 1847.
165 NTA Western District, Dublin Branch/DTPS Account book January 1845 – May 1849, p. 20.

on 24 December. In a branch of slightly over 300 members the burden of such a rate of unemployment was huge; it is not certain to what extent the diminution of numbers in claimants towards the end of the year reflects a genuine picking up in trade or merely journeymen going out of benefit because they had reached the limit of benefit receivable in the six month period.[166] The efforts to continue to pay benefit put enormous stress on members in employment and was to lead to the secession of the Dublin branch from the National Typographical Association.

Although the continued double rate of subscription brought in substantial funds, by April 1847 the Dublin branch was obliged to seek money from the District Board, obtaining £50 in that month, and £41 in May and £10 in June. By the end of May the Western District Board was in financial difficulties and a deputation from it attended a special meeting of the Dublin branch on 28 May at which correspondence 'of a nature rather cheerless and disheartening' was read out.[167] The deputation stated that the District Board 'could not guarantee the payment of the claimants any longer unless the Dublin Society imposed upon itself a voluntary levy'. The deputation thought an additional 6d, making a total subscription of 1s 6d for those in full employment, would be sufficient along with the remittances from other Boards, and urged the summoning of a delegate meeting. The Dublin committee believed it lacked power to enforce such a levy and that it must continue to rely on the District Board for sufficient funds to pay benefits at the settled rate. The secretary's account records that 'the interview terminated, having been anything but satisfactory'. The committee meeting on 31 May saw the first tangible sign of crisis, when the order passed by the committee on 25 May to the District Treasurer for £10 was returned £2 short of what was requested. The committee resolved to hold a delegate meeting 'for the purpose of considering the present alarming position of the Association generally, but especially for the purpose of providing funds to meet the demands of the Dublin claimants at the present crisis; no hope having been held out by the Board on Friday evening last, or since, of receiving money from any other quarter'.

At the delegate meeting on 2 June the chairman gave the gloomy news to the members.[168] He gave details of the recent negotiations with the District Board which urged the local society to levy the treble subscription on itself, 'that money should be raised here to prevent the necessity of drawing heavily upon other districts, so as to enable them to maintain the Edinburgh men, by which course … the whole Society would be upheld throughout the present struggle'. The executive's order for

---

[166] Figure taken from NTA Western District, Dublin Branch Delegate meeting 2 August 1847 when 317 members voted in the choice of a representative to attend a meeting in Liverpool. DTPS Minutes of Committee meeting 28 May 1847.

[167] NTA Western District, Dublin Branch Committee meeting 28 May 1847.

[168] NTA Western District, Dublin Branch Delegate meeting 2 June 1847.

a treble subscription issued on 17 April had been rescinded on 18 May after widespread objection.[169] The committee recommended to the meeting that the treble levy should be paid, until 1 July and that the payment should be placed to the credit of members [i.e. regarding it as a loan to the society]. It further recommended calling on the District Board to ensure that all branches should be on a similar financial footing in the future. The meeting was adjourned for one day to allow voting on the recommendations which were accepted on the following evening.

On 5 June the number of claimants reached ninety-three at a cost to the Society of £28 4s 7½d compared to a subscription income of £14 11s 6½d.[170] The District Treasurer could only send £10 to the committee in response to its request for £15. At their meeting on 8 June the committee resolved to hold a delegate meeting on 10 June to consider 'the propriety of laying on a further voluntary levy to meet the present increased outlay and the committee are of opinion, that, in order to do so double the present subscription will be required', i.e. at the rate of 3s for members on establishment wages. The committee also asked for £25 from the District Board, but was informed on 10 June 'that at present there are not funds'. The sixfold subscription rate was accepted by a majority at the delegate meeting on 10 June, and renewed by vote at weekly meetings until the end of July. There was not universal acceptance of the rate, for instance; on 23 June the delegate from the *Dublin Evening Post* read a resolution from that chapel refusing to pay such a subscription until it was levied equally over the whole Association by the executive, or until the executive declared itself incompetent to so order. The members of the chapel stated they would continue to pay the subscription rate ordered by the Executive of 1s 6d a week until 1 July. Nonetheless, in voting the next evening, 24 June, on the question of continuing the levy there were 180 votes in favour and 41 against. That same evening the meeting was informed that the District Board had no hope whatever of being able to supply funds — no matter how small — to any society in this District.

The District Board was considering possible economies including the limitation of benefit allowances to £3 per half year to each claimant. For those claiming at the maximum rate of 6s. this would allow only 10 weeks of benefit payable. The half years began respectively on 1 January and 1 July thus breaking up the peak unemployment season of the summer months. While possible savings were considered by the District Board, the Dublin branch had to institute immediate economies. On 19 June the 90 claimants had been paid a total of £27 17s 11d, while income only amounted to £23 15s 7d. The committee decided on 24 June to pay claimants 1s short of their entitlement to benefit, and to class men on strike pay as equivalent only to the top out-of-work benefit class of 6s; men entitled to 6s would now receive only 5s. On

[169] Musson, *Typographical Association*, p. 73.
[170] NTA Western District, Dublin Branch/DTPS Account book January 1845 – May 1849, pp. 23, 26.

26 June ninety-three members claimed benefit, but due to the reduced level of benefit the payment amounted only to £21 12s 0½d compared with subscription income of £25 15s 7d. The committee was clearly aware that the massive levy could not be continued for any great length of time, and upon the District Board producing its proposals for the limitation of benefit to £3 per half year and the establishment of an emigration fund at the committee meeting on 28 June, one member observed that if the proposals were not acted upon by the Executive he saw no alternative to secession and reorganisation as an independent society. This opinion was endorsed at a meeting of the unemployed men on 21 July. Similar sentiments were being widely expressed throughout the Association, a great many branches in other Districts being under financial stress.

A further delegate meeting of the Dublin branch on 30 June appointed a committee to investigate the willingness of the various District Boards to have an equal rate of subscription throughout the Association, and also to raise the question of mutual recognition of cards in the event of the Dublin branch seceding from the Association. The meeting also called on the Western District Board to warn other branches that as Dublin was forced to fund its liabilities entirely from its own resources members of other societies could not expect relief from it. The instantaneous compliance of the District Board, in sending out a circular to this effect on 1 July, was disavowed by a resumed delegate meeting that evening as 'having a tendency towards disconnecting us rather prematurely from the General Amalgamation', and the meeting took two seemingly inconsistent decisions, the first to send a circular to other Irish branches announcing that no distinction would be made between Dublin members and those presenting certificates from outside the city, the second to notify Irish branches that on and after 10 July men with certificates would not be relieved 'pending the reorganisation of the Association'. The pressure on finances continued to be heavy; on 16 July the committee cut the benefit by 1s 6d, i.e. men entitled to 6s received 4s 6d; a week later the cut was 1s off the entitlement. Despite this the expenditure for the month ran to £116 10s, which exceeded the subscription income by 14s 6d. A total of 433 claims were met during the month.

The frenzied pace of committee and delegate meetings in June and July ceased at the beginning of August when the Executive summoned a Grand Delegate Meeting in Liverpool in an attempt to save the Association which by now was effectively bankrupt.[171] The Dublin branch secretary Charles Ross attended and reported back to a delegate meeting on 6 September. The new rules agreed at Liverpool affected both the financial and organisational structures. To cope with the financial crisis

---

[171] Musson, *Typographical Association*, p. 74.

severe cuts were made in the levels of benefit payable, with the maximum out-of-work benefit being set at 4s per week, and payable only up a limit of £3 per half year. A tramp allowance of £4 per year was instituted, which thereby acknowledged defeat of one of the original aims of the Association. The rate of subscription was fixed at one penny in every 3s earned for the period to 31 December 1847 and thereafter one penny in every 4s earned. The suspensions of the weekly delegate meetings which had endorsed the sixfold levy meant that the subscription paid by members shrank to the level set by the executive in June, i.e. 1s 6d, per member on full establishment wages. The consequent reduction in income forced the committee to cut the benefits paid even more severely, until in the weeks following 17 August claimants were being paid 3s less than their entitlement under the rules.

The shortage of work forced the committee to become flexible in its attitude to members taking work in non-union houses. In September 1847 the committee gave permission to Mr Nolan to go to work for Pattison Jolly 'solely and alone, in consequence of the present very distressed state of the business, and the uncertainty of adequate funds to meet the weekly expenditure'.[172] But the permission was only given on condition that if the committee required Nolan to leave Jolly's employment at any time he should not have any entitlement to benefit. Similar permissions were granted to Messrs Lowell and O'Neill a month later to work for J. Browne,[173] and for Samuel Gribbon to work for A. Thom.[174]

When the new rules agreed at Liverpool became public knowledge, the unemployed men in Dublin met on 7 September and sent a request to the committee that double the set subscription rate be paid for a few weeks to enable benefit to be paid at 4s, the additional amount levied above the rule to be regarded as a loan to the society. The committee issued a circular dated the same day urging 'one more effort to carry us through our difficulties', and proposing what the unemployed members had suggested. It is evident from the number of votes cast on the issue on 10 September that there was a waning of sympathy as only 124 members voted: eighty-eight in favour, thirty-six against, compared with over 220 votes on the subscription issue on 24 June. The poor response obliged the committee to pay the unemployed men 1s short of the 4s that they were entitled to on 11 September, the eighty-eight claimants receiving a total of £12 6s 1d. Under the new rules the level of subscription income shrank rapidly. The receipts had been £26 3s 6d on 12 June, the best week of the sixfold subscription; by the end of August with the membership paying 1s 6d, the receipts amounted to £14 14s 1d on 28 August. Following the change of method of assessment of subscription to 1d in every 3s earned, the total shrank to

---

172 NTA Western District, Dublin Branch Committee meeting, 7 Sept. 1847.
173 Ibid., 19 Oct. 1847.
174 Ibid., 26 Oct. 1847.

£9 16s 5d on 25 September. A further cut in benefit was imposed on 3 October: men entitled to 4s received 2s. A committee decision of 2 November ruled that claimants could not be paid more than 2s a week until further notice, but permitted them to earn a further 2s in casual work without loss of benefit; beyond that level they would only receive the difference between earnings and 4s. Payment continued at this low level until the end of April 1848.

A delegate meeting was called for 27 September to discuss the financial situation and to vote on matters arising out of the alterations in the rules agreed at Liverpool. Delegates were advised to come with authority to vote on whether the Dublin branch should remain within the National Typographical Association. This was decisively agreed by a majority of 156 votes in favour to 44 against. They had also to decide on the composition of a District Committee as, under the resolutions agreed at Liverpool, District Boards were abolished from 25 September. The meeting ordered that the local committee should also fulfil the role of the District Board. The changes merely lasted a month and in that time the attitude of the Dublin branch changed radically. Yet another delegate meeting was summoned to meet on 26 October 'for the purpose of hearing a statement of the true position of the affairs of the Association, and to consult as to the best mode of averting the dangers which at present appear to threaten us'. Three propositions were put to this meeting by the committee: I, to secede completely from the National Typographical Association, and to re-establish the Dublin Society as an independent entity; II, to take up a separate subscription on which a separate society could be funded, but waiting to see if the National Typographical Association should survive, and if it did, to continue as part of it; III, to go on with the National Typographical Association for the time being. The first proposition was approved by the delegates and the meeting adjourned to 1 November so that the members of the chapels could vote on the resolution. On 1 November the votes were 158 in favour of, and 51 against, secession from the NTA.

The break was to be immediate and absolute. A delegate asked the question 'Would certificates of the National Typographical Association be paid?' The reply was 'Certainly not'. The meeting took several resolutions towards the formation of an independent society. On financial matters they instructed the committee to take up subscriptions for the dual purpose of helping those currently unemployed and raising a fund for the payment of benefits by the new society six months in the future i.e. from 1 May 1849; members in debt to the National Typographical Association were not to be in benefit until the debts were paid off, and as the debts were paid off, the money was to be allocated to the burial fund which had been used to support the unemployed. The new society was to be regulated by the rules of the DTPS, with the exception of those relating to the payment of benefit, etc., until new rules as proposed by the committee had been adopted by the membership. The subscription was to continue at the level set by the Liverpool Delegate Meeting in August, i.e. 1d in each 3s earned up to maximum subscription of 1s. Finally, an explanation of the

Society's motives and action was to be sent to the English and Scottish societies, and also to the local branches of the NTA in Ireland.

A copy of the circular to the Irish societies is included in the DTPS committee minute book following the minutes of the meeting on 2 November. It explained that by the end of August the National Typographical Association had incurred debts of £1,500, that large numbers of members had deserted, 'in London out of upwards of 2,000 there remained but 800'; that London, Liverpool and Edinburgh could not meet their weekly liabilities nor could Dublin 'from the dearth of business, for there were no seceders here'. Not everyone was happy with the decision to secede. Alex Sinclair, the former secretary of the Western District Board, went to the Midland District Committee on 16 November 1847, complaining that those who voted to secede at the Delegate Meeting in Dublin on 26 October had not, in fact, represented a majority of members of the branch.[175] The Midlands District Committee resolved that those Dublin printers still in favour of the association with the NTA should reform the branch and advise the various Districts of the names of officers. The various Midlands committees felt it imperative to 'dishonour all Dublin cards or certificates issued by any other authority than the Dublin branch or District officers dated on or after the 8 November (the date of the Dublin Address and secession)'. Nothing came of this proposal. The National Typographical Association had been tottering towards disaster since August. The Edinburgh strike finally collapsed on 13 October.[176] It had cost the Association about £2000.[177] The Executive decided to suspend the payment of unemployment and strike benefit from 1 November and to devote the subscription income to the payment of debts owing.[178] This decision arrived in Dublin after the branch had voted for secession.[179]

The new Dublin committee was immediately in action. It met on 2 November and concentrated initially on financial matters. It also resolved that all who presented NTA certificates to the Secretary would be considered as members of the reconstituted society. A week later the committee ordered a slightly higher admission fee for newly qualified journeymen of 10s; these would not be in benefit until 26 weekly subscriptions had been paid. By late January the new rules had been drawn up and on 25 January the committee ordered the Secretary to issue a circular to other societies, a copy of which is contained in the committee minutes. The principal points were provision for the admission to the Dublin Society at half the regular rate

---

[175] NTA Midlands District Committee meeting, 16 November 1847 (University of Warwick MS 39A/TA/1/1/1.).

[176] S. C. Gillespie, *A Hundred Years of Progress: The Record of the Scottish Typographical Association 1853 to 1952*, Glasgow, 1953, pp. 38–39.

[177] Musson, *Typographical Association*, p. 74.

[178] Ibid., p. 74.

[179] Printed circular dated 8 November 1847 from Charles Ross, Secretary to the DTPS, to Irish branches of the NTA explaining the motives for the secession of the Dublin branch.

for members of Societies which recognised the Dublin cards, the relief of tramps at the rate of 5s on one occasion in a year, and the establishment of an emigration allowance of £8 for travel to America, the colonies or a foreign country with a card conspicuously exhibiting the words 'foreign emigration'. The circular requested that anyone asking for relief in Great Britain using such a card should not be recognised without reference to the Dublin Secretary. The secretary asked if the other societies would recognise Dublin cards, and on what terms. Positive responses from London and Glasgow were announced at committee meetings on 29 February and 7 March.

A delegate meeting on 9 February 1848 took measures to tidy the financial aspects of reorganisation even further. It was agreed that the new rules should come into operation on 19 February. The delegates affirmed the continuity of authority by deeming those who had been in debt to the Dublin branch of the NTA to be indebted to the new Society for the same amount. Subscriptions for the earlier society counted towards qualification for benefit. Benefit levels for the first twelve months of the new society's existence were to be held to 4s per week, and emigration allowances were only to be paid at half the rate stated in the rules. In a further step to consolidate the finances, no member to whom the society was indebted was to be repaid anything until funds exceeded £200, and then only at the discretion of the committee.

Due to the slashing of the unemployment benefit to 2s and a gradual reduction in the numbers claiming benefits (which fell below thirty in December, and down to nine on 24 December) the finances began to improve during the winter of 1847. In the July to September quarter the income was £230 4s 6½d, the expenditure £225 16s 6½d, leaving a minute surplus of £4 8s.[180] The change in subscription rates reduced income in the last quarter to £107 13s 3d but rigorous economy kept expenditure down to £66 14s 1d and the DTPS began 1848 with a surplus of £40 19s 2d. At the end of March the surplus stood at £76 4s 4½d. This was the second last month of payment of benefit at its lowest level, and although the numbers of claimants were only 8 on 22 April and 7 on 29 April this was a consequence of members exceeding the threshold of benefit payable of £6 between 1 March 1847 and 1 May 1848, rather than an improvement in employment.[181] Writing in the *Typographical Protection Circular* in January 1849 Charles Ross, secretary of the DTPS reported: 'Two seasons have now passed during which the depression in our business has been extreme. In the Spring of last year there was literally nothing doing in the book department.'[182] Dublin was not alone, for in the same issue was a report from Glasgow that 'the trade has been unprecedently depressed here for a considerable time past.'[183]

---

[180] NTA Western District, Dublin Branch DTPS Account book January 1845 – May 1849, pp. 28–31.
[181] DTPS Resolution of Delegate meeting 9 February 1848.
[182] *Typographical Protection Circular*, no. 1 (January 1849), p. 2.
[183] Ibid., p. 2.

At the start of May 1849 with benefit being paid at 4s per week, the numbers rose sharply with twenty-five claiming on 6 May and thirty-seven on 27 May. In early June there was another leap in unemployment with forty-nine claimants on 3 June, but the number fell away by the end of the month and did not exceed forty-one in July. Unemployment increased again in August and September, there being sixty-four claimants on 19 August, and fifty-eight on 23 September. There was a dramatic fall in October from fifty-one on 7 October to eleven on 28 October; the highest number to claim in November was eleven on 11 November, and in December eighteen on 30 December. As Charles Ross observed 'in the autumn, the preparation for almanacks usually issued at the close of the year took up many hands.'[184] Again, some long-term unemployed could have exceeded the benefit allowance of £4 a year, which at the weekly rate of 4s would last only 20 weeks, and this may also account for some of the fall at the end of the year.

The higher rate of benefit and larger number of claimants put the finances under renewed pressure. The surplus which at the end of April 1849 stood at £111 14s 4½d rose marginally to £115 8s 7d at the end of May, then shrank to £94 4s 7d at the end of June, the expenditure having included five burial grants of £3 each and three emigration allowances to England of £1 each.[185] By 16 August the committee had to order the sale of £30 stock to meet current expenses as the treasurer had only £9 in hand. The treasurer reported to the committee on 11 October that the balance in hand on 1 October had shrunk to £63 4s 6d. In fact, matters improved greatly in the last quarter and the society retrieved its position ending up £127 16s 8d in credit. Demand for labour continued buoyant in the early months of 1849 and the number of claimants was low until the end of April, not going beyond 21 on 10 February.[186] There were, in fact, only 189 claims in the first quarter of the year, and only forty-six in April. On 1 April 1849 the society had £173 3s 8d in hand and by May the membership totalled 356.[187] As a consequence of this improvement, proposals for changes to the rules were made to a delegate meeting on 18 April.[188] The committee proposed that claimants be paid 6s and that the emigration allowance be paid at half the rate specified in the rule book. The chapel in Bull's office proposed an increase in the emigration allowance for England to £4 instead of £2, with the proviso that the number of solvent sureties be raised from two to four. One member, Thomas Leonard, proposed the establishment of a benevolent fund for the provision of an allowance to such members 'as may be permanently incapacitated, by old age or

---

[184] Ibid., p. 2.
[185] NTA Western District, Dublin Branch/DTPS Account book January 1845 – May 1849, pp. 42–46.
[186] Ibid., p. 63.
[187] *Typographical Protection Circular*, 6 (June 1849), p. 21.
[188] A printed copy of the proposed changes dated 5 April 1849 is pasted into the DTPS Committee Minute book February 1847 to July 1852 under 17 April 1849.

infirmity, from exercising their trade'. This was to be funded from a subscription of a halfpenny a week to be paid in addition to the subscription by members to the provident fund. The delegates approved the 6s unemployment benefit, an £8 emigration allowance to America or Australia, an £2 allowance for travel to England. The vote on Thomas Leonard's proposal was not mentioned in the account of the meeting.

In June 1849 the DTPS was yet again undergoing a financial crisis. Expenditure exceeded the income for April and May by £21 and on 1 June the treasurer had insufficient funds in hand to pay the claimants due on the following day. Mr Harlow, the Treasurer, appears to have embezzled £47 5s 5d. An abject letter from him was read to a delegate meeting on 5 June, offering to hand over 'any or all his furniture' to help pay off the debt. More practically he handed over two bills, payable at three and six months respectively. The meeting took emergency action to stem the outflow of funds by reducing the foreign emigration allowance to £4, and keeping the English one at £2. Foreign emigration had become a particularly heavy item of expenditure; a report written in July stated that the society had spent £75 10s 3d in the preceding two months on emigration allowances, and had 'sent eight of our members to America and Australia'.[189] The reduction in the emigration allowance did little to alleviate the financial pressure, and despite the sale of Government stock authorised by the committee on 1 June, further remedial action had to be taken. The committee proposed two actions to the membership, a cut in the amount paid to tramps from 5s to 3s for a period of six months, and a levy for two months of an extra 50% on the subscription, to be repaid to subscribing members within four months of the end of the levy. These were accepted by large majorities at a delegate meeting on 1 August but the continuing parlous state of the funds was underlined by the refusal by the committee on 28 August to grant an emigration allowance for England to John Kenny on the grounds of a 'want of funds'. The levy ended in the first week of October. Although at a delegate meeting on 17 October, the chapel of Corbett's office proposed a continuation of the levy until all the Society's debt should be discharged and, deeming 'this the most fitting time for such a levy, as there may be a likelihood of many of our present claiming members falling into employment', this did not meet with approval. Instead, a subcommittee was set up to consider the use of the funds. Among its recommendations which were accepted by a delegate meeting, probably that held on 11 December 1849, were the reduction in the tramp allowance to 2s 6d, the abolition of the foreign emigration allowance, and a disbarring of a member from benefit unless he had paid four months subscription the previous year.[190]

---

[189] *Typographical Protection Circular*, no. 8 (August 1849), p. 30.
[190] Ibid., no. 16 (April 1850), p. 79.

However, following the dismissal of six men from the *Railway Gazette* for refusal to sign 'a document pledging themselves to remain on the paper no matter what might occur', the decision of a delegate meeting on 13 November to give strike pay to all of them for ten weeks committed the society to an expenditure of £5 2s a week. This meeting also gave approval to a further levy of a penny on each three shillings earned for eight weeks.

The employment situation for members of the DTPS improved over the winter. While this was no doubt due to the usual winter upturn in trade an added factor was the award to Grierson, the Queen's printer, of the Government book printing contract (i.e. reports, papers and books required for the public service including school-books) early in 1850. This contract had previously been held by the non-union house of Alex Thom, a long-term antagonist of the union. Grierson, upon being awarded the contract, negotiated concessions with the DTPS to reduce the labour costs. According to an unauthorised and critical report by Charles Ross in the *Typographical Protection Circular* in April 1850, there were ten society men employed on the work.[191] Ross's comments were disowned by the committee on 23 April. In the autumn, having come under fire from other businesses which were also seeking concessions, the committee gave a long justification of their conduct to a general meeting on 2 November and claimed 'for the last eight months thirty men, on an average, have had constant employment in that house, for the most part upon the establishment, whilst the general trade of the city had been for the greater part of that time in a state of the greatest depression'.

Notwithstanding the high cost to the DTPS of the lack of business during the summer, the additional employment during the winter left the society in credit to the amount of £102 17s 10d at 31 March 1850, and a delegate meeting on 17 April decided that the August 1849 levy should be repaid commencing on 18 May. Income continued to be satisfactory and there was a balance in hand of £157 15s 3d at the end of June. Despite the usual summer difficulties the funds continued to grow, albeit slowly, and having a credit balance of £168 0s 5d standing at the end of September the quarterly delegate meeting on 16 October 1850 decided to reinstate the foreign emigration allowance at £4 per member, who had to be 'clear [of debt] on the Society's books, and two years in benefit', on condition of a two years' absence from the United Kingdom, and guarantees from three sureties, each of whom had to be in full benefit.

The society was once again in a position to be sympathetic to appeals from other societies, and voted in October to lend £10 to the typefounders who had gone on strike at Caslon and Figg in London. The notice from the committee recommending

---

[191] Ibid., no. 16 (April 1850), p. 79.

the loan to the members noted that the employers had recruited strike-breakers, including fifteen Frenchmen, four French women, one Dutchman, and one English woman. They especially deplored 'the dangerous principle of the introduction of female labour to supersede that which rightly pertains to *men* — and which, if successful in this case might be too readily transferred to ourselves'.[192]

Towards the end of the year the committee became concerned about a slackness in the payment of subscriptions and issued a notice to members on 29 November, pointing out the penalties provided in the rules for late payment of subscriptions and fines.[193] By these a member two weeks in arrears was expelled. The rate of payment of fines was regulated at 6d a week, in addition to the weekly subscription, when a member's earnings exceeded 12s, and at a shilling a week if earnings exceeded £1. The secretary was instructed to put the rules into strict operation from 7 December. The half century ended with the society's finances again healthy. With £233 8s 6d in hand at the end of 1850, the committee resolved on 10 January 1851 to recommend to the Delegate Meeting on 15 January that the sixfold levy of 1847 be repaid in two installments, in mid-February and mid-May, and two repayments amounting to £100 were made in the first half year.[194]

In England the question of forming a larger union had been aired almost immediately following the collapse of the National Typographical Association. The Manchester Society had drafted and circulated rules for a 'Provincial Typographical Union' in October 1848.[195] Rival proposals were issued by the Liverpool Society and delegates were invited from other societies to a meeting in Sheffield on 4 June 1849 to consider them. The DTPS was among the societies invited, and the committee issued a circular asking for the votes of the chapels on the question of sending a delegate.[196] However, the Dublin men voted against sending a representative.[197] It was proposed that the new union should be on the general basis of the former Northern Union. Local societies could make their own laws, subject to a general harmony with the interests of the union. A fixed proportion of the subscriptions would be credited to the executive to defray all the costs of the relief of tramps, and of strike pay. The Provincial Typographical Association was established following the meeting and eventually came to dominate the trade in Great Britain in the

---

[192] A printed copy of the circular is pasted into the DTPS Committee Minute book February 1847 to July 1852 under date 22 October 1850.

[193] Ibid., under date 29 November 1850.

[194] DTPS Committee meeting, 8 April 1851.

[195] Musson, *Typographical Association*, pp. 104–05.

[196] A printed copy of the circular dated 17 May 1849 is pasted into the DTPS Committee Minute book February 1847 to July 1852 under date 22 May 1849.

[197] DTPS Committee meeting, 25 May 1849.

twentieth century. Despite the refusal of the DTPS to join the new grouping, recognition of cards issued in Dublin was made under the provisions of Rule 29 of the PTA which allowed for the honouring of cards for tramp relief issued by societies 'which we know to be established upon good principles'.[198]

Organised labour in Dublin was renowned for the vigour with which industrial disputes were conducted in the early nineteenth century.[199] Writing in the *Quarterly Review* in 1859 Samuel Smiles observed: 'If strikes and combinations could elevate the condition of labour, Dublin must now have been the paradise of working men. The operatives there, with true Celtic vehemence, have thrown themselves heart and soul into the unions, and have fought their battles with a devotion worthy of a better cause. Moreover, they have been almost uniformly successful; but their victories have been even more disastrous than defeats. Dublin was formerly the seat of numerous extensive and highly prosperous trades'.[200] The claim that trade union activity was damaging to Dublin's prosperity had by then a long history. It was certainly aired in the *Dublin Journal* on 9 January 1818. Reporting an assault on John Gregory, one of its printers, the paper observed that the attack 'originated in one of those abominable species of combination which has so materially injured and depressed the trade of this city'.

Perhaps the most forceful expression of this view came at the meeting of the Trades Political Union addressed by Daniel O'Connell on 6 November 1837.[201] He fulminated against those Dublin societies which limited the number of apprentices and which insisted on uniform rates of pay. He singled out the printing, bookbinding and shipbuilding unions for particular opprobrium blaming them for the loss of business to other cities.[202] Within a couple of days Thomas Daly, secretary of the DTPS, replied in the columns of *Saunders's Newsletter* laying the responsibility for the loss of printing business on the master printers' insistence on high profit margins.[203] O'Connell returned to the attack at another meeting of the Trades Political Union on 8 January 1838, denouncing three aspects of union activity, apprentice limitation, setting of wage levels and coercion of employers to establish a closed shop.[204] Thomas Daly again replied on behalf of the printers, noting that most reputable master printers had agreed to the restriction in apprentice numbers and

---

[198] Printed Abstract of the rules of the Provincial Typographical Association pasted in the DTPS Committee minute book February 1847 to July 1852 in the minutes of the Delegate Meeting 18 July 1849.

[199] E. O'Connor, *A Labour History of Ireland 1824–1960*, Dublin, 1992, pp. 14–18.

[200] *Quarterly Review*, 106, no. 212 (October 1859), p. 515.

[201] For a study of O'Connell's attitudes and the Dublin working class response see P. Holohan, 'Daniel O' Connell and the Dublin trades: a collision, 1837/8', *Saothar*, 1, no. 1 (1975), pp. 1–17.

[202] *Saunders's Newsletter*, 7 November 1837.

[203] Ibid., 9 November 1837.

[204] *Freeman's Journal*, 9 January 1838.

that such restriction had only been considered when employment opportunities for journeymen were seriously threatened, and that the proportion of apprentices to employed printers was in the ratio of three to one. Daly emphatically denied that violence or intimidation was used to secure co-operation with that restriction.[205]

It is evident from the DTPS committee minutes that the policy in industrial disputes was to attempt negotiation by sending a deputation from the committee and in a majority of cases this rapidly produced a settlement of the issues in question. In the event of negotiation failing the withdrawal of labour and the blacking of jobs was resorted to.[206] In fact the minutes of the DTPS committee and council indicate that comparatively few disputes were long drawn out. The generally precarious state of DTPS funds combined with the regular annual cycles of fuller employment in autumn and winter and slackness in summer made the prospect of long disputes uninviting. Prospects for success in any dispute depended greatly on the extent to which the DTPS could prevent strike breaking either by outsiders or by members. Three disputes, one with newspapers in 1829 and the other two in 1840 involving Alex Thom and J. S. Folds tested the union's resolve and resources severely.

The dispute with the newspapers in 1829 arose from a decision of the DTPS committee to demand higher salaries, and it defined norms of work from 14 March.[207] The objectives were a salary of £1 17s per week on morning papers with work limited to setting 300 long primer lines per post, and on evening papers a salary of £1 12s 6d a week with setting limited to 530 long primer lines per post. The committee prepared carefully for any confrontation, promising to pay, if need be, unemployment benefit of £1 per week for seven weeks and 15s per week for a further six weeks and a sum of £6 in the event of a member emigrating. Other members of the DTPS who were employed in book houses were prohibited from newspaper work on penalty of expulsion.[208] In accordance with the committee's resolution the journeymen were to ask for an increase on 2 March to take effect on 14 March. Disputes ensued particularly with the *Morning Register* and the *Freeman's Journal*. On 21 March the committee heard that eight strike-breaking Scots had arrived to work on the *Morning Register*. Realisation that the strike might be lengthy prompted the Committee to propose an increase in the subscription of 6d a week for six months to which a general meeting agreed on 4 April. The committee also circulated a copy of its resolution ordering those eligible to join to do so within one month.[209]

---

[205] Ibid., 13 January 1838.
[206] *Second Report from the Select Committee on Combinations of Workmen* (UK Parliamentary Papers. 1838. VIII p. 421), p. 101.
[207] DTPS Council meeting, 28 February 1829, recording dispatch of the Resolution.
[208] Copy of resolution pasted in DTPS Council Minute Book 1827–1830.
[209] DTPS Committee meeting, 2 May 1830.

Early in May Michael Staunton, proprietor of the *Morning Register*, made peace overtures, being clearly in financial difficulties.[210] He had reduced the size of his newspaper from twenty columns to sixteen on 9 April. He proposed employing six compositors and a sufficient number (unspecified) of apprentices to enable him to get the newspaper out. While the committee was prepared to agree on six compositors it was not prepared to permit more than four apprentices. For various reasons, almost certainly including strike breaking by Dublin journeymen, the positions of the DTPS and the employer were reversed within a week. The DTPS was prepared to compromise, resolving that 'under the circumstances it is prudent that the chapel of the Register should be permitted to make the best terms they can with their employer respecting the number of apprentices (holding however to the present recognised salary, & to the proposed number of men — viz. six)' but the employer was not interested.[211] The DTPS felt the need to issue another warning against strike breaking.[212] By mid-June Staunton felt confident enough to dismiss three members of the DTPS.[213] The strike dragged on through the summer and by mid-September the DTPS was in financial difficulties. It regarded the continuation of the raised subscription rate as the only way to prevent a complete collapse of the society.[214] The worsening position forced a surrender, with the committee resolving on 14 November that 'the compositors should accept the sum of £1 12s, per week, and that all compositors be at liberty to accept of a like sum on the other morning papers'.

Early in July the strike at the *Freeman's Journal* ended with the men being permitted to accept 're-engagement at the regulated salary', but being cautioned to adhere to the limitation on the setting of lines.[215] Following the surrender to the *Morning Register*, however, pay levels came under further pressure from the employers with both the *Morning Register* and the *Freeman's Journal* offering jobs at £1 10s per week. This the committee continued to resist, ordering in March 1830 two men who had taken this wage on the *Freeman's Journal* to quit or face expulsion from the DTPS.[216] The increasing financial difficulties of the DTPS coupled with the poor financial state of the newspapers prompted the chapel of the *Star of Brunswick* to propose in July that the newspapers be opened to members at £1 10s per week. On this, however, the committee stood firm.[217]

---

[210] Ibid., 19 May 1829.
[211] Ibid., 23 May 1829.
[212] Ibid., 30 May 1829.
[213] Ibid., 20 June 1829.
[214] Ibid., 17 September 1829.
[215] Ibid., 6 July 1829.
[216] Ibid., 24 March 1829.
[217] Ibid., 3 July 1830.

The formation of the Irish Typographical Union in 1836 did not lead to any change in policy for the management of disputes. The aim was to succeed by negotiation wherever possible. The hands of local branches were strengthened by Rule 6 of the ITU which provided for notification by a local secretary to the ITU secretary of names of individuals who went to work in closed offices. Such names could then be circulated around the union and the individuals appropriately treated in all branches. The fifth annual report of the ITU observed that:

as disputes with employers are often attended with consequences of an unpleasant or injurious character they should and have been, as much as possible, avoided. It was only when an amicable adjustment could not be obtained without a sacrifice of principle that your committee, like their predecessor in office, allowed any of their brethren to proceed to such an undesirable extremity.[218]

The difficulties in 1840 involved two of the larger book houses in the city, those of Alexander Thom, who employed up to 20 men and J. S. Folds who had 22 on his payroll.[219] Although the principal issue in both cases was apprentice numbers the disputes were not directly related.[220] Thom in addition was also in dispute over working hours. During the 1830s pressure to reduce hours had come from the DTPS and some success had been achieved by 1838. Originally the number of hours worked each day in the six-day working week had been eleven, but one employer, P. D. Hardy, had accepted the ten hour day by 1838.[221] It still had not been universally accepted by 1840. The fourth annual report of the Irish Typographical Union noted that:

the adjustment of working time and over hours engaged the attention of the committees of the Dublin Society during the past two years: they considered it to be an injustice to themselves, and many of their employers, to allow the men in some offices to work for eleven hours each day, while those in others were employed only ten.[222]

The DTPS negotiated with the employers but Thom stood out against the charge and tried to get his men to sign a one-year contract with him. The men gave notice and left; the committee made its case to journeymen in Edinburgh and the attempt to recruit strike breakers there was unavailing.[223] Thom's office was to remain closed to the trade until at least July 1841.[224]

---

[218] *Second Report from the Select Committee on Combinations of Workmen* (UK Parliamentary Papers. 1838. VIII. p. 421), p. 101.
[219] *The Compositors' Chronicle*, no. 1 (7 September 1840), p. 2.
[220] Ibid., p. 2.
[221] *Second Report on Combinations of Workmen*, p. 41.
[222] *The Compositors' Chronicle*, no. 7 (1 March 1841), p. 49.
[223] Ibid.
[224] Ibid., no. 12 (2 August 1841), p. 91.

In July 1840, just three months after Thom's office was closed, J. S. Folds announced his intention of taking on more apprentices than the DTPS would countenance. The men withdrew their labour. Unemployment among printers rose to about 80 men.[225] Folds recruited men on three-year contracts to replace them, principally from London, but had difficulty in fulfilling contracts.[226] By September he was rumoured to have brought stereotype plates to London to be printed there.[227] By November some of the strike breakers had left Folds, and he was recruiting again in London but simultaneously making approaches to the DTPS which were, however, rejected.[228] By 1 January 1841 he was employing twenty-two journeymen and had twelve apprentices.[229]

A fire broke out early on 2 January 1841 and destroyed the Folds' printing house. In the circumstances arson was suspected; the premises were uninsured; the premium being about to be paid. Damage was estimated at £5000.[230] The DTPS moved at once to distance itself from any association with criminal behaviour. Thomas Daly, the secretary, writing to *Saunders's Newsletter*, expressed a belief that the dispute would have been amicably settled that week and offering a reward of £50 for the discovery and conviction of the perpetrator. The hearings before the city Grand Jury in search of compensation revealed that there had been some intimidation of workmen.[231] The eventual settlement was very much in favour of the DTPS position, Folds accepted apprentice limitation, the DTPS to be recruited as required and the strike breakers whose contracts could not be broken 'except for neglect or misconduct' to be kept on 'but should an opportunity for dismissal occur, they would not be retained'.[232]

The management of the strike from the DTPS view point was satisfactory. They received support from the London Union of Compositors to the tune of £100 and the Northern Typographical Union to the same amount.[234] Solidarity came from Scotland, the fourth annual report of the General Typographical Association of Scotland noting that no Scotsman had accepted a job in Dublin.

The DTPS was relieved to record a peaceful time in the following year reflecting that 'no collision of importance occurred'.[235] During the second half of the 1840s the

---

[225] Ibid., no. 1 (7 September 1840), p. 2.

[226] Ibid., p. 2.

[227] Ibid., p. 5.

[228] Ibid., no. 4 (7 December 1840), p. 28.

[229] *Saunders's Newsletter*, 5 January 1841.

[230] Ibid., 4 January 1841.

[231] Ibid., 27 April 1841.

[232] *The Compositor's Chronicle*, no. 12 (2 August 1841), p. 91.

[233] Ibid., no. 1 (7 September 1840), p. 3.

[234] Ibid., p. 7.

[235] *Fifth Annual Report of the Irish Typographical Union* reprinted in *The Compositor's Chronicle*, no. 21 (1 May 1842), p. 161.

ability of the union to effect compliance with regulations on wages and apprentice limits was severely affected by the general unemployment and consequent pressure on funds. The DTPS was, however, prepared to declare businesses closed to members to enforce its decrees. By 2 November 1850 there were twelve of these.[236] The temporary weakness of the DTPS was reflected in the permission given by the committee to individual members to work in them pending a revival of its fortunes and the trade generally.

Underlying the journeyman's life there was always the threat of financial insecurity from unemployment, as well as pressure from employers unwilling to accept the limitations on apprenticeship imposed by the union or the pay levels agreed by employers and journeymen.

---

[236] Printed extract of Report adopted by General Meeting, 2 November 1850.

Chapter Four: The Journeyman Bookbinder

JOURNEYMEN BOOKBINDERS had an even greater amount of insecurity than journeymen printers in this period. In their case the insecurity came on the one hand from the loss of government business following the extinction of the Irish Parliament in 1800 and on the other hand from the 1820s changes in technology which led to the development of publishers' case bindings. The journeymen bookbinders in Dublin were strongly organised with up to seventy per cent belonging to a union in 1836.[1] The Dublin journeymen bookbinders' society had joined the Bookbinders' Consolidated Relief Fund or Union in 1835 and Dublin became the headquarters of this union from 1843 to 1848 when an acrimonious dispute over money resulted in its removal to Liverpool.

A survey of the trades in Dublin, compiled in 1834 to provide Daniel O'Connell with ammunition for his campaign for repeal of the Act of Union, included a gloomy assessment of the bookbinding trade among its reports.[2] The report looked nostalgically at the pre-Union years as a golden age of high employment, good wages and artistic achievement. There is no doubt that the craft then flourished at the highest levels and the quality of the best bindings matched in design and execution those of any other European country.[3] Of course, most of the bookbinding done in the early nineteenth century was purely utilitarian with little, if any, decoration and there was also an extensive business in binding commercial account books.

From the perspective of the trade unionist compilers of the 1834 report, the rate of decline in the trade seemed to be accelerating as the years passed. Certain markets, previously the source of good employment, had disappeared, including the Irish parliament and the export trade in books to America. They lamented the dearth of craftsmen of real artistic ability as a factor which limited the amount of fine work done.[4] The decline in employment opportunities was elaborated in evidence to the Poor Inquiry. Specific problems were then seen as were the removal in 1821 of

---

[1] F. D'Arcy, 'Dublin Artisan Activity, Opinion and Organisation, 1820–1850'. Unpublished M.A. thesis N.U.I. 1968.
[2] 'Reports on trades and manufactures [in] Dublin 1834', pp. 184–93.
[3] The best survey is M. Craig, *Irish Bookbindings 1600–1800*, London, 1954 but see also J. McDonnell and P. Healy, *Gold-Tooled Bookbindings Commissioned by Trinity College Dublin in the Eighteenth Century*, Leixlip, 1987 and J. McDonnell, *Five Hundred Years of the Art of The Book in Ireland*, Dublin, London, 1997.
[4] 'Reports on trades and manufactures [in] Dublin 1834', pp. 184–85.

Custom House work to England (with the loss of some twenty to twenty-eight jobs) and the loss in 1827 of binding work for the Bible Society. It was claimed that the principal binding work remaining in Dublin was done for the Kildare Place Society. It was also claimed that the bookbinders were getting binding done in England because of more favourable credit terms given to them.[5]

CHANGES IN TECHNOLOGY

Technological change in book binding had already begun in the London trade and this was to lead to a further loss of business.[6] Up to the 1820s all the operations involved in binding a book were done by hand. The sheets were collated, folded, beaten, sewn, rounded, boarded and covered manually. The boards were laced on to the cords on which the gatherings of the book were sewn. Most of the binding was done at the bookseller's shop rather than at the publisher's premises. The practice both in England and Ireland at the start of the nineteenth century was that books were supplied to the booksellers in quires: 'the London publishers *invariably* have all their works delivered to them by their printers made up in perfect books in quires of from 15 to 20 sheets each, each octavo volume making one or two quires according to its thickness. The reasons for this are various; in the first place, they wish to incur no more expence that [*sic*] necessary, in the next, that the books may always have a fresh appearance, they have them done up only as they are required to meet the sale'.[7] A further attraction in the case of Dublin was the relative cheapness of binding compared with London prices: 'there is a difference of a penny to two-pence a volume in binding a school-book, and three-pence to four-pence on a larger book, between Dublin and London; leather is much cheaper in Dublin, and labour also'.[8]

The earliest labour saving machinery was the rolling press introduced in 1823 to replace the hand beating of the folded gatherings; Gaskell claims that this machine reduced the amount of male labour required for pressing by a factor of six.[9] The Dublin men claimed 'this machine does as much in one day as four men do in a week.'[10] The crucial change in the bookbinding structure was the development in the early 1820s of the prefabricated cloth casing containing the boards and hollow

---

[5] *First Report of Commissioners for Inquiring into the Condition of the Poorer Classes in Ireland* (UK Parliamentary Papers 1836. XXX. p. 538), p. 486.

[6] The nineteenth-century developments are summarised in P. Gaskell, *A New Introduction to Bibliography*, Oxford, 1972, pp. 231–37.

[7] Longman and Co. to B. Crompton, 28 May 1821. Longman Correspondence I, 101, no. 142.

[8] Evidence of W. Wakeman in *Third Report of the Commissioners of Inquiry into the Collection and Management of the Revenue arising in Ireland* (UK Parliamentary Papers 1822. XIII. 1219), p. 15.

[9] P. Gaskell, op. cit., p. 235.

[10] *First Report of Commissioners for Inquiring into the Condition of the Poorer Classes in Ireland* (UK Parliamentary Papers. 1836. XXX. p. 538), p. 48c.

spine into which the bookblock was pasted and the union of the parts was strengthened by the addition of the endpapers. It mattered not that this operation produced
a weaker structure than with the old process. In the early 1820s successful experi-
ments were made in calendaring the calico cloth with dyed starch, and about 1830
an embossing machine was developed to give relief patterns to the cloth. In 1832
came the arming (or embossing) press which enabled the spines and covers to be
blocked in blind or gilt. It seems that the Dublin trade was somewhat slow to adopt
new methods and machinery, for the bookbinders complained publicly in November
1837 that embossing, die-sinking and cover making were not done by the Dublin
masters.[11] However, the auction of the bankrupt William Challoner's stock in trade
on 17 December 1835 included an Imperial Arming Press by Sherwin and Cope.[12]
The introduction of these new machines made possible the establishment in London
and in other centres of large binding factories, such as Westley and Clark's in London
where up to 200 women and even more men were employed in the busy season
during the early 1840s.[13] It also led to the large-scale importation to Dublin of books
already bound in publishers' bindings.

NUMBERS EMPLOYED

The number of people employed in binding in Dublin at the end of the eighteenth
century was recorded as 213 men and 170 women, working for thirty-six named
employers and an unspecified number of petty masters.[14] It was claimed that
American orders kept thirty men busy while a further forty were employed on
government work for Parliament, the Custom House, the Four Courts and the Stamp
Office.[15] Figures given to the Poor Inquiry in 1836 suggest a continuing decline in
the number of journeymen from 150 in 1806 to 120 in 1814 and to not more than
eighty in 1834.[16] Union sources, in their evidence, given in 1834, gave the current
number as sixty-eight journeymen.[17] W. J. Battersby, himself a bookbinder, had
claimed in 1830 that the numbers in the trade had been reduced from a total of
between 300 and 400 before the Act of Union to 160.[18]

---

[11] *Saunders's Newsletter*, 14 Nov. 1837.

[12] Ibid. 14 Dec. 1835.

[13] The best description of a binding factory is in G. Dodd, *Days at the Factories, Series 1*, London, 1843, pp. 363–84.

[14] 'Reports on trades and manufactures [in] Dublin 1834', p. 184. Absolute accuracy cannot be relied on for these numbers.

[15] Ibid., p. 184.

[16] *First Report of Commissioners for Inquiring into the Condition of the Poorer Classes in Ireland* (UK Parliamentary Papers. 1836. XXX. p. 538) p. 48c; ibid. (p. 538), p. 48c.

[17] Ibid. (p. 495), p. 5c.

[18] W. J. Battersby, *Repeal, or Ruin for Ireland, or, A Speech Delivered … 18th November, 1830, at a Most Numerous Meeting of the Bookbinders of Dublin, to Petition for the Repeal of the Union*, Dublin, 1830, p. 32.

Battersby's figures for 1830 are close to the total of 180 male bookbinders, aged 20 years and upwards, recorded in Dublin city and county in the Census of 1831, for that figure included masters, journeymen and appropriately aged apprentices.[19] For the 1841 Census different criteria were used and a total of 251 males and 167 females, aged 15 years and over, were recorded for the city and county, as well as a further nine boys and eight girls under 15 years.[20] This represents a large increase on the total of eighty-six men, forty females and about 100 apprentices given in the 'Reports on trades and manufactures [in] Dublin 1834'.[21] It is possible that the great success of the primary school text-books published by the Commissioners of National Education may account for some of this change.[22] In April 1846 the Dublin Journeymen Bookbinders' Society claimed that in the recent past forty women and twenty-five to thirty men had been employed on the Commissioners' work.[23]

WAGES

In June 1845 the Dublin Journeymen Bookbinders' Society claimed that 105 journeymen, '88 good men and 17 rats,' were working in the city,[24] and the Society had 104 members when it was suspended in June 1848.[25] The Census of 1851 recorded an increase, particularly in female employment, compared with that of 1841 producing a total of 266 males and 300 females aged 15 years and over, and fourteen boys and twenty-two girls under 15 years, for the city and county.[26] These figures are strongly at variance with trade union evidence in 1850 which records the names of only forty-nine journeymen, whether trade unionists or not.[27]

Such evidence as exists for wages points to a gradual decline in the prosperity of the trade following a boom during the Napoleonic wars. In 1806 a forwarder earned between £1 10s and £1 15s a week, and a finisher between £2 and £3.[28] In 1814 a forwarder's earnings were in the range of £1 12s 6d and £1 18s a week, and a finisher

---

[19] *Population of Ireland* (UK Parliamentary Papers 1833. XXXIX. pp. 14, 24), pp. 74, 86.

[20] *Population (Ireland)* (UK Parliamentary Papers. 1843. XXIV. pp. 22, 34), pp. 130, 142.

[21] Ibid., p. 184; the figure for men is at odds with the union figure given to the Commissioners for inquiring into the condition of the poorer classes in Ireland.

[22] For the scale of the commercial success of the Commissioners' school books in the 1840s see J. M. Goldstrom, 'The correspondence between Lord John Russell and the publishing trade', *Publishing History*, XX, 1986, pp. 5–59.

[23] 'Dippings into divers subjects,' by Duodecimo. 'No. 1. Our union, what it was,' *Bookbinders' Consolidated Union Trade Circular*, III, no. 23 (26 March 1868), p. 408.

[24] Ibid., no. 21 (26 September 1867), p. 366.

[25] *Bookbinders' Consolidated Union Circular*, no. 10 (26 March 1849), p. 39.

[26] *Census of Ireland: General Report* (UK Parliamentary Papers 1856. XXXI. pp. 29–30, 44–45), pp. 173–74, 188–89.

[27] *A Report of the Correspondence between the Dublin Local Society and the Central Committee of the Consolidated Union of Bookbinders in Liverpool*, Dublin, 1850, pp. 5–6.

[28] *First Report of the Commissioners for Inquiring into the Condition of the Poorer Classes in Ireland* (UK Parliamentary Papers 1836. XXX. p. 495), p. 5c.

between £1 16s and £2 2s a week, but the level had fallen by 1824 to £1 4s for forwarders and £1 6s for finishers.[29] An anonymous master bookbinder gave evidence
to the Poor Inquiry that in 1826 the lowest wage he paid to a journeyman was £1 6s
or £1 7s while a foreman received £2 2s, but that by 1834 such wages had shrunk to
£1 and £1 10s respectively for a 65-hour working week.[30] Evidence given by the
journeymen to the same Commissioners drew on a wider sample and reported wage
rates for forwarders as 18s to £1 4s and for finishers between £1 4s and £1 15s.[31] The
journeymen bookbinders complained in an open letter that Dublin wages in 1837
were about 10s below those in London, and not even as high as in provincial towns
in England and Scotland.[32] Near the same time Gerald Bellew claimed to have paid
one of his workmen £1 12s a week in January 1837, and to have paid his successor
£1 14s a week.[33]

In 1846 Frederick Pilkington and John Mowat were recruiting journeymen binders
in order to fill their contract for binding school books for the Commissioners of
National Education. They advertised in Dublin and Edinburgh positions at £1 5s per
week, conditional on applicants not belonging to any trade society, but the Dublin
bookbinders urged a boycott of the jobs, claiming that there were 'more than enough
of men here for the work, and willing to do it for 24s. per week'.[34]

Neither of the two agreements for partnerships in the bookbinding business, one
in the 1820s and the other in the 1840s, suggest a lavish profitability. In the partnership established in 1823 between Thomas Tucker and Richard Beere it was agreed
that Tucker would take a weekly wage of £1 14s 1½d for managing the business.[35] In
1846 neither Pilkington nor Mowat proposed to reward themselves particularly
highly for managing the business; the partnership agreement limited them to £2 a
week each.[36] In both cases there were profit-sharing clauses.

Women working in the trade were paid substantially less than men and were
generally employed on the operations of folding, sewing and capping. Wages before
1800 were in the range of 10s to 20s a week.[37] Evidence from trade union sources to
the Poor Inquiry suggested a range of 10s to 15s a week was current in 1814 with a
decline to between 6s 6d and 8s by 1834.[38] This is considerably less than the level

---

[29] Ibid. (p. 538), p. 48c.
[30] Ibid. (p. 494), pp. 4c, 5c.
[31] Ibid. (p. 495), p. 5c.
[32] *Saunders's Newsletter*, 14 Nov. 1837.
[33] Ibid., 20 Jan. 1837.
[34] 'Dippings into divers subjects,' by Duodecimo, 'No. 1. Our union, what it was', *Bookbinders' Consolidated Union Trade Circular*, III, no. 23 (26 March 1868), pp. 408–09.
[35] Memorial of deed of partnership dated 21 May 1823. Registry of Deeds Memorial no. 781/469/529004.
[36] Memorial of deed of partnership dated 3 July 1846. Registry of Deeds Memorial no. 1846/11/201.
[37] 'Reports on trades and manufactures [in] Dublin 1834', pp. 184.
[38] *First Report of Commissioners for Inquiring into the Condition of the Poorer Classes in Ireland* (UK Parliamentary Papers. 1836. XXX. p. 538), p. 48c.

reported to the same commissioners by a master bookbinder who employed fourteen women whose average wage was 10s a week in 1834.[39] The range was 6s to 13s in a report done for Daniel O'Connell.[40] Although there was some limited casual work for the wives of journeymen, the latter were reluctant to apprentice their daughters to a declining business.[41]

Unemployment appears to have been endemic in the trade. The annual cycle mirrored that of printing with unemployment always rising in the summer months. The rates of unemployment were high, being cited as 20% in 1814, at least 33% in 1824 and about the same in 1834.[42] Emigration to England and America was of noticeable frequency.[43] An open letter in 1834 on the poor prospects for journeymen bookbinders lamented that 'wages [are] reduced to little lower than labourers — and work, even at that wages, very difficult to be obtained.'[44] Matters did not improve much in the 1840s. In the course of the dispute between the journeymen bookbinders and Pilkington and Mowat in 1846, P. Fitzpatrick, secretary of the Dublin society, wrote on 23 April 1846 to the secretary of the Edinburgh Journeymen Bookbinders' Society that 'Mowat now has eight Scotchmen, twelve boys, and four nondescripts, that no other person would employ here. Not a society man has gone to him, although many are idle, and several have gone away.'[45] There was a general depression in the book trade in the United Kingdom in 1847–1848, and the Central Committee of the Bookbinders' Consolidated Union lamented that 'on every hand men have been out of employment, and many still are.'[46]

One of the more successful master bookbinders, Gerald Bellew, attributed most of the problems to an excess of poorly trained apprentices and to the restrictive practices enforced by the trade union. On 19 January 1838 a letter he wrote to Daniel O'Connell was read at a meeting on workmens' combinations held at the Corn Exchange:

I never saw a good workman to want employment unless he was a drunkard. The consequence is, I have refused as much work during the last month as would keep five additional men employed sooner than run the risk of getting a drunkard or a botch ... I have never found more than one good workman to every five.[47]

---

[39] Ibid. (p. 495), p. 5c.

[40] 'Reports on trades and manufactures [in] Dublin 1834', p. 184.

[41] *First Report of Commissioners for Inquiring into the Condition of the Poorer Classes in Ireland* (UK Parliamentary Papers. 1836. XXX. p. 538), p. 48c.

[42] Ibid. (p. 538), p. 48c.

[43] 'Reports on trades and manufactures [in] Dublin 1834', p. 184.

[44] *Freeman's Journal*, 22 January 1834.

[45] Quoted in 'Dippings into divers subjects,' by Duodecimo, 'No. 1. Our union, what it was', *Bookbinders' Consolidated Union Trade Circular*, III, no. 25 (26 September 1868), p. 445.

[46] *Bookbinders' Consolidated Union Circular*, no. 4 (26 June 1848), p. 13.

[47] *Saunders's Newsletter*, 20 January 1838.

Apprentices to the business served a seven-year apprenticeship. In 1806 the trade had been considered eminently respectable and fees for apprenticeships were in the range of £50 to £100.[48] By the mid-1830s it was no longer so and the journeymen bookbinders issued a warning to parents against apprenticing their children to the trade, deploring 'the avaricious conduct of some master bookbinders, who, by false representations of the goodness of the trade, have induced many people to bind children to them, giving premiums with them, by which means the trade is now completely overstocked with hands', and claiming that there were over ninety apprentices and only sixty journeymen.[49] Gerald Bellew denounced 'chamber masters, and other unprincipled persons, who have little or no knowledge of the bookbinding business, who take apprentices, and very often get fees from their parents, and are not capable of teaching them the business'.[50] He believed that proper training could not be obtained in more than ten of the Dublin establishments. J. O. Bonsall, who had been in the bookselling and publishing business in Dublin between 1817 and 1836, took a cynical view of the journeymen bookbinders' restrictive practices:

their object in this is to prevent all who are not descended from bookbinders from being apprenticed to that trade. I have known few instances of good and sober men of the bookbinding trade being out of employment.[51]

TRADE UNIONISM

Although much is made in employers' statements during the 1830s of the iniquity of the practices of the bookbinders' union, evidence of earlier activity is sparse. It would seem that a society was well established by the early 1820s when a man named Saw was believed to have been its secretary in 1821–1824.[52] The society's papers were seized by magistrates at some point before the repeal of the combination laws in 1825; they were quickly returned.[53] In 1827 the Dublin bookbinders corresponded with the Edinburgh Journeymen Bookbinders' Union Society about a trade dispute in progress in Dublin.[54] A notice in the *Freeman's Journal* of 17 November 1830 which

---

[48] *First Report of Commissioners for Inquiring into the Condition of the Poorer Classes in Ireland* (UK Parliamentary Papers. 1836. XXX. p. 495), p. 5c.

[49] *Freeman's Journal*, 22 January 1834.

[50] *Saunders's Newsletter*, 20 January 1838.

[51] *First Report of Commissioners for Inquiring into the Condition of the Poorer Classes in Ireland* (UK Parliamentary Papers. 1836. XXX. p. 242.), p. 18.

[52] Ibid. (p. 494), p. 4c.

[53] 'To the public. From the Journeymen Bookbinders of the City of Dublin', *Saunders's Newsletter*, 14 November 1837.

[54] Edinburgh Journeymen Bookbinders' Union Society. Committee meeting, 14 February 1827.

called for a public meeting of journeymen bookbinders to be held the next day to petition Parliament for a repeal of the Act of Union was signed by fifty bookbinders. The petition, among many others, was brought to the House of Commons on 9 December 1830.[55] It is reasonable to assume that they were all members of a union.

The activities of organised labour in the trade become clearer in the investigations of the Poor Inquiry. A series of 32 queries, designed to elicit the effect of 'combination' in the trade, was put to the journeymen.[56] The answers make melancholy reading. The existence of a union, to which nearly all workmen belonged, was admitted. It had as its major objective the maintenance of fair wages with mutual assistance as a subsidiary aim. Although there had been a trade fund for supporting the unemployed this no longer existed and support in the case of sickness or death was given through a special contribution of 6d per man. The regular weekly contribution to the organisation was 4d.

The evidence of a master bookbinder to the Commissioners suggests a growing militancy among the journeymen in the early 1830s. The latter had begun operating a bar-book system for employment. The master bookbinder stated,

within the last three months they sent me a regular notice, stating, that if at any time I wanted a fresh hand, that I must send to their house-of-call for him, and that I must take whomsoever they chose to send, without reference to his fitness.[57]

Gerald Bellew deplored the practice:

First, as to the employment of men in our trade, no man is allowed to look for employment; any employment wanting a man, is obliged to put his [name] on the journeymens' books, stating the sort of workman he wants ... It is my opinion that everyman should be paid according to his ability, and it was the case in my trade until the last four years. Whenever I have had to put my name on their books, I have had to change five or six times, before I could get a man to suit me, giving each a trial, and each spoiling my work, and I obliged to pay each their standard wage.[58]

Employers were coerced into acceptance of this system. When in November 1835 Bellew declined to employ a man named Ward 'who was after treating Mr. Mullen, in my trade, very ill', the journeymen resolved that no one should enter Bellew's employment for two months unless he employed Ward.[59]

The Dublin Journeymen's Society continued to operate the bar-book system into the 1840s, finding that it strengthened the arguments for journeymen to continue

---

[55] *Journals of the House of Commons*, vol. 86, London, 1831, p. 161.

[56] *First Report of Commissioners for Inquiring into the Condition of the Poorer Classes in Ireland* (UK Parliamentary Papers. 1836. XXX. p. 538), p. 48c.

[57] Ibid. (p. 495), p. 5c.

[58] *Saunders's Newsletter*, 20 January 1837.

[59] Ibid.

their membership. In September 1845 it became a source of friction with the Manchester Branch of the Consolidated Bookbinders' Union which complained that it was virtually impossible for a tramp to obtain employment in Dublin since as the bar-book system operated on a first come, first served basis, no tramp could remain in Dublin long enough to get to the top of the list.[60] An unfavourable comparison was drawn with the Manchester system where there was no restriction on tramps seeking employment; indeed, the relieving officer gave each tramp a list of the employers. The exchange of letters ended with an offensive reply from the Dublin branch secretary Peter Fitzpatrick:

Let us see what your great personal accommodation for tramps has done — your no-bar and employers' lists, etc … The last registry showed that we registered 88 good men and only 17 rats — two of which have joined since — whilst you registered 45 men good men and 23 rats. Is this the fruit of your accommodation and no-bar list? We think it is.

Nonetheless in November 1845 the Dublin branch felt compelled to issue a circular defending its position, claiming that in the previous four months six out of eight tramps had managed to find employment.

Apart from the imposition of the bar-book employment system, the Dublin men also showed a marked reluctance to allow immigrant journeymen to work in the city.[61] Bellew had suffered from this. In January or February 1837 he had recruited a journeyman in Liverpool but some union members 'jealous that I could act independent of them, got around him, kept him drinking three days a week until I was obliged to send him back'.[62] The attitude caused understandable resentment in other journeymen's societies. Responding to a plea from Dublin for support in a dispute with Pilkington and Mowat, Samuel Haig, secretary of the Edinburgh Journeymen Bookbinders' Union Society, wrote to the Dublin secretary on 16 April 1846: 'the men of this town have not received such kindness at your hands as to justify them in refusing advantageous situations merely that the members of your society may have it all their own way. Several years ago, and at different times, men from Edinburgh have received engagements to full situations in Dublin but were compelled to return home in consequence of your men refusing to work along with them.'[63]

The increased level of trade-union activity in Dublin occurred against a background of moves towards amalgamation of societies on a United Kingdom basis.

---

[60] 'Dippings into divers subjects', by Duodecimo, 'No. 1. Our union, what it was', *Bookbinders' Consolidated Union Trade Circular*, III, no. 21 (26 September 1867), pp. 366–67; III, no. 22 (26 December 1867), pp. 387–88.

[61] *First Report of Commissioners for Inquiring into the Condition of the Poorer Classes in Ireland* (UK Parliamentary Papers. 1836. XXX. p. 495), p. 5c.

[62] *Saunders's Newsletter*, 20 January 1837.

[63] 'Dippings into divers subjects', by Duodecimo, 'No. 1. Our union, what it was', *Bookbinders' Consolidated Union Trade Circular*, III, no. 23 (26 March 1868), p. 410.

Negotiations were held in Manchester on 19–20 October 1835 and in Birmingham on 26–27 October 1835 with the aim of establishing a national union.[64] As a result of these meetings the Bookbinders' Consolidated Relief Fund or Union was established in order 'to afford proper and suitable relief to bookbinders travelling to seek for work'; any surplus arising could 'be applied to remedy any abuses that exist, or to bettering the condition of the journeymen bookbinders'.[65] The headquarters of the new body, from which the journeymen in the two major cities, Edinburgh and London, stood aloof, was in Manchester, and the Central Committee and General Secretary were drawn from the ranks of the Manchester men.

The initial tasks when the Central Committee assembled on 7 November 1835 were to draw up administrative procedures and to establish the membership on a sound footing. The various local societies were called on to pay a registration fee of 1s per member before 1 January 1836 and a monthly subscription of 1s. Thereafter the fee for an individual to enter the union increased to one guinea. Reforms were immediately instituted in the system of relieving peripatetic journeymen. The system whereby a tramp carried the card of his original society and received a variable sum from the secretary of the society in whatever town he visited was abolished. Tramps received instead the union's General Parchment Document and became entitled to relief at the rate of a penny a mile travelled and a bed at the station town. Should a tramp wish to rest on the Sabbath he was entitled to the sum of 1s 6d and a bed. 'Water carriage' was arranged on the basis of union payment of deck passage and 2s per day during the voyage.[66] Three routes were approved for travel between Great Britain and Ireland: Glasgow to Belfast, Liverpool to Dublin and Bristol to Cork.[67]

In some quarters enthusiasm for the union waned early: the quarterly report for the period to 31 March 1836 blacklisted eighty-four men.[68] The Central Committee attempted to drum up membership by decreeing in December 1836 that after 1 January 1837 any individual journeyman who had been a journeyman prior to 1 January 1836 and now wished to join would have to pay a guinea entrance fee and subscription of 1s a month, backdated to 1 January 1836. Where entire societies joined, membership would be granted on the original terms.[69]

Within four years there were moves made by the London Society of Bookbinders to form a new union for the whole kingdom. The London Society had fought a major

---

[64] Ibid., II, no. 20 (26 December 1859), p. 207. The present account of the development of the union is heavily dependent on the successive articles published under this title at intervals until 1871.

[65] Ibid., p. 207.

[66] Ibid., p. 208.

[67] E. Howe and J. Child, *The Society of London Bookbinders 1780–1851*, London, [1952], p. 144.

[68] 'Dippings into divers subjects', by Duodecimo, 'No. 1. Our union, what it was', *Bookbinders' Consolidated Union Trade Circular*, II, no. 20 (26 December 1859), p. 208.

[69] Ibid., p. 210.

strike between January and August 1839 over apprentice limitation which was complicated by the determination of the Master Bookbinders to crush the Society. The strike, which ended in partial victory for the journeymen, left the Society with debts of £1,668 9s 1d which were not fully discharged until 1848.[70]

During the course of 1839 a committee of the London Society was appointed to consider plans for the union for the whole kingdom and for the consolidation of the London Society, then composed of three lodges. These lodges amalgamated in May 1840 as the Consolidated London Lodge of Journeymen Bookbinders. Early in 1840 proposals for a union were circulated and at least two societies, Derby and Dublin, published detailed responses.[71] A delegate meeting attended by 26 representatives was held in Manchester on 13–15 April 1840 and agreed the constitution of the new body, the Bookbinders' Consolidated Union. The primary objective was the relief of out of work members, providing them with travelling money; it was also intended to provide rapid support for branches whose members were threatened by employers.[72] It was agreed that the seat of government of the Union should move to London on 20 December 1840 and that, on assuming the government, the London Lodge should be able to charge half of its expenses to the general fund. Not all societies agreed to join; Edinburgh voted against by a small majority.[73] Financial difficulties in London prevented the transfer from Manchester and at the end of the year the London Lodge was suspended from participation in the Union until it could meet its obligations.[74]

Quite apart from the difficulties in London, the succeeding years saw further financial problems in the Bookbinders' Consolidated Union, partly due to sloppy accounting in various branches. Late in 1842 the Dublin branch voiced its discontent in a circular published on 28 December condemning the poor management of affairs.[75] It had resolved on 17 November 'to suspend all payment to the Consolidated Union from the above date, until such time as we are furnished with a registered list of the members paying into its funds'. The very existence of the Union was called into question as the Manchester branch had determined to quit as organisers of the Central Committee. A Provisional Committee was established with directions to manage affairs until the other societies decided on the appropriate path for the Union.

---

[70] E. Howe and J. Child, *The Society of London Bookbinders 1780–1851*, London, [1952], pp. 114–39.

[71] 'Dippings into divers subjects', by Duodecimo, 'No. 1. Our union, what it was', *Bookbinders' Consolidated Union Trade Circular*, II, no. 25 (26 March 1861).

[72] Howe and Child, *The Society of London Bookbinders*, pp. 142–43.

[73] Edinburgh Journeymen Bookbinders' Union Society. Extraordinary meeting 18 June 1840.

[74] C. J. Bundock, *The story of the National Union of Printing, Bookbinding and Paper Workers*, Oxford, 1959, pp. 15–16.

[75] 'Dippings into divers subjects', by Duodecimo, 'No. 1. Our union, what it was', *Bookbinders' Consolidated Union Trade Circular*, III, no. 2 (26 December 1862), p. 20.

The Dublin Society intervened in decisive fashion, issuing a circular on 17 March 1843 in which they offered to take over the running of the union subject to certain conditions being fulfilled. These dealt mainly with financial matters. The principal requirements were that each society should furnish a registered list of members for future publication; that there should be equal payments made by each member in employment throughout the Union; that there should be prompt compliance with calls from the Central Committee for cash in due proportion to the funds in hand at each society; that there should be a general settlement of accounts at the end of each half year. By 5 May the Provisional Committee had announced its intention to transmit all relevant papers to Dublin, and on 29 May Henry Searson as General Secretary to the new Central Committee issued the first circular of the Dublin executive.[76]

The circular was intended to effect a financial restructuring of the Union. It called on all branch secretaries to supply lists of members and subscriptions for the month of May before 14 June, as well as a list of the non-union journeymen. It announced the intention to re-open all relief stations as soon as practicable but wished it to be clearly understood that 'no document was to be issued, nor relief given at any station' until they had officially announced that the organisation of the Union was once more complete. The Dublin executive disclaimed responsibility for any money owed by the former Central Committee arguing that as they did not ask for any arrears owing to the Union they should not hold themselves responsible for any claims that might be made against it.

It took some months for the reorganisation of branches to be completed. The successful outcome was announced in a circular dated 8 September 1843. The call for a shilling per member subscription had produced £15 6s indicating a total of 306 members. Membership had fallen away greatly since October 1840 when the numbers had been 707 London-based members, and 630 from the rest of the United Kingdom.[77] Severe problems were evident in two places, Birmingham and Bristol, both of which had to cope with considerable numbers of tramps. In Birmingham there were only seven union men out of twenty-seven journeymen, and in Bristol only six out of thirty. Given that little income could be generated in these towns, economies had to be instituted; a tramp arriving in Birmingham was allowed only 1s and a bed, irrespective of the distance he might have travelled; in Bristol, a tramp arriving from Cork was allowed 5s and a bed, and if arriving there from any English town his cash allowance was calculated at half the usual mileage rate and, of course,

---

[76] Ibid., III, no. 3 (26 March 1863), pp. 39–42.
[77] Howe and Child, *The Society of London Bookbinders*, p. 144.

a bed. Furthermore the Central Committee recommended that in these towns tramps should seek work 'in the Ratshops on any terms'.[78]

The full registration of members was not accomplished until June 1845, and was not achieved without some friction with the Manchester branch over its failure to forward the details of registration compiled at the time of amalgamation in 1840. The list of members issued in June 1845 contained 423 names with details of the date of entrance and place of registration. It also contained the names of 180 non-union journeymen.[79]

The parlous state of the general funds of the union was an underlying factor in a long running dispute between the Central Committee in Dublin and the branches in Manchester and Liverpool over the remuneration of the local branch secretaries.[80] The Central Committee raised the issue in their report of 12 October 1844, having found nothing in the rules to justify charging the general funds with any such expense and feared ruination for the funds if all branches were to do the same. The quarrel rumbled on until 1846. The essence of the case made by the Liverpool and Manchester branches was that the duties in each were exceptionally onerous. Liverpool claimed, furthermore, that three years previously the executive in Manchester had queried and then allowed the claim. On 31 October 1845 the Central Committee issued a second circular on the question, expressing a reluctance to make the practice of subsidising secretaries' pay a general one, but holding that the practice must either be made general or abolished. The Central Committee proposed that it be abolished from 1 January 1846 as it had never been sanctioned by the members of the Union. If this proposal were voted down the Central Committee would consider the Manchester branch to be under an obligation to draft a new rule on the subject which could be put to members. The matter of the drain on the general funds was again alluded to. The issue was not resolved and in March 1846 the Manchester branch proposed that in future only half of the entrance fee be paid over by each society to the credit of the Union and the balance retained locally to defray running costs.[81] This was apparently never voted upon.

Superficially the outlook for the Bookbinders' Consolidated Union looked good in the mid-1840s. The Bradford and Glasgow Societies, the latter including bookbinders at Paisley, made overtures in 1846 and the Central Committee proposed their admission on payment of 1s each per member, subject to the branches agreeing not to issue any documents for three months; this proposal was accepted after some delay.[82] At the beginning of 1847 the Union was further strengthened by the addition

---

[78] 'Dippings into divers subjects', by Duodecimo, 'No. 1. Our union, what it was', *Bookbinders' Consolidated Union Trade Circular*, III, no. 3 (26 March 1863), p. 41.

[79] Ibid., III, no. 4 (26 June 1863), p. 53. No copy of this list has been located.

[80] Ibid., III, no. 17 (September 1866), pp. 289–91 and III, no. 18 (December 1866), pp. 307–08.

[81] Ibid., III, no. 19 (26 March 1867), pp. 333–34.

[82] Ibid., III, no. 21 (26 September 1867), p. 365.

of the bookbinders of Edinburgh and Coldstream, the branches containing 34 and 10 members respectively.[83] The powers of the Union were considerably strengthened by an agreement announced in July 1847 between it and the London Consolidated Lodge of Journeymen Bookbinders whereby unpaid fines levied on members by one society would be collected by the other society if the defaulter sought admission to it.[84]

Despite these signs of interest in the Union there were serious financial problems. In Dublin the dispute with Pilkington and Mowat had made serious demands on resources and in England some of the relief stations, among them Warrington, Shrewsbury and Wrexham, were out of funds at the start of 1847.[85] The Liverpool branch had lost confidence in the Central Committee in general and in the Chief Secretary, Henry Searson, in particular. In April the Liverpool branch called on him to resign for a failure to fulfil his duties. Attacks on him continued and culminated in a circular from the Liverpool branch to the trade dated 10 August expressing their lack of confidence, and urging all other branches to voice their opinions.[86] At least fourteen others had sentiments similar to Liverpool's. Searson announced his resignation in a public letter to members of the union dated 24 September 1847, stating 'I have the satisfaction of seeing that I leave the Union much better than I found it.'[87] In fact this was not so and no financial reports had been issued since mid-1846.

A proposal that the seat of the Central Committee be removed to Liverpool by 20 February 1848 was approved and acted upon.[88] The new Central Committee found the funds at a very low ebb and was forced to appeal to the branches for immediate assistance. Manchester sent £10; Dublin could only manage £2.[89] In fact, neither Dublin's record-keeping nor its contributions to the union funds had been maintained and although the Central Committee had received an apology from the Dublin secretary in March, it noted in June that 'if the law is not acted up to, the suspension of the society will be the result'.[90] The Dublin society was in fact suspended that month.

In September it became evident that £50 of union funds had been misappropriated during the dispute with Pilkington and Mowat and used to bribe Scottish journeymen to return home.[91] The Central Committee was prepared to lift the suspension

[83] Ibid., III, no. 27 (26 March 1869), pp. 481–82.
[84] Ibid., p. 484.
[85] Ibid., III, no. 29 (26 September 1869), p. 517.
[86] Ibid., p. 518.
[87] Ibid., III, no. 30 (26 December 1869), p. 541.
[88] Ibid., III, no. 34 (26 December 1870), pp. 611–12.
[89] *Bookbinders' Consolidated Union Circular*, no. 4 (26 June 1848), pp. 13–14.
[90] Ibid., p. 14.
[91] *A Report of the Correspondence between the Dublin Local Society and the Central Committee of the Consolidated Union of Bookbinders in Liverpool*, Dublin, 1850, p. 15.

subject to the immediate payment of a quarter of the deficit and an undertaking to pay the balance by regular installments. The Dublin branch, hit by many defections since 1846, sought to ensure that the remaining members should not be saddled with the entire debt.[92] In March 1849 it forwarded the names of 104 men who were members, details as to when the funds were spent, and a list of twenty-seven men who had been paying subscriptions to the branch since its suspension.[93]

A year later the suspended branch, with a membership of twenty (as against twenty-nine 'non-society' men), was still negotiating with the Central Committee pleading for fair play, either to be received as members in good standing individually or to be reconstituted as a legitimate branch.[94] Some urgency was injected into the discussions as the Dublin secretary understood that the Central Committee had 'authorised a Mr McIntosh from Scotland to open a station here on behalf of the Bookbinders' Society of Dublin'.[95] A brisk exchange of letters included a list of former Dublin members and the dates of their expulsion from the branch for failure to pay debts. But the Central Committee took a firm line, the Chief Secretary, W. Fearnall, writing on 22 April 1850, that:

we gave your society every opportunity of again becoming members, and did all we could to induce them to do so; and, as I stated before, if they had complied with our request, viz: the payment of 12s 6d, and arrears, they would have been immediately brought into benefit … We have made what we consider to be a just demand, *and are determined that not one* of the members of the late Dublin Society shall again be admitted into the union, unless every member of that society pays a due proportion of the sum deficient.[96]

The nub of continued Dublin objections was not to the repayment of a portion of the missing funds, but to the demand for arrears of subscription for the time the branch was suspended and its members deprived of the benefits of union.[97]

Although the Central Committee announced that the Dublin position was regularised by September 1851 with a new branch organised by Peter McIntosh, the evidence of disunion clearly remained. The branch had but 16 voting members, and only one of these had been a member of the suspended branch in 1850.[98] Numbers were slow to grow with only thirty-five men being listed as in good standing by September 1857.[99]

---

[92] *Bookbinders' Consolidated Union Circular*, no. 8 (28 December 1848), p. 30.
[93] Ibid., no. 10 (26 March 1849), p. 39.
[94] *A Report of the Correspondence between the Dublin Local Society and the Central Committee of the Consolidated Union of Bookbinders in Liverpool*, Dublin, 1850, p. 6.
[95] Ibid., p. 7.
[96] Ibid., p. 11.
[97] Ibid., p. 15.
[98] *Bookbinders' Consolidated Union Circular*, no. 10 (26 September 1851), p. 4.
[99] *Bookbinders' Consolidated Union Trade Circular*, II, no. 11 (26 September 1857), p. 96.

The decline in unionised labour from 104 in 1846 to thirty-five in 1857 reflects many factors other than animosity among journeymen. Book publishing in Dublin was in serious decline as the industry became concentrated in London, Edinburgh and Glasgow. The development of publishers' trade bindings cut out the greater part of the Dublin journeymen's work, leaving those with skills little alternative but migration to the centres of publication.

Conclusion

T HE COMPARATIVE LACK OF INTEREST in the early nineteenth century Dublin book trade compared with that of the eighteenth century can be attributed in part to the disparaging comments made by contemporary observers and in part to the relatively unattractive appearance of many of the books produced. Although these writers were correct in decrying the low level of literary publication in the first few decades following the introduction of the Copyright Act in 1801, there was, after an uncertain start, an increasing business in utilitarian publication for schools and the university, in works to fulfil the religious needs of Protestants and Catholics and in works of local political controversy. Examination of surviving printers' ledgers shows many works being produced in editions of considerable size. The quantity of publication by subscription is evidence of the existence of enterprising publishers and of extensive, largely middle class, patronage.

Two features distinguished Dublin publishing activity from other centres in the United Kingdom. There was a big demand for Catholic religious literature to satisfy the needs of the large Catholic majority in the city and the island generally, and there was publication of works aimed at Irish nationalists. The demand for Catholic religious literature is notable in the proportion of overtly Catholic works published by subscription in the first two decades of the century and in the edition sizes of Catholic books commissioned by Patrick Wogan from the printers Graisberry and Campbell. While there had been some publication of nationalist literature through the early decades such as chapbook biographies of Lord Edward Fitzgerald and Robert Emmet, the identification of the true potential of the market did not occur until the 1840s when the Young Ireland writers associated with the *Nation* established a publication programme as the 'Library of Ireland' with James Duffy as their agent. Despite certain successes in the export market, particularly in school-book publishing, Dublin publishing was largely limited to a provincial trade.

The Dublin booksellers had to change the source of their supply of most books from Dublin to the United Kingdom at the start of the century when the unauthorised reprinting of British publications became illegal. The scale of growth of the market during the Napoleonic Wars was spectacular despite many of the more prominent booksellers having recurrent cash flow problems and some, indeed, falling into bankruptcy. The length of credit given to favoured customers was one source of difficulty particularly when they were dealing with a man like Christopher Dillon Bellew who collected on the grandest scale. The impression of a healthy trade given by the increased figures of imports shown in the Customs ledgers in the period 1801-1818 is at variance with the expressions of economic difficulties in booksellers' letters to Bellew.

Book printing was only one aspect of printing activity and the economic and administrative life of the country was underpinned by printed matter ranging from regimental returns to railway tickets. Changes in printing technology occurred first in England with the production of the Stanhope iron hand press in 1800 and then with the application of steam power in 1814. Stanhope presses were being used here by 1810 but no steam press was in use in Dublin before 1834. Steam presses were most economic when employed on regular long production runs. They were best suited to newspaper work but most Dublin newspapers did not have sufficient circulation to justify their use.

A measure of the increasing use of print in Dublin is to be seen in the increasing number of journeymen printers recorded in census figures and trade union membership. While underemployment was endemic and unemployment occasionally catastrophic the increase suggests that printing was seen as a comparatively attractive career option. From the 1820s Dublin printers were heavily unionised and the rates of pay agreed between journeymen and master printers put those who had full employment at the top end of the artisan pay league. Although Dublin had a reputation for trade union militancy in the 1820s the printers do not appear to have been involved in more than a handful of violent outrages. Their organisation, the Dublin Typographical Provident Society was one of the bodies which formed the Irish Typographical Union in the mid-1830s. The attempts, as part of this body, to impose restrictions on apprentice numbers led to some long running industrial conflicts and to the printers being publicly castigated by Daniel O'Connell for their restrictive practices. The evidence on printing in Dublin given to the Select Committee on Combinations of Workmen (the establishment of which was promoted by O'Connell), gives a remarkable overview of the industrial relations within the trade.

Once the DTPS had established itself as a dominant force among the journeymen it was able to use withdrawal of labour to promote its aims, but its preferred tactic was negotiation and by the late 1840s most disputes were quickly solved. Where withdrawal of labour occurred most employers quickly caved in and only one employer was obdurate in resisting employing unionised labour.

In 1845 the Dublin Typographical Provident Society joined the English-based National Typographical Association which had members in the principal towns outside London. One of the prime objectives of the NTA was to cope in a satisfactory way with migrant workers. It is evident from DTPS sources that there was extensive movement of labour not merely within the United Kingdom but also to America, principally the United States, and to Australia and that not all emigration was permanent. The NTA suffered severe financial difficulties in 1847, compounded so far as the Irish branches were concerned by the economic disruption caused by the famine when up to 25 per cent of printers were unemployed. Nonetheless the 1851 Census showed a greater number of printers in Dublin than in 1841. Employment for journeymen was most regular on newspapers with their fixed publication schedule and finite quantity of space to be filled. In other employment there was a broad annual pattern of activity with business brisk at the beginning of the year, falling away in the summer months and picking up in the autumn, being generally busiest in November and December.

Journeymen bookbinders were far more affected by changes in technology than the printers. The advent of publishers' case bindings in the late 1820s and 1830s diminished the quantity of work to be done on imported books which had hitherto been imported unbound. To some extent this loss of work was balanced by the employment in binding schoolbooks but a survey in the mid-1830s looked nostalgically back to the pre-Union days as an era of plentiful high quality work. The Dublin journeymen bookbinders' society played an active role in the 1840s in the affairs of the Consolidated Union of Bookbinders whose membership covered the United Kingdom, and in 1843 took on the role of providing headquarters for the Union.

The period of Dublin rule of the Union lasted until 1848. It was ended by sustained allegations of financial irregularity. The headquarters were transferred to Liverpool and the Dublin branch was then suspended and a new one instituted but the records of the Consolidated Union of Bookbinders suggest that trade union loyalty among the journeymen bookbinders was seriously weakened by the bitterness caused by the suspension.

There is an overall pattern of growth in the Dublin booktrade in the first half of the nineteenth century. Recovery from the disruption caused to publishing by the Copyright Act began to take place in the second decade of the century although literary publishing, particularly of fiction, did not recover until the 1840s and even then was only briefly of more than domestic significance. Business in bookselling was healthy with some booksellers remaining in business for several decades. In common with other parts of the British Isles, interest in reading was also promoted by the large-scale charitable distribution of religious and improving literature, the production of which contributed to the prosperity of journeyman printers and bookbinders.

Bibliography

I. MANUSCRIPT MATERIAL

DUBLIN

Dublin City Archives
MSS FR/Reg/3–5 Dublin Corporation Freedom Registers 1774–1864.

Dublin Corporation Libraries
Gilbert Library MSS 278–289 Madden Papers.

Friends Historical Library
MSS Box 32–a Correspondence of E. Carbutt.

Irish Print Union
Dublin Typographical Provident Society Council Minutes 1827-1830; Council Minutes 1843, 1845; Committee 1845; National Typographical Association. Western District. Dublin Branch Committee Minutes 1845–1847; Dublin Typographical Provident Society Committee Minutes 1847–1860; Account book 1845–1849.

The King's Hospital
Register of pupils 1675–1819; Register of pupils 1823–1882; List of pupils 1766–1829.

National Archives
Official Papers OP 161 (9) Petitions for licenses as stamp sellers 1803.
Ordnance Survey OS 2 Correspondence Registers.
Ordnance Survey OS 12/1–5 Engraving Journals.
Ordnance Survey OS 5/8 Nominal return of civil assistants employed at Mountjoy … 11th May 1846.
Ordnance Survey OS 5/355 Return showing the pay and qualifications of civil assistants employed on the Trigonometrical Survey under Captain Cameron 27 Sept. 1847.

Protestant Orphan Society 999/1045/5/1 Register of orphan case histories; 999/1045/7/2 Register of apprentices 1835–1850; 999/1045/7/6 Masters' applications for apprentices; 999/1045/5/2 Register of application for elections of orphans 1837–1848, 1848–1857.

National Library of Ireland
MSS 139 R. D. Webb/Webb and Chapman wages book.
MSS 141 Webb and Chapman bill book 1846–1850.
MSS 7522–7523 Larcom Papers.
MSS 12126–128 Guild of St. Luke the Evangelist. Transactions 1785–1841.
MSS 12131 Guild of St. Luke the Evangelist. Record of admission of apprentices.
MSS 27293, 27295, 27301, 27304, 27306, 27309, 27311–27317, 31993. Bellew Papers.

Registry of Deeds. Dublin
Book of Anonymous Partnerships. Memorials of Deeds.

Representative Church Body Library
Baptismal and marriage registers of the parishes of St. Audoen 1801–1853, St. Catherine 1793–1859, St. George 1827–1852, St. James 1836–1854, St. Mark 1801–1856, St. Mary 1801–1853, St. Peter 1801–1853.

Royal Irish Academy
MSS 4.b.2 Reports on trades and manufactures [in] Dublin 1834.

Trinity College Dublin
MSS 10310 O'Kelly, J. J. 'The house of Gill' typescript.
MSS 10315 Graisberry and Campbell Ledger 1797–1806.
MSS 11037 Graisberry and Campbell bill book 1812–1815.
MSS 5659-5661 Incorporated Society for the promotion of English Protestant Schools in Ireland. Schools general register of apprentices 1798–1814.
MSS 5662–5664 General register of apprentices 1812–1838.
MSS 5667 Applications for apprentices.

ENGLAND

British Library
Strahan Archive Add. MSS 48906B, 48906C.

The National Archives, Kew
CUSTOMS 15, Ledgers of imports and exports, Ireland, 1698–1829.

University of Reading
Longman Archives 1/98–102, Correspondence

EDINBURGH

National Library of Scotland
Mf. Sec. MSS 239 Acc. 4395 Edinburgh Journeymen Bookbinders' Union Society. Committee Minutes.
The John Murray Archive: John Murray Letter book 1803–1823.

II. PRINTED COLLECTIONS OF LETTERS AND PAPERS

Calendar of Ancient Records of Dublin, Gilbert, Sir J. T. and Gilbert, R. M. eds, Dublin, 1889–1922. 18 v.
Maxwell, Sir H., *The Life and Letters of George William Frederick, Fourth Earl of Clarendon, K.G., G.C.B.*, London, 1913. 2 v.

O'Connell, D., *The Correspondence*, ed. O'Connell, M., Shannon and Dublin, 1972–1980.

Printing Patents. *Abridgement of Patent Specifications relating to Printing 1617–1857*. London, 1969.

The Registers of Christ Church Cathedral, Dublin, Refaussé, R. and Lennon, C. eds, Dublin, 1998.

Registers of the French Conformed Churches of St. Patrick and St. Mary, Dublin, Digges La Touche, J. J. ed., Dublin, 1903.

St. Michael's [C. of I.] Parish Register 1749–1872. Printed in *The Irish Builder*, XXXIII and XXXIV (1891 and 1892).

III. British Parliamentary papers

Third Report of the Commissioners of inquiry into the collection and management of the revenue arising in Ireland (UK Parliamentary Papers 1822. XII).

Fifth Report from Select Committee on Combination Laws (UK Parliamentary Papers 1824. V).

First Report of the Commissioners of Education in Ireland (UK Parliamentary Papers 1825. XII).

Population of Ireland (UK Parliamentary Papers 1833. XXXIX).

First Report of Commissioners for Inquiring into the condition of the poorer classes in Ireland (UK Parliamentary Papers 1836. XXX).

Second Report from Select Committee on Combinations of Workmen (UK Parliamentary Papers 1837–1838. VIII).

First Report from the Select Committee on Postage (UK Parliamentary Papers 1837–1838. XX).

Report of the Commissioners appointed to take the Census of Ireland, for the year 1841 (UK Parliamentary Papers 1843. XXIV).

The Census of Ireland for the year 1851. Part VI. General Report (UK Parliamentary Papers 1856. XXXI).

IV. Printed works published before 1900

Battersby, W. J., *Repeal or Ruin for Ireland*, Dublin, 1830.

Birch, J., *Plaintiff: A Full Report of the Proceedings in the Record Case of James Birch, Proprietor of The 'World' Newspaper against the Right Hon. Sir William M. Somerville, Bart., Tried at Nisi Prius, Queen's Bench ... 5th And 6th Of December, 1851*. Dublin, 1851.

Black, A., *Memoirs*, Edinburgh, 1885.

[Browne, T.], *The Parson's Hornbook*, Dublin, 1831.

Carleton, W., *Traits and Stories of the Irish Peasantry*, Dublin, 1842, 3 v.

Chapman, J., *Cheap Books and How to Get Them*, London, 1850.

Clymer, G., *Additional Testimonials Respecting the Patent Columbian Printing Press*, London, 1820.

Clymer, G., *The Patent Columbian Printing Press*, London, 1818.

Commissioners of Stamp Duties. *Retailers Licensed to Sell Stamps. 3 May 1813*, [Dublin, 1813].

Compositors' Scale of Prices. Revised and Adopted, March, 1870, Dublin, 1877.

Constable, T., *Archibald Constable and his Literary Correspondents*, Edinburgh, 1873. 3 v.

Dibdin, T. F., *The Library Companion*, London, 1824.

Dodd, G., *Days at the Factory*, London, 1843. Series I.

The Dublin directory [Wilson's]. Dublin, 1800–1832.

Dublin Typographical Provident Society, *Constitution*, Dublin, 1833.

Dublin Typographical Provident Society, *Constitution*, Dublin, 1842.

Duffy, Sir C. G., *Four Years of Irish History, 1845–1849*, London, 1883.

Duffy, Sir C. G., *Young Ireland: a Fragment of Irish History*, London, 1880.

Eagar, F. J., *A Genealogical History of the Eager Family*, Dublin, 1861.

Fitzpatrick, W. J., *The Sham Squire, and the Informers of 1798*, Dublin, 1866.

Gilbert, Sir John T., *A History of the City of Dublin*, Dublin, 1854–59. 3 v.

Hansard, T. C., *Typographia*, London, 1825.

Holroyd, J. B., Lord Sheffield, *Observations on the Manufacture, Trade and Present State of Ireland*, London, 1785. 3rd ed.

Hudson, J. W., *The History of Adult Education*, London, 1851.

[Knight, C.], *The Printer*, London, [1850].

Liberal Annuity Company of Dublin, *Deed of Agreement*, Dublin, 1832.

A List of the Constituency of the City of Dublin, as Registered Prior to the City of Dublin Election, in January 1835. Arranged in dictionary order by T. M. Ray. Dublin, [1835].

List of voters at the city of Dublin election … [25 29 January 1842], Dublin, 1842.

McLennan, J. F., *Memoir of Thomas Drummond*, Edinburgh, 1867.

Madden, R. R., *The History of Irish Periodical Literature*, London, 1867. 2 v.

Magee, J., *Defendant. The Trial of John Magee, Proprietor of the Dublin Evening Post, for Publishing an Historical Review of the Duke of Richmond's Administration, Tried, in the Court of King's Bench, on the 26th and 27th July*, Dublin, 1813.

Moxon, J., *Mechanick Exercises on the Whole Art of Printing*, London, 1683–1684 reprinted London, 1962.

Murray, P. J., *The Life of John Banim*, London, 1857.

Nichols, J., *Literary Anecdotes*, London, 1812–1815. 9 v.

Pettigrew and Oulton, *The Dublin Directory*, Dublin, [1833–1847].

Pigot, J. and Co., *City of Dublin and Hibernian Provincial Directory*, London and Manchester, 1824.

Pigot, J. and Co., *The Commercial Directory of Ireland, Scotland … for 1820–21 & 1822*, Manchester, 1820.

Post Office, *Annual Directory*, Dublin, 1832–1833, 1836–1838, 1840.

Preston, W., 'Essay on the natural advantages of Ireland', *Transactions of the Royal Irish Academy*, IX (1803), pp. 161–428.

Prices of Printing Work agreed upon by the Employers and Journeymen of the City of Dublin, commencing January 1 1800, [Dublin, 1799].

Prices of Printing Work agreed upon by the Employers and Journeymen of the City of Dublin, commencing July The First, 1808, [Dublin, 1808]. [Printed in *Irish Book Lover*, 20 (1932), pp. 35–38].

Proceedings at the Election for the City of Dublin, which commenced on Monday, January the 12th, and Terminated on Saturday, the 17th, 1835, Dublin, 1835.

Ray, T. M., *A Correct List of the Poll of Voters at the City of Dublin Election in August, 1837*, Dublin, 1838.

Rees, A., *The Cyclopaedia*, London, 1819. 39v.

A Report of the Correspondence between the Dublin Local Society and the Central Committee of the Consolidated Union of the Bookbinders in Liverpool, Dublin, 1850.

A Scale of Prices for Compositors and Press Men, agreed upon by the Employers and Journeyman Printers of the City of Dublin, February 9, 1829, Dublin, 1842.

Savage. W., *A Dictionary of the Art of Printing*, London, 1841.

Shaw, H., *New City Pictorial Directory*, Dublin, 1850.

Smiles, S., *A Publisher and his Friends: Memoir and Correspondence of the Late John Murray*, London, 1891. 2 v.

Society for promoting the education of the poor of Ireland. *Reports*. Dublin, 1818–1820.

Stower, C., *The Printer's Grammar*, London, 1808.

The Temple of Fame, Dublin, 1820.

Thom, A., *Irish Almanac and Official Directory*, Dublin, 1844–1851.

To Master Printers [Dublin, 1832].

[Tufnell, E. C.], *Character, Object, and Effects of Trades' Unions*. London, 1834.

Ullathorne, W., *The Autobiography*, London, 1891–1892. 2 v.

Wakefield, E., *An Account of Ireland, Statistical and Political*, London, 1812. 2 v.

Warburton, J., Whitelaw, J., Walsh, R., *History of the City of Dublin*, London, 1818. 2 v.

Webb, A. J., *A Compendium of Irish Biography*, Dublin, 1878.

Willis, T., *Facts connected with the Social and Sanitary Condition of the Working Classes in the City of Dublin*, Dublin, 1845.

V. Printed works published after 1900

Andrews, J. H., *A Paper Landscape: The Ordnance Survey in Nineteenth-Century Ireland*, Oxford, 1975.

Aspinall, A., *Politics and the Press c. 1780–1850*, London, 1949.

Barnes, J. J., *Free Trade in Books*, Oxford, 1964.

Barrow, G. L., *The Emergence of the Irish Banking System*, Dublin, 1975.

Bell, B., 'Pioneers of literature: the commercial traveller in the early 19th century', Isaac, P. and McKay, B., eds, *The Reach of Print Making, Selling and Using Books*, Winchester, 1998.

Benson, C., 'Printers and booksellers in Dublin 1800–1850' in R. Myers and M. Harris, eds, *Spreading the Word: Distribution Networks of Print 1550–1850*, Winchester, 1990, pp. 47–59.

Black, R. D. C., *A Catalogue of Pamphlets on Economic Subjects Published between 1750 and 1900 and Now Housed in Irish Libraries*, Belfast, 1969.

Bundock, C. J., *The Story of the National Union of Printing Bookbinding and Paper Workers*, Oxford, 1959.

Burtchaell, G. D., and Sadleir, T. U., *Alumni Dublinenses*, Dublin, 1935.

Butler, P., *The Brocas Collection*, Dublin, 1997.

Casteleyn, M., *A History of Literacy and Libraries in Ireland*, London, 1984.

Centenary of the Cork Typographical Society 1806–1906, Cork, 1906.

Clarkson, J. D., *Labour and Nationalism in Ireland*, New York, 1925.

Coakley, D., *Irish Masters of Medicine*, Dublin, 1982.

Craig, M., *Irish Bookbindings, 1600–1800*, London, 1954.

Dickson, D., 'The demographic implications of Dublin's growth, 1650–1850', Lawton, R., and Lee, R., eds, *Urban Population Development in Western Europe from the Late-Eighteenth to the Early-Twentieth Century, Liverpool*, 1989, pp. 178–89.

Downey, E., *Charles Lever*, London, 1906. 2 v.

Eliot, S. E., *Some Patterns and Trends in British Publishing 1800-1919*, London, 1994.

Gaskell, P., *A New Introduction to Bibliography*, Oxford, 1974.

Gillespie, S. C., *A Hundred Years of Progress. The Record of the Scottish Typographical Association 1853 to 1952*, Glasgow, 1953.

Goldstrom, J., 'The correspondence between Lord John Russell and the publishing trade', *Publishing History*, xx (1986), pp. 5–59.

Griffin, S., 'The Catholic Book Society and its role in the emerging system of national education 1824-1834', *Irish Educational Studies*, 11 (1992), pp. 82–98.

Harrison, R. S., *Richard Davis Webb: Dublin Quaker Printer (1805–72)*, [s.l.], 1993.

Harvey, K., *The Bellews of Mount Bellew*, Dublin, 1998.

Hill, J., *From Patriots to Unionists: Dublin Civil Politics and Irish Protestant Patriotism, 1660–1840*, Oxford, 1997.

Holohan, P., 'Daniel O'Connell and the Dublin trades: a collision 1837/8', *Saothar*, 1, no. 1 (1975), pp. 1–17.

Holroyd, J., *George Robertson of Melbourne, 1825–1898: Pioneer Bookseller & Publisher*, [Melbourne], 1968.

Houfe, S., *The Dictionary of 19th-Century British Book Illustrators and Caricaturists*, revised edition, Woodbridge, 1996.

Howe, E., *The London Compositor*, London, 1947.

Howe, E. and Child, J., *The Society of London Bookbinders 1780–1951*, London, 1952.

Howe, E. and Waite, H. E., *The London Society of Compositors*, London, 1948.

Hunt, C. J., *The Book Trade in Northumberland and Durham to 1860*, Newcastle upon Tyne, 1975.

Inglis, B., *The Freedom of the Press in Ireland*, London, 1954.

Kennedy, L. and Dowling, M. W., 'Prices and wages in Ireland, 1700–1850', *Irish Economic and Social History*, XXIV (1997), pp. 62–104.

Kinane, V., *A History of the Dublin University Press 1734–1976*, Dublin, 1994.

Kinane, V. and Benson, C., 'Some late 18th- and early 19th-century Dublin Printers' Account Books: the Graisberry Ledgers', Isaac, P., ed., *Six Centuries of the Provincial Book Trade in Britain*, Winchester, 1990, pp. 139–50.

Levistone Cooney, D. A., 'A pious Dublin printer', *Dublin Historical Record*, XLVI, no. 2 (Autumn 1993), pp. 74–100.

McCormack, W. J., *Sheridan Le Fanu and Victorian Ireland*, Oxford, 1980.

McDonnell, J., *Five Hundred Years of the Art of the Book in Ireland*, Dublin, London, 1997.

McGuinne, D., *Irish Type Design: A History of Printing Types in the Irish Character*, Dublin, 1992.

Methodist Centenary Church. A Commemorative Record, Dublin, 1943.

Moody, T. W., Martin, F. X., Byrne, F. J., eds, *A New History of Ireland*, v. VIII, Oxford, 1982.

Moran, J., 'The Columbian Press', *Journal of the Printing Historical Society*, 5 (1969), pp. 1–23.

Moran, J., *Printing Presses*, London, 1973.

Murphy, S. ed., *Bully's Acre and Royal Hospital Kilmainham Graveyards: History and Inscriptions*, Dublin, 1989.

Musson, A. E., *The Typographical Association*, London, 1954.

Myers, R. 'Writing for the booksellers in the early nineteenth century', Myers, R. and Harris, M., eds, *Author/Publisher Relations during the Eighteenth and Nineteenth Centuries*, Oxford, 1983.

North, J. S., *The Waterloo Directory of Irish Newspapers and Periodicals, 1800-1900*, Waterloo, 1986.

Ó Casaide, S., 'Watty Cox and his publications', *Bibliographical Society of Ireland*, V, no. 2 (1935), pp. 21–38.

Ó Gráda, C., *Ireland: A New Economic History 1780–1939*, Oxford, 1994.

Ó Ciosáin, N., *Print and Popular Culture in Ireland, 1750–1850*, London, 1997.

O'Connor, E., *A Labour History of Ireland 1824–1960*, Dublin, 1992.

O'Donoghue, D. J., *The Poets of Ireland*, Dublin, London, 1912.

Plant, M., *The English Book Trade*, London, 1974. 3rd ed.

Pollard, M., *Dublin's Trade in Books 1550–1800*, Oxford, 1989.

Pollard, M., 'John Chambers, Printer and United Irishman', *Irish Book*, 3 (1964), pp. 1–22.

Powicke, Sir F. M. and Fryde, E. B., *Handbook of British Chronology*, London, 1961.

Public Records of Ireland. *The Thirtieth Report of the Deputy Keeper of the Public Records and Keeper of the State Papers in Ireland. Appendix*, Dublin, 1899.

Public Records of Ireland. *The Fifty-fifth Report of the Deputy Keeper of the Public Records and Keeper of the State Papers in Ireland. Appendix*, Dublin, 1928.

Public Records of Ireland. *The Fifty-sixth Report of the Deputy Keeper of the Public Records and Keeper of the State Papers in Ireland*, Dublin, 1931.

Public Records of Ireland. *The Fifty-seventh Report of the Deputy Keeper of the Public Records and Keeper of the State Papers in Ireland*. Dublin, 1936.

Ramsden, C., *Bookbinders of the United Kingdom*, [London], 1954.

Sadie, S. ed., *The New Grove Dictionary of Music and Musicians*, London, 1980, 20 v.

Sadlier, M., *XIX Century Fiction*, Cambridge, 1951, 2 v.

Sayle, C. E., *A Catalogue of the Bradshaw Collection of Irish books in the University Library Cambridge*, Cambridge, 1916, 3 v.

Scragg, B., *Thomas Haydock, 1772–1859, Catholic Bookseller*, Newcastle upon Tyne, 1999.

Stephen, L. and Lee, S., eds, *Dictionary of National Biography*, London, 1908–1909, 22 v.

Strickland, W. G., *A Dictionary of Irish Artists*, Dublin, 1913, 2 v.

Wall, T., *The Sign of Doctor Hay's Head*, Dublin, 1958.

White, P., 'The printing trade in Dublin: the University Press, Trinity College Dublin', *Irish Printer*, 3, no. 11 (June 1908), pp. 8–10; 3, no. 12 (July 1908), pp. 8–9; 4, no. 1 (August 1908), pp. 6–8.

Wilson, C. and Reader, W., *Men and Machines. A History of D. Napier and Sons Engineers Ltd. 1808–1958*, London, 1958.

VI. NEWSPAPERS AND PERIODICALS

Bankrupt and Insolvent Calendar, 1846–1850

Bookbinders' Consolidated Union Trade Circular, Liverpool, London, 1848–1872

Bookbinders Trade Circular, London, 1850–1857

Carrick's Morning Post, April 1814–1820

The Compositors' Chronicle, London, 1840–1843

Correspondent, July–December 1807, January–March 1808, 1821–1822

Dublin Correspondent, 1823–1824

Dublin Evening Express, 5 January – 28 April 1824

Dublin Evening Herald, February 1821 – January 1822

Dublin Evening Mail, February–December 1823, 1833, 1846, 1849

Dublin Evening Post, 1801–1802, 1807 – June 1812, 1816, 1828–1850

Dublin Gazette, 1801–1850

Dublin Journal, 1801, 1805, 1809–1815, 1821

Dublin Monitor, 1838–1845

Dublin Morning Post, 1822, 1826–1827, 1832

Dublin Morning Press, 9 February – 2 April 1842

Dublin Penny Journal, 1832–1836

Dublin Times, November 1831 – May 1832

Dublin Weekly Messenger, November 1808–1810

Evening Herald, 1806

Evening Packet, 1828

Freeman's Journal, 1801–1806, 1812, 1813–1815, 1820, 1826, 1834–1836, 1841

Hibernian Journal, March–July 1801, 1804, 1805

Hibernian Magazine, 1801–1812

The Irish Book Lover, 1909–1957

The Irish Printer, 1903–1908

Irish Times, 15 October 1823 – 18 July 1825

Irishman, January–May 1850

Morning Register, 1828, 1831
Nation, October 1842–1851
Saunders's Newsletter, 1802, 1805, 1808, 1816–1854
Stewart's Telegraphic Despatch and Daily Advertiser, 1832–1835
Typographical Gazette, London, 1846–1847
Typographical Protection Circular, London, 1849–1853
Warden, 1828
World, May 1840–1843

VII. Unpublished theses

D'Arcy, F., 'Dublin artisan activity, opinion and organisation, 1820–1850', National University of Ireland M.A. thesis 1968.

Harrison, Richard S., 'Dublin Quakers in business 1800–1850', Trinity College Dublin M. Litt. thesis 1987.

Hislop, H., 'The Kildare Place Society 1811–1831: an Irish experiment in popular education', Trinity College Dublin Ph.D. thesis 1990.

O'Neill, C. M., 'A short title catalogue of Dublin printed periodicals 1801–1825', Library Association of Ireland Fellowship thesis 1985.

Wheeler, W. G., 'Libraries in Ireland before 1855', University of London Diploma in Librarianship thesis 1957.

VIII. List of books published in Dublin by subscription 1801–1850

All at Home; or, The Irish Nieces. A Comedy, Dublin, 1804.
Brief Memorials of the Rev. B. W. Mathias, Dublin, 1842.
The Dublin Magazine, Dublin, 1812–1813.
Gleanings of Literature, Dublin, 1805.
The Life of St Columb-kille, Dublin, [*c.*1810].
Life of the Holy Mother, St. Teresa, Dublin, 1809.
The Literary and Masonic Magazine, Dublin, 1802–1803.
Tales by an Unwilling Author, Dublin, 1822.
The Works of Spencer, Campion, Hanmer, Dublin, 1809.
Atkinson, A., *The Irish Tourist*, Dublin, 1815.
[Archdeacon, M.] *Connaught in 1798: A Historical Tale*, Dublin, 1830.
[Archdeacon, M.] *Everard: An Irish Tale*, Dublin, 1835.
[Archdeacon, M.] *Legends of Connaught*, Dublin, 1839.
Bayly, T., *Miniature Lyrics*, Dublin, [1823].
Boiardo, M. M., *The Expedition of Gradasso*, Dublin, 1812.
Bossuet, J. J., *A Discourse on Universal History*, Dublin, 1811.
Bourdaloue, L., *Spiritual Retreat*, Dublin, 1801.
Brenan, M. J., *An Ecclesiastical History of Ireland*, Dublin, 1840.
Brooke, C., *Reliques of Irish Poetry*, Dublin, 1816.
Brooks, H., *The Victories of the Sutlej: A Prize Poem*, Dublin, 1848.
Brown, J., *A Historical, Geographical, Chronological, Etymological, and Critical Dictionary of the Bible*, Dublin, 1801 [i.e. 1802].
Buchan, W., *The Domestic Medicine*, twentieth edition. Dublin, 1807.

Burdy, S., *Ardglass*, Dublin, 1802.

Butler, A., *The Life of the Most Illustrious … Saint Augustin, Bishop of Hippo*, Dublin, 1813.

Butler, A., *The Lives of the Fathers*, third edition, Dublin, 1802.

Butler, A., *Meditations and Discourses on the Sublime Truths and Important Duties of Christianity*, second edition, Dublin, 1815.

[Catholic Church] *The Catechism*, Dublin, 1816.

[Catholic Church] *An Exact Reprint of the Roman Index*, ed. R. Gibbings, Dublin, London, 1837.

Caussin, N., *The Holy Court*, Dublin, 1815–1816.

Challoner, R., *The Life of the Holy Mother St. Teresa*, Dublin, 1828.

Challoner, R., *The Unerring Authority of the Catholic Church*, Dublin, 1829.

Chester, R. and W. B., *Poems: Historical and Miscellaneous*, Dublin, 1849.

Cloney, T., *A Personal Narrative of 1798*, Dublin, 1832.

Comins, P., *The Science of Commerce*, Dublin, 1814.

Cummins, E., *The Miscellaneous Poetic Works*, Dublin, 1808.

D'Alton, J., *The Memoirs of the Archbishop of Dublin*, Dublin, 1838.

D'Alton, J., *The History of Drogheda*, Dublin, 1844.

D'Alton, J. ,*The History of Ireland*, Dublin, 1845.

Deighan, P., *A Complete Treatise of Arithmetic*, Dublin, 1804.

Donnelly, P., *Love of Britain*, Dublin, 1824.

Doyle, G., *A Compendium of the History of Rome*, Dublin, 1821.

Edkins, J., ed., *A Collection of Poems*, Dublin, 1801.

Ennis, F., *A Complete System of Modern Geography*, Dublin, 1816.

Erck, J. C., *An Account of the Ecclesiastical Establishment*, Dublin, 1830.

Erck, J. C., *The Ecclesiastical Register*, Dublin, 1820.

Fitzpatrick, R., *The Bard's Museum*, Dublin, 1809.

Fitzsimons, E. J. B., *Irish Minstrelsy*, Dublin, London, [1814].

Fletcher, W. L., *The Frequented Village*, Dublin, 1844.

Fletcher, W. L., *The Frequented Village*, second edition. Dublin, 1845.

Gautier, C., *Idioms, or Proverbial Expressions of the French Language*, Dublin, 1807.

Gordon, J. B., *A History of Ireland*, Dublin, 1805.

Grey, H. and J., *Arithmetical Excellencies*, Dublin, 1822.

Grey, H. and J., *Arithmetical Excellencies*, third edition. Dublin, 1824.

Grey, H. and J., *Arithmetical Excellencies*, fourth edition. Dublin, 1825.

Grey, H. and J., *Practical Arithmetic*, fifth edition. Dublin, 1825.

Grey, H. and J., *Practical Arithmetic*, tenth edition. Dublin, 1830.

Grou, J. N., *The School of Christ*, Dublin, 1801.

Hargrove, G., *An Account of the Islands of Walcheren and South Beveland*, Dublin, London, 1812.

Hawarden, E., *Charity and Truth*, Dublin, 1809.

Hawarden, E., *The True Church of Christ*, Dublin, Kilkenny, 1808.

Henry VIII, *Defence of the Seven Sacraments*, Dublin, [1815?].

Hodgson, P. J., *The Commercial Revenue Guide*, Dublin, 1801.

Humphreys, T., *The Irish Builder's Guide*, Dublin, 1813.

Hunter, R., *The Racing Calendar*, Dublin, 1801–1850.

Jamelin, J., *A New Manual of Prayer*, Dublin, 1805.

Jennings, J., *Book-Keeping*, Dublin, 1802.

[Jennings, W.] *A General System of Attack and Defence*, Dublin, 1808.

Johnson, S., *The Works*, Dublin, 1816–1817.

Josephus, F., *The Jewish War*, Dublin, 1813.

Keenan, J. C., *The Standard of Christianity*, Dublin, 1805.

Kingsley, J., *Preparations for the Session of 1839, on the Criminal Returns of Ireland*, Dublin, 1839.

Knox, A., *The Irish Watering Places*, Dublin, London, 1845.

Lamb, R., *An Original and Authentic Journal of Occurrences during the Late American War*, Dublin, 1809 [–1810].

Lanigan, J., *An Ecclesiastical History of Ireland*, Dublin, 1822.

Leadbeater, M., *Poems*, Dublin, London, 1808.

Leadbeater, M., *Cottage Dialogues*, Dublin, 1811.

Ledwich, E., *The Antiquities of Ireland*, Dublin, London, Bath, Bristol, Liverpool, 1804.

Leet, A., *A Directory to the Market Towns … in Ireland*, second edition, Dublin, 1814.

Lysaght, E., *Poems*, Dublin, 1811.

MacGeoghan, J., *History of Ireland*, Dublin, 1831–1832.

Mackey, J., *Compositions in Verse*, Dublin, 1819.

McKinley, J., *The Giant's Causeway*, Dublin, 1821.

MacNally, L., *The Justice of the Peace for Ireland*, Dublin, 1808.

[Macpherson, J.] *Fingal: An Epic Poem*, London, Edinburgh, Dublin, 1844.

Magrath, A. J., *Blossoms of Genius*, Dublin, 1834.

Marcus, B., *Segtile*, Dublin, 1841.

Massillon, J. B., *Select Translations of the Beauties of*, Dublin, 1812.

Moody, J., *Sermons*, Dublin, 1814.

Moore, T., *A Selection of Irish Melodies*, Dublin, London, [1807].

Morgan, S. O., *Poems*, Dublin, London, 1801.

Murphy, B., *Sermons*, Dublin, 1808.

Neligan, J., *The Bible in Miniature*, Dublin, 1808.

Neligan, J., *Sacred Poetry*, Dublin, 1820.

O'Conor, C., *Dissertations on the History of Ireland*, Dublin, 1812.

O'Flaherty, C., *Poems*, Dublin, 1813.

O'Hegerty, C., *Contes Moraux*, Dublin, 1812.

O'Halloran, S., *An Introduction to and an History of Ireland*, Dublin, 1803.

O'Kelly, P., *The Eudoxologist*, Dublin, 1812.

O'Kelly, P., *The Hippocrene*, Dublin, 1831.

O'Kelly, P., *Poems on the Giant's Causeway*, Dublin, 1808.

O'Reilly, E., *Sanas Gaoidhilge-Sagsbhearla*, Dublin, 1817.

Patrick, Saint, *Synodi, Canoni, Opuscula*, Dublin, 1835.

Persius Flaccus, A., *Satires*, Dublin, 1827.

Proyart, L. B., *The Life of Princess Louisa*, Dublin, 1812.

Quigley, C., *Poems*, Dublin, 1813.

Reeve, J., *Practical Discourses on the Perfections and Wonderful Works of God*, second edition, Dublin, 1840.

Reid, J., *Emma: or, the Victim of Despair*, Dublin, 1821.

Rodriguez, A., *The Practice of Christian Perfection*, Dublin, 1831.

Ryan, E., *The History of the Effects of Religion on Mankind*, second edition, Dublin, 1802.

Ryan, J., *The History and Antiquities of the County of Carlow*, Dublin, 1833.

Ryan, J., *The Life of William the Third*, Dublin, 1836.

Ségur, L. P. de, *The Four Ages of Life*, Dublin, London, Edinburgh, 1826.

Sleater, M., *Introductory Essay to a New System of Civil and Ecclesiastical Topography*, Dublin, 1806.

Steele, S,. *Eva, an Historical Poem*, Dublin, 1816.

Bibliography

[Stewart, J.?] *Roll of a Tennis Ball through the Moral World*, Dublin, 1812.

Stewart, W., *Precedents of Law Forms in the Courts of Dublin, Queen's Bench*, Dublin, 1838–1840.

Taylor, A. C., *Designs for Agricultural Building*, Dublin, 1841.

Taylor, J., *A Speech Delivered at the Historical Society*, Dublin, 1814.

Templeton, J., *Poems*, Dublin, 1809.

Templeton, J., *Poems on Several Occasions*, Dublin, 1801.

Thomas a Kempis, *Viator Christianus*, Dublin, 1804.

Ussher, M. N., *A Latin Grammar*, Dublin, 1823.

Ussher, M. N., *Synonymous Terms in the English Language Explained*, Dublin, 1816.

Villanueva, J., *Ibernia Phoenicea*, Dublin, 1831.

Villanueva, J., *Poesias Escogidas*, Dublin, 1833.

Ward, T., *Errata of the Protestant Bible*, Dublin, London, 1807.

Waylett, H., ed., *The Beauties of Literature*, Dublin, 1804.

West, M., *Female Heroism*, Dublin, 1803.

West, M., *Sermons*, Dublin, London, 1819.

Weyman, D., *Melodia Sacra*, Dublin, [1814].

White, A., *Confutation of Church of Englandism*, Dublin, London, 1841.

White, H., *Twenty Sermons*, Dublin, 1834 [J. Ryan, *The Life of William the Third*, Dublin, 1836 claims that White's book was published by subscription]

White, J., *An Essay on the Indigenous Grasses Of Ireland*, Dublin, 1808.

NOTE: All the lists in H. and J. Grey's arithmetic books seem remarkably similar.

Appendix I: Updated Bibliography

A listing of relevant works on the Irish book trade most of which have appeared since the finishing of the thesis in 2000

Adams, J. R. R., *The Printed Word and the Common Man: Popular Culture in Ulster 1700–1900*, Belfast, 1987.

Archbold, Johanna, 'Irish periodicals in their Atlantic context, 1770–1830: the monthly and quarterly magazines of Dublin, with comparison to those of Edinburgh and Philadelphia' (Trinity College Dublin, unpublished Ph.D. thesis, 2008).

Arndt, Sarah Crider, 'The book trade and print culture: a comparative analysis of Belfast and Baltimore 1760–1825', (Trinity College Dublin, unpublished Ph.D. thesis, 2012).

Arndt, S. C., 'Bringing books into Baltimore: tracing networks of textual importation, 1760–1825', *Book History*, 16 (2013), pp. 62–88.

Barnard, Toby; Ó Cróinín, Dáibhí; Simms, Katharine (eds), *A Miracle of Learning: Studies in Manuscripts and Irish Learning: Essays in Honour of William O'Sullivan*, Aldershot, 1998.

Barnard, Toby, *Brought to Book: Print in Ireland, 1680–1784*, Dublin, 2017.

Benatti, Francesa, 'Dublin Penny Journal' in Brake, Laurel; Demoor, Marysa (eds), *Dictionary of Nineteenth-Century Journalism*, London, 2009, pp. 182–83.

Benson, Charles; Fitzpatrick, Siobhán (eds), *That Woman! — Studies in Irish Bibliography, a Festschrift for Mary 'Paul' Pollard*, Dublin, 2005.

Boran, Elizabethanne (ed.), *Book Collecting in Ireland and Britain 1650–1850*, Dublin, 2018.

Caball, Marc; Carpenter, Andrew (eds), *Oral and Print Cultures in Ireland 1600–1900*, Dublin, 2010.

Clyde, Tom, *Irish Literary Magazines: An Outline History and Descriptive Bibliography*, Dublin, 2003.

Cole, Richard Cargill, *Irish Booksellers and English Writers 1740–1800*, London, 1986.

Cunningham, Bernadette; Kennedy, Máire (eds), *The Experience of Reading: Irish Historical Perspectives*, Dublin, 1999.

Cunningham, Bernadette; Fitzpatrick, Siobhán (eds), *Treasures of the Royal Irish Academy Library*, Dublin, 2009.

Daly, Mary E., *Dublin, the Deposed Capital: A Social and Economic History 1860–1914*, Cork, 1984.

Daly, Mary; Dickson, David (eds), *The Origins of Popular Literacy in Ireland: Language Change and Educational Development 1700–1920*, Dublin, 1990.

Davison, Peter (ed.), *The Book Encompassed: Studies in Twentieth-Century Bibliography*, Cambridge, 1992.

Dickson, David, *Dublin: The Making of a Capital City*, Dublin, 2014.

Donnelly, James S.; Miller, Kerby A. (eds), *Irish Popular Culture 1650–1850*, Dublin, 1998.

Fanning, Martin; Gillespie, Raymond (eds), *Print Culture and Intellectual Life in Ireland 1660–1941: Essays in Honour of Michael Adams*, Dublin, 2006.

Farmar, Tony; Kostick, Conor, *The History of Irish Book Publishing*, Dublin, 2018.

Fenning, Hugh, 'Dublin imprints of Catholic interest, 1800–09', *Archivium Hibernicum*, 61 (2008), pp. 246–324.

Finkelstein, David, 'Nineteenth-century print on the move: a perilous study of translocal migration and print skills transfer', in McElligott, Jason; Eve Patten (eds), *The Perils of Print Culture: Book, Print and Publishing History in Theory and Practice*, Basingstoke, 2014, pp. 150–66.

Finkelstein, David, *Movable Types: Roving Creative Printers of the Victorian World*, Oxford, 2018.

Fox, Peter (ed.), *Treasures of the Library, Trinity College Dublin*, Dublin, 1986.

Fox, Peter, *Trinity College Library Dublin: A History*, Cambridge, 2014.

Gillespie, Raymond; Hadfield, Andrew (eds), *The Irish Book in English, 1550–1800* (The Oxford History of the Irish Book, 3), Oxford, 2006.

Graham, Colin; Litvack, Leon (eds), *Ireland and Europe in the Nineteenth Century*, Dublin, 2006.

Gray, John; McCann, Wesley (eds), *An Uncommon Bookman: Essays in Memory of J. R. R. Adams*, Belfast, 1996.

Hayley, Barbara; McKee, Enda (eds), *Three Hundred Years of Irish Periodicals*, Dublin, 1987.

Hinks, John; Armstrong, Catherine; Day, Matthew (eds), *Periodicals and Publishers: The Newspaper and Journal Trade 1740–1914*, New Castle, DE, and London, 2009.

Howell, John Bruce, *A History of the Dublin Library Society, 1791–1881*, Halifax, NS, 1985.

Hunt, Arnold; Mandelbrote, Giles; Shell, Alison (eds), *The Book Trade and its Customers 1450–1900: Historical Essays for Robin Myers*, Winchester, 1997.

Jackson, Timothy R. (ed.), *Frozen in Time: The Fagel Collection in the Library of Trinity College Dublin*, Dublin, 2016.

Jessop, Norma; Nudds, Christine (eds), *Guide to Collections in Dublin Libraries: Printed Books to 1850 and Special Collections*, Dublin, 1982.

Kavanagh, Robin, 'Stereo-typed to stereotype: illustrations, "The most influential novelty" in the nineteenth-century Irish and British press', in Carrera, Maria José; Carrera, Anunciación; Cámara, Enrique; Dapía, Celsa (eds), *The Irish Knot: Essays on Imaginary/Real Ireland*, Valladolid, 2008, pp. 147–60.

Kelleher, Margaret; O'Leary, Philip (eds), *The Cambridge History of Irish literature*, 2 vols, Cambridge, 2006.

Kelly, James, 'Regulating print: the state and control of print in eighteenth-century Ireland', *Eighteenth-Century Ireland*, 23 (2008), pp. 142–74.

Kelly, James, 'Print and the provision of medical knowledge in eighteenth-century Ireland', in Gillespie, Raymond; Foster, R. F. (eds), *Irish Provincial Cultures in the Long Eighteenth Century: Essays for Toby Barnard*, Dublin, 2012, pp. 33–56.

Killen, John, *A History of the Linen Hall Library, 1788–1988*, Belfast, 1990.

Kinane, Vincent, 'A galley of pie: women in the Irish book trades', *Linen Hall Review*, 8, no. 4 (1991), pp. 10–13.

Kinane, Vincent, 'Printers' apprentices in 18th and 19th century Dublin', *Linen Hall Review*, 10, no. 1 (1993) pp. 11–14.

Kinane, Vincent; Walsh, Anne (eds), *Essays on the History of Trinity College Library Dublin*, Dublin, 2000.

Kinane, Vincent, *A Brief History of Printing and Publishing in Ireland*, Dublin, 2002.

Kirk, John; Brown, Michael; Noble, Andrew (eds), *Cultures of Radicalism in Britain and Ireland*, London, 2013.

Kissane, Noel (ed.), *Treasures from the National Library of Ireland*, Dublin, 1994.

Loeber, Rolf; Loeber, Magda; Burnham, Anne Mullin, *A Guide to Irish Fiction, 1650–1900*, Dublin, 2006.

Long, Gerard (ed.), *Books Beyond the Pale: Aspects of the Provincial Book Trade in Ireland before 1850*, Dublin, 1996.

McCarthy, Muriel; Simmons, Ann (eds), *The Making of Marsh's Library: Learning, Politics and Religion in Ireland, 1650–1750*, Dublin, 2004.

McCarthy, Muriel; Simmons, Ann (eds), *Marsh's Library a Mirror on the World: Law, Learning and Libraries, 1650–1750*, Dublin, 2009.

McElligott, Jason; Eve Patten (eds), *The Perils of Print Culture: Book, Print and Publishing History in Theory and Practice*, Basingstoke, 2014.

McGuire, James; Quinn, James (eds), *Dictionary of Irish Biography: From the Earliest Times to the Year 2010*, Cambridge, 2018.

McKitterick, David, *The Invention of Rare Books: Private Interest and Public Memory, 1600–1840*, Cambridge, 2018.

McManus, Antonia, *The Irish Hedge School and its Books, 1695–1831*, Dublin, 2004.

Maddock, Philip, *Exquisite and Rare: Bookbindings from the Library of Benjamin Guinness, 3rd Earl of Iveagh*, Dublin, 2013.

Manley, K. A., *Irish Reading Societies and Circulating Libraries Founded before 1825: Useful Knowledge and Agreeable Entertainment*, Dublin, 2018.

Moore, Sean D. (ed.) *Eighteenth-Century Studies*, 45, no. 3, special issue, Ireland and Enlightenment (Spring 2012).

Murphy, J. H. (ed.), *The Irish Book in English, 1800–1891* (The Oxford History of the Irish Book, 4), Oxford, 2011.

Murtagh, Timothy, 'Dublin's artisans and radical politics 1779–1803', (Trinity College Dublin, unpublished Ph.D. thesis, 2015).

Murtagh, Timothy, 'The shadow of the pikeman: Irish craftsmen and British radicalism, 1803–20' in McElligott, Jason; Conboy, Martin (eds), *The Cato Street Conspiracy: Plotting, Counter-Intelligence and the Revolutionary Tradition in Britain and Ireland*, Manchester, 2020, pp. 135–52.

Myers, Robin; Harris, Michael (eds), *Spreading the Word: The Distribution Networks of Print 1550–1850*, Winchester, 1990.

Myers, Robin; Harris, Michael; Mandelbrote, Giles (eds), *Books for Sale: The Advertising and Promotion of Print since the Fifteenth Century*, New Castle, DE, and London, 2009.

Neligan, Agnes (ed.), *Maynooth Library Treasures: from the Collections of Saint Patrick's College*, Dublin, 1995.

Niall Ó Ciosáin, *Ireland in Official Print Culture 1800–1850: A New Reading of the Poor Inquiry*, Oxford, 2014.

Ó Gráda, Cormac, *Ireland: A New Economic History 1780–1939*, Oxford, 1994.

Phillips, James W., *Printing and Bookselling in Dublin 1670–1800*, Dublin, 1998.

Pollard, A. W.; Redgrave, G. R., *A Short-Title Catalogue of Books Printed in England, Scotland, & Ireland*, 3 volumes, London, 1986, 1976, 1991.

Pollard, M., *A Dictionary of Members of the Dublin Book Trade 1550–1800*, London, 2000.

Raven, James, *The Business of Books: Booksellers and the English Book Trade 1450–1850*, New Haven, CT, 2007.

St Clair, William, *The Reading Nation in the Romantic Period*, Cambridge, 2004.

Sharpe, Richard, 'Irish poetry in print in Cox's 'Irish Magazine' 1808–1810', *Journal of the Cork Historical and Archaeological Society*, 121 (2016), pp. 64–80.

Sher, Richard B., *The Enlightenment and the Book*, Chicago, IL, 2006.

Suarez, Michael F.; Turner, Michael L. (eds), *The Cambridge History of the Book in Britain. Vol. 5, 1695–1830*, Cambridge, 2009.

Suarez, M. F.; Woudhuysen, H. R. (eds) *The Oxford Companion to the Book*, 2 v., Oxford, 2010.

The University of the People: Celebrating Ireland's Public Libraries. The Thomas Davis Lectures 2002, Dublin, 2003.

Tilley, Elizabeth, *The Periodical Press in Nineteenth-Century Ireland*, London, 2020.

Vaughan, W. E. (ed.), *The Old Library Trinity College Dublin 1712–2012*, Dublin, 2013.

Westerhof, Danielle (ed.), *The Alchemy of Medicine and Print. The Edward Worth Library, Dublin*, Dublin, 2010.

Happiest with his nose in a book: Charles
Benson and grandson Charles Louis
Michael Benson, 2015.

Appendix II: a bibliography of the writings of Charles Benson

compiled by Lydia Ferguson and Siobhán Fitzpatrick

Mary Pollard and Charles Benson, '"The rags of Ireland are by no means the same": Irish paper used in the Statutes at large' *Long Room*, 2 (autumn–winter 1970), 18–35.

'A friend of the [Trinity College Dublin] library, 1759', *Long Room*, 9 (spring–summer 1974), 40.

'A note on the printer of a Dublin edition of *The Orators* [by Samuel Foote]', *Long Room*, 9 (spring–summer 1974), 40.

'"Wild oats" in New Ross: theatre in an Irish country town, 1789–95', *Long Room*, 22–23 (1981), 13–18.

'The curious use of [George] Berkeley's *Alciphron* printed in 1755', *Long Room*, 28–29 (spring–autumn 1984), 17–27.

'Early printed books and special collections: notes on selected accessions', *Long Room*, 26–27 (spring–autumn 1983), 37–38.

'Early printed books and special collections: notes on selected accessions', *Long Room*, 28–29 (spring–autumn 1984), 45–46.

'Anatomizing early printed books in Trinity College, Dublin' in 'Notes', *Eighteenth-Century Ireland*, 1 (1986), 195–99.

'"Here's fine work! Here's fine suicide, paracide and simulation"' in Peter Fox (ed.), *Treasures of the Library: Trinity College Dublin* (Dublin, 1986), 148–57.

'"Probationary starts and unprovok'd rants": the drama collection at Trinity College Dublin', *Antiquarian Book Monthly Review*, 14 (June 1987), 216–18.

'The Irish contribution to ESTC', *Factotum: Newsletter of the XVIIIth century STC*, 29 (1989), 3–4.

'Printing and booksellers in Dublin 1800–1850' in Robin Myers and Michael Harris (eds), *Spreading the Word: The Distribution Networks of Print 1550–1850* (Winchester, 1990), 47–59.

Vincent Kinane and Charles Benson, 'Some late 18th- and early 19th-century Dublin printers' account books: the Graisberry ledgers' in P. Isaac (ed.), *Six Centuries of the Provincial Book Trade in Britain* (Winchester, 1990), 139–50.

'Trinity College: a bibliographical essay' in Charles Holland (ed.), *Trinity College Dublin and the Idea of a University* (Dublin, 1991), 357–71.

'Aldritt printing press:[a note]' in 'Bibliophile's diary', *Long Room*, 36 (1991), 12–13.

'Research resources in Trinity College Dublin', *The East-Central Intelligencer*, n.s. 5(1) (1991), (noticed in 'Recent publications' *An Leabharlann / The Irish Library*, ser. 2, 9 (1) (1992), 21).

'Thomas Mullen: "the cheapest and the best book-binder in Dublin"', *Long Room*, 36 (1991), 18–19.

Charles Benson and Norma MacManaway, '"A sceliton with taffety hangings": the early college library' in David Scott (ed.), *Treasures of the Mind: A Trinity College Dublin Quatercentenary Exhibition Catalogue* (London, 1992), 143–50.

Charles Benson and Mary Pollard, 'The silken purse: bibliography in Ireland' in Peter Davison (ed.), *The Book Encompassed: Studies in Twentieth-Century Bibliography* (Cambridge, 1992), 200–05.

A Checklist of Plays in the English Language Printed Before 1700, held in Trinity College Library Dublin (Dublin, 1993).

'A Dublin printer's strike of 1840–41' *Long Room*, 39 (1994), 43–47.

Charles Benson and Helen F. Mulvey, 'Bibliography' in W. E. Vaughan (ed.), *A New History of Ireland. Vol. 6: Ireland under the Union, pt. 2, 1870–1921* (Oxford, 1996), 764–879.

[Review of the state of bibliographical research in Ireland, originally delivered at the 1995 AGM of the Book Trade History Group] *Book Trade History Group Newsletter* (27 March 1996), 3–5.

'Trinity's hidden treasure' *Cara*, 32(4) (July-August 1999), 52–58.

'A Dictionary and Investigation of the Dublin Book Trade, 1801–1850' (Trinity College Dublin, unpublished PhD thesis, 2000).

'Department of Early Printed Books: a review of accessions 2001–2002', *Long Room*, 47 (2002), 9–12.

Charles Benson and Paul Corrigan, *Trinity College Library, Dublin* (Dublin, 2003).

'Bruce, William (1702–1755), bookseller' entry in *Oxford Dictionary of National Biography* (print and online versions) (23 September 2004).

'Joy, Francis (1697–1790), printer and paper manufacturer', entry in *Oxford Dictionary of National Biography* (print and online versions) (23 September 2004).

'Thom, Alexander (1801–1879), printer and writer', revision of original entry by C. L. Falkiner, *Oxford Dictionary of National Biography* (print and online versions) (23 September 2004).

'TCD Department of Early Printed Books: a review of accessions 2003–2004', *Long Room*, 49 (2004), 9–12.

'TCD Department of Early Printed Books: a review of accessions 2005–2006', *Long Room*, 50–51 (2005–2006), 11–16.

Charles Benson and Iain Beavan, '"Your side of the water": nineteenth-century Scottish printers and their wholesale trade with Dublin', *Long Room*, 50–51 (2005–2006), 22–40.

Charles Benson and Siobhán Fitzpatrick (eds), *That Woman!: Studies in Irish Bibliography: A Festschrift for Mary 'Paul' Pollard* (Dublin, 2005).

'Introduction' in Benson and Fitzpatrick (eds), *That Woman!: Studies in Irish Bibliography: A Festschrift for Mary 'Paul' Pollard* (Dublin, 2005), 8–13.

'Libraries in university towns' in Giles Mandelbrote and K. A. Manley (eds), *The Cambridge History of Libraries in Britain and Ireland. Vol. II, 1640–1850* (Cambridge, 2006), 102–21.

'Ireland' in Bill Bell (ed.), *The Edinburgh History of the Book in Scotland. Vol. 3: Ambition and Industry 1800–80* (Edinburgh, 2007), 418–29.

'The reward for honest toil: wages in the printing trade in early nineteenth-century Dublin', *Journal of the Printing Historical Society* n.s. 12 (Winter 2008), pp. 47–60.

'The journeymen bookbinders in early 19th-century Dublin', *Long Room*, 52–53 (2008), 37–48.

'"Eminently calculated for the public good": the Dublin Society's statistical surveys' in Fergus Mulligan (ed.), *Auguri: to Mary Kelleher* (Dublin, 2009), 56–63.

'The Irish trade' in Michael F. Suarez and Michael L. Turner (eds), *The Cambridge History of the Book in Britain. Vol. 5: 1695–1830* (Cambridge, 2009), 366–82.

'Many good books: advertising and the book trade in early nineteenth-century Ireland' in Robin Myers, Michael Harris, and Giles Mandelbrote (eds), *Books for Sale: The Advertising and Promotion of Print since the Fifteenth Century* (New Castle (DE) and London, 2009), 109–22.

'Some private libraries in early eighteenth-century Ireland' in Danielle Westerhof (ed.), *The Alchemy of Medicine and Print: The Edward Worth Library, Dublin* (Dublin, 2010), 48–56.

'Nabobs, soldiers and imperial service: the Irish in India', *History Ireland*, 18 (4) (July–August 2010), 6–7.

'The Irish book trade in the Romantic period' in Jim Kelly (ed.), *Ireland and Romanticism: Publics, Nations and Scenes of Cultural Production* (London, 2011), 163–71.

'The Dublin book trade' in James H. Murphy (ed.), *The Oxford History of the Irish Book. Vol. IV: The Irish Book in English 1800–1891* (Oxford, 2011), 27–46.

'Workers in printing and bookbinding' in James H. Murphy (ed.), *The Oxford History of the Irish Book. Vol. IV: The Irish Book in English 1800–1891* (Oxford, 2011), 88–97.

Charles Benson and Siobhán Fitzpatrick, 'Pamphlets' in James H. Murphy (ed.), *The Oxford History of the Irish Book. Vol. IV: The Irish Book in English 1800–1891* (Oxford, 2011), 139–43.

'A friend of the Library in 1759 (1974)', *Long Room*, 54–55 (2012), 49–50.

'Building a library', *Irish Arts Review*, 29 (1) (Spring (March–May 2012)), 110–13.

'"Must do better": enhancing the collections of early printed books and special collections' in W. E. Vaughan (ed.), *The Old Library, Trinity College Dublin 1712–2012* (Dublin, 2013), 437–44.

Pollard, Mary ('Paul'), entry in *Dictionary of Irish biography* online (June 2015).

Charles was the main compiler of 'Bibliophile's Diary', nos 1–18 which appeared in *Long Room*, 34 (1989) to 52–53 (2007–2008). These were notices and commentaries on contemporary bibliographical developments, publications and matters of interest to bibliographers, collectors and librarians.

Exhibition catalogues

Helga Robinson-Hammerstein and Charles Benson, *A Bohemian Refuge: Irish Students in Prague in the Eighteenth Century: An Exhibition in the Long Room, Trinity College, Dublin, December 1997 to May 1998* (Dublin, 1997).

Napoleon: Emperor of the French. Issued in conjunction with 'Napoleon', an exhibition in the Long Room of the Old Library, Trinity College Dublin, 18 June – 2 November 2009 (Dublin, 2009).

The Irish in India: Nabobs, Soldiers & Imperial Service [Dublin, 2010].

Troubled Magnificence: France under Louis XIV. Booklet accompanying an exhibition at Trinity College Dublin Library, 12 October 2011 – 1 April 2012 (Dublin, 2011).

Reviews

Bibliography of George Berkeley, Bishop of Cloyne: His Works and his Critics in the Eighteenth Century by Geoffrey Keynes (London, 1976), *Irish Booklore*, 3 (2) (1977), 135–37.

Charles Benson and Elizabeth Gleeson, *A Bibliography of Eighteenth Century Legal Literature: A Subject and Author Catalogue of Law Treatises and all Law Related Literature Held in the Main Legal Collections in England* by J. M. Adams and G. Averley (Newcastle upon Tyne, 1982), *Irish Jurist*, n.s. 17 (1) (1982), 180–84.

A History of Libraries and Literacy in Ireland by Mary Castelyn (Aldershot, 1984) *An Leabharlann / The Irish Library*, ser. 2, 1 (4) (1984), 127–28.

Irish Booksellers and English Writers, 1740–1800 by Richard Cargill Cole (London etc., 1986), *Eighteenth-Century Ireland*, 2 (1987), 230–31.

A History of the Dublin Library Society 1791–1881 by J. B. Howell (Halifax, 1986), *An Leabharlann / The Irish Library*, ser. 2, 4 (1) (1987), 26.

The Printed Word and the Common Man: Popular Culture in Ulster, 1700–1900 by J. R. R. Adams (Belfast, 1987), *Irish Historical Studies*, 26, no. 101 (Cambridge, 1988), 108–09.

Eighteenth-Century British and Irish Promptbooks by Edward H. Langhans (New York, 1987),
    Eighteenth-Century Ireland, 4 (1989), 182–83.

*A Dictionary of Members of the Dublin Book Trade, 1550–1800, based on the Records of the Guild
    of St Luke The Evangelist, Dublin* by Mary Pollard (Oxford, 1989), *The Papers of the Biblio-
    graphical Society of America*, 96 (1) (March 2002), 133–35.

Index